David A. Lowndes

TIME AND THE HOUR

BY THE SAME AUTHOR

The Social Structure of Medieval East Anglia
Feudal Documents from the Abbey of Bury St Edmunds
The Domesday Monachorum of Christ Church Canterbury
English Scholars
William the Conqueror
The Norman Achievement
The Norman Fate 1100–1154

TIME AND THE HOUR

Some Collected Papers of
David C. Douglas

Fellow of the British Academy
Emeritus Professor of History
in the University of Bristol
Honorary Fellow of Keble College, Oxford

EYRE METHUEN · LONDON

First published 1977
© 1977 David C. Douglas
Printed in Great Britain for
Eyre Methuen Ltd
11 New Fetter Lane, London EC4P 4EE
by Butler & Tanner Ltd, Frome and London

ISBN 0 413 31830 3

To
W. E. B.
and
L. C. L.
In Grateful Memory

Contents

Introduction

The articles which are reprinted in this book have been selected and adapted from the more extensive literary production for which I have been responsible, and which is summarized below in a select bibliography. And that bibliography in its turn reflects much of my own development as a student of history. The stages in that development could in fact easily be summarized. Thus it was my father who first made me aware of the fascination of historical study, and while still at school, Neville Gorton, then a school master and later to be Bishop of Coventry, made me conscious for the first time of the ethical questions which must always be inherent in the study of the past. Later, at Keble College, Oxford, where I am now proud to be an Honorary Fellow, I was taught by J. E. A. Jolliffe that historical interpretation must always depend strictly upon the original evidence on which history is based. By him, too, my interests were directed towards the Middle Ages, and I was privileged to be introduced to the criticism of medieval texts by E. A. Lowe and Reginald Lane Poole. At the same time I had the further good fortune to become a research pupil of Sir Paul Vinogradoff, and was thus brought into contact with the traditions which the great Russian scholar had inherited from Stubbs and Maitland. In these circumstances it is not surprising that my earliest work should have been concerned with the agrarian and social organization of the various provinces of England during the earlier Middle Ages. And this work, which was represented in several of my early articles, eventually took shape in my book on the *Social Structure of Medieval East Anglia* which was published in 1927.

The study of Domesday Book had thus been made to loom very largely in my early work, and about this time I began to profit from the friendship and the instruction of Frank Merry Stenton. I had, moreover, come to believe that Domesday studies had become strictly dependent upon the investigation of other texts which were themselves closely related to Domesday Book itself. These 'satellite surveys', as I ventured to call them, were mainly concerned with the estates of the greater English monasteries. I had therefore already printed surveys from Ely and Abingdon, and I now determined to take more extensive publication of the records of Bury St Edmunds. With this in mind, I issued an edition of the *Feudal Book of Abbot Baldwin*, who was abbot of Bury St Edmunds from 1065 to 1098, and at the same time I edited a large number of early charters relating to the same monastery. These texts were all included in my *Feudal Documents from the Abbey of Bury St Edmunds* which was published by the British Academy in 1932.

In the meantime I was attempting to enlarge my historical interests, and with this aim in mind I began to plan the general survey of the earlier centuries of medieval growth, which in 1935 found a place in the third volume of the *History of European Civilization* under the editorship of Edward Eyre. These more general studies were in fact to be continued by me during the years when I served as Professor of History, successively at Exeter, Leeds and Bristol. And partly for the same reasons I also, at this time, began to address myself to a wider circle of readers with the encouragement of Sir Bruce Richmond, then Editor of *The Times Literary Supplement*. As will appear, many of my articles were to be published in that periodical.

During these years, moreover, I was becoming ever more conscious of the debt which modern students of medieval England owed to their predecessors, and this debt I believed to have been imperfectly recognized. It was partly to rectify this, but more specifically to enlarge my own intellectual horizons, that I began a study of English medieval scholarship in the seventeenth and eighteenth centuries. This was expressed in addresses to the Royal Historical Society and to the University of Glasgow, and it was eventually embodied in my *English Scholars* (1939), the book which reflects, perhaps more intimately than any other, my own scholarly aspirations and emotions.

All this work had of course been dependent upon a study of the original sources of history so that it was natural that I should also attempt to make some of those sources more widely available. I therefore became General Editor of a series of volumes in which there might be presented the basic sources of English history in a form which would enable them to be fully used by readers of English. The publication of original texts in a popular form and if necessary in translation is of course attended with difficulties, but the undertaking was none the less put into operation, and the plan was formed to cover the whole of English history in this manner from the fifth century to the present day. The publication of *English Historical Documents* began in 1953, and now eleven of these large volumes have been published. They appear to be widely used, and I am indeed proud that so many scholars of high distinction have been willing to contribute to the enterprise which is now nearing completion.

Already, however, my interests had become concentrated on what from the start had been a focal point in my research. As early as 1928 I had written a pamphlet on the Norman Conquest for the Historical Association, and followed this with a short text-book on the 'Age of the Normans' in English history. Much of my work on Domesday Book had similarly been concerned with the structure of feudal society, and with the social influence which the Normans had in this respect exercised upon this country. The origins of feudalism in England thus fell to be particularly considered, and under the guidance of Lewis Loyd I sought to relate my feudal studies to the history of the greater families of Norman origin which were established in England in the last quarter of the eleventh century. In 1946, in the David Murray Lecture which I delivered to the University of Glasgow, I considered some of the previous work which had been done on this subject.[1] Later I investigated the rival claims to the English throne which were put forward in 1066 by William Duke of Normandy and Harold Earl of Wessex. The campaign by the Duke in England during the autumn of 1066, and the men who took part in it as 'companions of the Conqueror', were also examined, and some of the propaganda which inspired them was discussed in a paper on the 'Song of Roland'. But all these studies could in a sense be considered as work supplementary to my book on *William the Conqueror* which was published in 1964, and in which I sought to display not only the Conqueror's life and reign but also the Norman impact upon England which was made under his dominating leadership.

I had, moreover, by now become convinced that the long debate about the Norman contribution to English growth could no longer be profitably sustained unless a fresh attempt was made to examine for its own sake the rise of Normandy as a factor in the making of Europe. This had in fact been the subject of my Raleigh Lecture to the British Academy in 1947,[2] and the same theme dominated many of my articles at this time such as those on Rollo, the first of the Norman Dukes,[3] and on the social organization of pre-conquest Normandy. Thus might be revealed (as I hoped) the basis of Norman strength in the last quarter of the eleventh century. It had, moreover, become clear to me that the Norman conquest of England ought to be placed in the wider setting of Norman endeavour, which had, for instance, already established Norman power in southern Italy and Syria. In other words, the Norman kingdom of England had to be studied in close comparison with the Norman kingdom of Sicily and the Norman principality of Antioch. Such was to be the theme of my later books, *The Norman Achievement* (1969) and *The Norman Fate* (1976). And it is on these comparative studies that I am at present engaged.

NOTES

[1] See below, pp. 57–76.   [2] See below, pp. 95–119.
[3] See below, pp. 121–40.

I

The Seamless Robe:
An Historian's Apology

Erat autem tunica inconsutilis, desuper contexta per totum. Dixerunt ergo ad invicem non scindemus eum sed sortiamur de illa cujus sit.

For a man to defend the studies to which he has devoted a great part of his working life is a hazardous undertaking. And still more hazardous would it be for him to explain – or perhaps even to excuse – the part which such studies might be expected to play in the general and cultural life of his country. This is assuredly a task to be undertaken only with very great diffidence. None the less, in the changing conditions of modern culture there may still be an excuse for posing once again the time-honoured question: 'Why read History?'

It must, however, at once be recalled that many eminent men have given a discouraging answer to that question. 'Read me anything but History for that must be false.' It is unlikely that Sir Robert Walpole ever said the words, but such was his sentiment, and he was not alone in its expression. Matthew Arnold, for example, likened History to a 'huge Mississippi of falsehood', and it would be easy to multiply such quotations. Moreover, this scepticism gains an added force at times of rapid change when the survival of a State may seem to depend upon the present and practical efforts of its members. Then, surely it would be egregious folly to pander to those whose foible it is to make literature out of dead empires. When your life is at stake why trifle with the 'dead junk' of Babbit? – or the 'bunk' of Mr Henry Ford?

By contrast, an intense interest in antiquity for its own sake has always been part of the make-up of many men who find therein a satisfaction of what Jeremy Taylor called 'a direct incontinency of the spirit', and such people have always refused to be ashamed of the personal refreshment that such studies afford. 'What song the Sirens sang, and what name Achilles assumed when he hid among women' are for them wholly

13

legitimate speculations, and it is their earnest hope that men will ever seek a glimpse of the 'face which launched a thousand ships'. Now, such curiosity may be held to be good or bad. It may be described as a gift of God or as a mental disease. It can (as I shall hope to show) be transformed into an impulse of incalculable value. But by itself, I would suggest, it cannot be cited as a defence for historical studies in a great university. To expect those who do not share such emotions none the less to applaud them might even appear impertinent. The private satisfaction of selected individuals is not necessarily a justification for academic endowments, or for the expenditure of public money. Devices of escape are always cowardly and usually ineffective. And if Clio be attacked, she certainly will not be rescued by amiable dilletante, unable to face the world around them, and taking their solace in past centuries.

The truth is so much more serious. G. H. Hardy in his apology for pure mathematics placed high among his arguments that the subject was 'harmless'. I can – alas – make no such plea for history. The correct use of historical study may be debatable, but the consequences of its abuse have been made plain for all the world to see. The propagandist use of history in the Germany of yesterday, in the Russia of today, is a fact of incalculable importance to the future fate of the world. An ignorance of history inviting its fabrication by the unscrupulous cannot be regarded simply as an innocuous academic failure. It has affected all our lives. It has led directly to Belsen and Buchenwald and Katyn Wood. It has contributed its full share to two major European disasters.

That is the immediate past. But the danger of historical ignorance and of historical distortion can hardly be regarded as less today when large populations made susceptible by literacy to new ideas but unable to discriminate among them present the most fertile field for propaganda that the world has ever seen. Viewed in the crudest and most general way it may therefore be suggested that the opportunities of the true and honest historian, and the responsibilities which are laid upon him, have never been greater than they are at the present moment.

If, however, the correct position of the historian as scholar and teacher is to be ascertained, some definition of the subject itself must be attempted. Yet, in truth, this is not easy, and as I hasten to assure you, one of the few merits of this lecture is that it will *not* attempt to decide the time-worn discussion whether history is an art or a science. I content myself merely with repeating on the one hand the invocation to 'Clio a Muse' made by G. M. Trevelyan, and on the other hand with citing to you the declaration of J. B. Bury that 'history is a science, no less and no more'. It is not for me to mediate between two eminent Regius Professors of History at Cambridge, but perhaps I may be permitted to think that the argument itself is somewhat fictitious. The distinct nature of his material makes the investigations of the historian radically different from those of the scientist, whilst, since he is concerned so largely with factual discovery, the historian can never be regarded as absolutely an artist. Does this seem to you a slipshod evasion of a difficult question? If so, I can only take comfort in the thought that a very notable Professor of Physics described his subject as 'a creative art'. At all events, I propose to leave the matter at that point.

Perhaps, indeed, there is excuse for so doing. The friendships that I have been privileged to hold with distinguished scientists and distinguished artists have led me to the belief that such men are too busy – and too interested in their proper work – to be much concerned with discussions as to its general nature. The working scientist (unless I have misunderstood him) is mainly concerned with his techniques – the means by which in his own particular field he can hope to add to the sum of human knowledge. The artist, in his turn, tends to be concerned not with the wider questions of aesthetics – that he leaves to the art-critics – but with the material for his expression and with the methods by which he can achieve creation. So, also, I suspect, is it with the historian. The philosophy of history is a fascinating and important subject, but with the rarest exceptions its chief English exponents have not been historians. Life is short, and the fervent historian has much to do. He has to discover; he has to create. The nature of his subject he must leave for others to discuss. 'I do not believe in the philosophy of history,' wrote the great William Stubbs, 'and therefore I do not believe in Buckle.'

Nevertheless, if history can be regarded absolutely neither as an art nor as a science, it partakes of the quality of both, and the investigation of the past can be dignified with the name of research. It must be dispassionate in the sense that I imagine all scientific research must be dispassionate: it must have as its objective the disinterested discovery of truth, using for that purpose all the available subordinate techniques such as palaeography, diplomatic, archaeological expertise, textual criticism, bibliography and so on. Historical research has indeed now become a highly technical business demanding a long and specialized training, and (as I wish to emphasize) its prosecution is certainly the most fascinating and probably the most rewarding task which lies open to the professional historian of today. Nor does its essential purpose need any elaboration; for this was never stated better, or more simply, than it was over two hundred years ago in the monastic meditations of Mabillon, the founder of modern documentary criticism. 'It is,' he says baldly, 'to proclaim certainties as certain, falsehoods as false, and uncertainties as dubious.'

So far so good. But the success of historical research in this respect must surely always be limited in a sense that a strictly physical investigation is not limited. It can never lead to the same 'certainties', because the material is here radically different, consisting of human nature and human motives. In other words, no historical event in its causes and consequences is ever precisely the same as any other event. To take a very crude example: after an investigation of the primary evidence, I might (if I was very lucky) be able to tell you with reasonable certainty that A killed B on the afternoon of 6 July 1040, and I might (with equal luck) be able to tell you in reasonably full detail the circumstances in which this took place, and the secular consequences of the action. But it would be with far less confidence that I would speak of the precise motives of the crime – or hazard any categorical opinion of what exactly A was thinking of when he slit his enemy's throat. And moreover (and this seems to me important) I could never generalize from all this to a murder of D by C in similar circumstances two centuries later. The cant phrase 'History repeats itself' is surely, on analysis, meaningless.

Yet research it is, and I myself could find no better definition of the primary motives which inspire it than those outlined by G. H. Hardy as the spurs to mathematical investigation. Firmly putting aside all verbiage about the 'betterment of humanity', he claimed that the motives for research were, normally, (a) personal ambition, (b) professional pride and (c) intellectual curiosity. I need not enlarge upon the first two of these, for they are common to all of us. But the intellectual curiosity which inspires the investigator of history is probably of a nature peculiar to himself, and so I must pause for a moment to consider it. It is certainly difficult to define. Perhaps I should describe it best if I called it an inherent – almost a passionate – conviction of continuity. A belief that those three elusive entities – the past, the present and the future – are woven together *as the seamless robe*, and form a trinity which is one and indivisible, and that of these three – the past, the present and the future – the present, which is here and gone even as I speak, is incomparably the least important.

I must be careful here for I am not unaware of the dangers of exaggeration – the danger of 'overtones of enthusiasm'. I must be careful – especially as I find in advance a full measure of reproof from an eminent scientist of the past. Was it not Thomas Huxley who expressed his horror of those who were guilty of 'plastering the fair face of truth with that pestilent cosmetic rhetoric'? To which a mere Arts man can only retort that that phrase might appear as one of the best plastered pieces of rhetoric in the English language. I must guard against all this. 'Good wine needs no bush.' And so without any cosmetic, but with the full force of an intimate conviction, I starkly voice my own belief that a sense of continuity is the sole thing that can raise historical 'research' above the level of a sophisticated detective problem, or an ingenious crossword puzzle. And no one who does not possess this conviction of continuity – and of its transcendent importance – should study history at any level. That is to say (for here I wish to be very precise) no one – inside this University or beyond its walls – should study history for any irrelevant reason – such as to find an 'escapist' device – or because 'old things are *so* interesting' – or to obtain a B.A. degree. The sole justification of historical study (if I may risk the necessary platitude) is a belief that – viewed in terms of time and eternity – such study is supremely worthwhile.

This notion of continuity must not, of course, be too rigidly applied. It is not necessary to the period closest to itself that an historically minded epoch will inevitably feel itself allied. The men of eighth-century Europe derived their inspiration from Christian Rome; the men of the Renaissance invoked Greek antiquity; the nineteenth-century Romantics called to the Middle Ages. It is a process which is constantly repeated, and perhaps I may offer a small example from my own experience. I well remember as an undergraduate at Oxford after the First World War the almost febrile disdain felt by every 'bright young thing' for Victorianism in all its forms. One touch of Strachey made the whole world kin – or at least the world *in statu pupillari* – and the waters of Isis ran foul with the efflux of Bloomsbury. And yet today Lytton Strachey is, I fancy, more out-moded than the men he satirized, and I seem everywhere to see a revived respect for the Victorians. I hear it in contrasted political utterances; I see it, albeit with an uninstructed eye, in feminine fashions of jewellery; and I have been told that the furniture which in the 1920s we cast out of our houses now fetches respectable prices in the antique shops of New York. Doubtless the reaction will in its turn go too far, and it is probable that men always tend to be more sympathetic to the ideals of their grandfathers than to the opinions of their fathers. None the less, the sense of sequence is there to be found, even though in such an instance it moves according to a different progression.

'Man,' says Dante, 'is as a horizon between two hemispheres,' and I am going to suggest that this personal sense of continuity, intimately felt, has always been the inspiration of all the greatest historical work. Today, when so much is heard about the 'organization of historical research', and its endowment, it deserves careful consideration whether the greatest productions of historical scholarship have not always been lit from an inward individual fire, and moved by an impulse which, in the last resort, is in its essence not didactic, or political, or educational but intensely subjective: the need on the part of the inquirer to explore for his own satisfaction the secrets of that continuity which he finds so important, and afterwards, perhaps – but still for his own self-fulfilment – to display according to his own desires the trophies of his fond adventuring. Not otherwise, it may be supposed, was Gibbon enabled to build his triumphant bridge across the centuries, or Maitland to elicit from our ninth-century ancestors their common thoughts about common things.

Mention of such names leads inevitably, in its turn, to a consideration of the relation of history to the Arts. For there can be no gainsaying that these men were artists if only in the obvious sense of being among the greatest writers of English prose. Nor would it be easy to deny that their importance as historians derived at least in part from this fact. The reflection is doubtless otiose, but it may, none the less, give us pause in view of assertions so frequently made, and still more frequently implied, that such achievement is strictly irrelevant to the high purpose of history. A very good friend of mine who was once Regius Professor of Modern History at Oxford, has in a remarkable lecture given voice to something like this point of view. 'The books we write,' he exclaims, 'are ephemeral, their usefulness must pass. The sources remain.' The prime purpose of the historian is thus to discover, to display, to edit the sources. It would ill become me to dispute such an opinion too vigorously, for (as it happens) I have spent a large part of my working life in editing historical sources. I am the last person, therefore, to decry the importance of such endeavours, and indeed their value to historical scholarship (I hope) hardly needs to be stressed. But, in my judgement, here is to be found only one part of the historian's task. Nor can his obligations be said to have been fully discharged when he has brought the edited documents from the Muniment Room to the reader's desk.

Any assertion that history is not a branch of literature seems to me to be belied by all the greatest historical work from Thucydides to Macaulay. Modern methods of specialized research have opened new doors upon historical reality, but the progress which has thus been achieved is often bought with a heavy price. Even the most consciously erudite monograph may fail of its purpose if the theme be insignificant and if its treatment be such as to repel perusal. And the best edited text, though it always contributes to scholarship, needs to be utilized before it can make its full contribution to knowledge. This is particularly true when the text itself is technical, or written in a language which most readers cannot comprehend. The proper relation between the reader and writer of history is not attained when the latter becomes a member of a learned esoteric clique, imparting the results of his research in language which none but his fellows can understand. To pander to a populace glutted with sensationalism is, of course, for the historian, to sin against the light. But it is not wholly the fault of the English reading public if English historians today exercise less influence than in the time of Green and Froude.

I would even suggest that the affinities between the historian and the creative artist are not to be envisaged solely in relation to literary achievement. The purpose of the historian is not merely to discover and present: it is also to elucidate. In other words, he must be concerned with creating patterns out of the past. To take one example of such a pattern in its very crudest form, we have the current distinction asserted as existing between 'political history', 'constitutional history', 'administrative history', 'economic history' and the like. So convenient indeed have such distinctions proved to students, teachers and examiners in a hurry, that in some quarters they have come to be regarded as possessing an absolute sanction, whereas in fact they may possibly serve merely to blur the truth about the past and mask its diversity. Personally I deprecate this practice. Historians, I am sure, 'incur grave danger of misconception if they divorce what are called political tendencies from the interplay of personal relations', and the logic of events is not derived from concentration upon isolated ideas in carefully selected minds. Again, institutions cannot be understood apart from the men who work them, and though man lives by bread, he does not live by bread alone.

More relevant to our present purpose, however, is the still more familiar pattern resulting from the division between 'ancient', 'medieval' and 'modern' history – a pattern which was in fact created by the humanist historians of the sixteenth century. And this too has proved so convenient for teaching and controversial purposes that in its turn it has come in many quarters to be regarded as possessing an absolute – and exclusive – validity. Yet of course this is not so. Equally cogent, and equally interesting, patterns could be made according to other interpretations, or by selecting other epochs of crucial transitional significance, at least in European history. Thus, it has been suggested that the critical period in the formation of medieval Europe came not in the fifth but late in the eleventh century when a new political grouping was formed in the West, when new cultural ideas were adumbrated and developed, and when the papacy could be seen advancing towards the political leadership of Western Europe. Even more significant is it perhaps that the cleavage in European development alleged to have occurred during the fifth and sixth centuries when the 'ancient world' was supposed to be coming to an end, appears to some to have been less important to the growth of Europe than the continuous process which took place during those years whereby the long pathway of the Roman genius began to be merged into the *Via Sacra* of the Cross.

Similar variations might be suggested for later periods. Undoubtedly the sixteenth century, which is traditionally cited as marking the beginnings of 'modern history', witnessed changes of enduring importance affecting the breakdown of an older social order, and the rise of secular states buttressed by national sentiment and claiming absolute authority. But it could also perhaps be argued that a more fundamental break occurred towards the end of the seventeenth century with the beginning of that revolution in scientific theory and achievement which has created the world in which we now live. Such variations could of course be lavishly illustrated. In the fourteenth century, for example, an instructive pattern of history was created by genius in the magnificent description of the flight of the imperial eagle which is embodied in the sixth canto of the *Paradiso* by Dante Aligheri. And we in our turn have been given infinite opportunities for similar endeavours. The history of the eastern Mediterranean during the first Christian millenium could for instance be portrayed with different but equally authentic perspectives if viewed from Rome, from Constantinople or from Aleppo. Again, the Norman conquests of the eleventh century could be exhibited with equal legitimacy, but with contrasted results, if considered from the angle of England or Sicily, or France or Syria. And today we need no reminder that it is possible to depict with equal sincerity but with opposed conclusions the history of Europe in the nineteenth century against a background of national fervour, of Christian ethics or of Marxian economics.

Now such patterns, to have any value, must of course be true to the facts. They must also be logically coherent, and logically impregnable. But I myself would further suggest (though perhaps I should find few to agree with me) that to attain their highest excellence such patterns should also provide an aesthetic satisfaction – a satisfaction akin to that given by the grouping of a full-scale Rembrandt composition – and more strictly allied to the '*beauty*' (and I use the word with the scientific authority of Whitehead) to be found in a mathematical problem of the first order. This is clearly not the place to enlarge on such an idea. Nor would I be competent to do so. I merely state the notion as another indication of the filiations which I am personally tempted to seek between history and the other arts and sciences. And certainly it is my view that a consideration of the relation of history to other intellectual disciplines is an essential prerequisite to any assessment of the part which historical instruction might be expected to play in the cultural life of a civilized people.

'Histories,' says Francis Bacon, make men 'wise', and all those addicted to the writing or reading of history must surely hope he was right. Historical instruction therefore should in its turn be concentrated not so much on technical training in historical research, as on a survey of broad trends of historical development coupled with an introduction to the canons of criticism upon which historical interpretation must be founded. The basis of all such teaching must in short be the belief that (in the old sense of the term) history is one of the 'humanities'. Historical studies may in other words provide an intellectual discipline leading to increased power of general judgement, and promoting what a great historian once described as 'speculative equity'. Perhaps it might also be asserted that history may not only possess its own intrinsic value but may in its turn open the door to the investigation of other subjects. Is there a great book of the past, whether poetry or prose, that is not in some degree rooted in its contemporary soil? Is there a great literature, ancient or modern, that can be studied apart from the history of the country from which it springs? Of the social sciences I speak with more diffidence, but I like to think that economic history may be of some assistance to the investigation of even the purest economics. With law, the connection is more obvious still. It deserves note perhaps that the greatest period of historical scholarship at Oxford occurred when the Schools of Law and History were combined, and as a pupil, however unworthy, of Sir Paul Vinogradoff, I am not likely to forget the mutual service that history and jurisprudence can render to each other. Perhaps I may also be permitted to add how much the lawyer can teach the historian about the use of evidence, and certainly *I* learnt most of the little I know about the criticism of medieval charters from a practising lawyer at work from ten to five in the office of the Treasury Solicitor.

I should myself like to go a stage further. I should like to confess a belief – or at any rate an aspiration – that history may now advance to a quite special position among the humane studies. The framework of our educational endeavour today clearly derives from two great movements of the past. The former of these was the humanistic revival of the sixteenth century, after which, until yesterday, a knowledge of the literature of Greece and Rome was regarded as the proof and test of an educated man. The second of these two movements (which condition our educational activities) was the scientific revival which began in the late seventeenth century and which has continued with increasing momentum, and increasing distinction, up to the present hour. I regard it as one of the tragedies of modern culture that there sometimes appears an antipathy – a mutual exclusiveness – between these two influences, and I believe that some new synthesis between them is now desirable and imperative. I speak here of course with very great diffidence but I should like to cite in my support, and with great admiration, some words used by Sir Edward Appleton in his Presidential Address to the British Association:

> Science has given back to the Universe that quality of inexhaustible richness and unexpectedness and wonder which at one time it seemed to have taken away from it. Science – pursued for its own sake – can enlarge men's horizons and invest the world with a deeper significance. But we must not forget that there are other values and other experiences. At the opposite pole from our scientific endeavour there are the ways of thought which do not change, whose concern is with what is not new, and with the things which will not be superseded; and today we stand in need of these enduring and sustaining values of the spirit.

Now, it was precisely with 'the things that are not new', with 'the enduring and sustaining values of the spirit', that the older classical studies at their best were concerned. Yet are they, today, in the modern circumstances of our educational life, still capable of satisfying the need so eloquently expressed by Sir Edward Appleton? They grew up and flourished when higher education was the prerogative of the few. They grew up and flourished when there existed among that minority a general knowledge of the classical tongues which now, alas, has lamentably passed away. Today, we, exponents of the Arts disciplines, sometimes seem to me to be living in the twilight of the Renaissance, and perhaps we shall be well advised to look in another direction for a new dawn. I am of course not unprejudiced in this matter, but I do feel that my own subject has here a vital contribution to make. And I do not think I am wholly mistaken when I note everywhere gaining in strength a tendency to substitute history for the classics as the perspective and common background in education. And if I am not wrong in my diagnosis I visualize as the end of this process a recognition of history not as the rival of the classics – heaven forbid – or of modern literature or of the natural sciences but rather as

the house in which they all can dwell; the cement which holds together all the studies relating to the nature and the achievements of man.

In my more optimistic moments therefore – and I hope with proper modesty – I sometimes wonder whether we may not now be on the threshold of a new Renaissance when we may need history to understand the modern world with its bewildering enrichment of fresh experience, just as the men of that other Renaissance four centuries ago went to the classics not only in search of the old wisdom but also to find the means of giving proper utterance to the new things that then needed to be said. Or if this is to put the matter too pompously, I might phrase it in terms of University education by hazarding the suggestion that, as an academic subject, history has perhaps now the opportunity of aspiring to the position once held for instance by the Oxford 'Greats' school – *litterae humaniores* – which served this country so long and so well. Here at least seems to me a great opportunity offered to all those who write or who study or who teach history. For historical education appears to me to possess the same large general character. It deals with men and women at all times, and in all their activities, with their problems and aspirations, with their thoughts, their beliefs, their achievements and their failures. *Nihil humani* is alien to this subject, for it is – or should be – as wide as life itself. It is thus essentially a unifying subject offering a meeting ground to other disciplines. Possessing its own standard of criticism it is as a subject catholic and comprehensive. That is why I make bold to claim for it in the circumstances of our time, at least the opportunity to become the basis of the humane education of the future.

At all events, if I am right in asserting that history is essentially one of the humanities, then the essential product of an historical education should be men and women of critical poise and enlightened intelligence. Men and women so equipped may even be said to have something of their own to offer to the welfare of the community to which they belong. Here, and not so much in any specialized knowledge or techniques, will, I fancy, be found their characteristic opportunity for service. For there is danger in this matter, in that men ever conscious of their present discontents are always apt to turn to the student of history in the fond hope that from his locker he may produce a nostrum of immediate potency. Thus does the desire for quick cure summon more quacks than physicians. I alluded earlier to the falsity of the cant phrase 'History repeats itself'. And personally, whenever I hear on the public platform, or read in the popular press, those four magic words 'History teaches us that', I view anything that follows with the utmost distrust and suspicion.

None the less, the study of history has, I think, its own contribution to make to the consideration of contemporary affairs. If history does not repeat itself, similar situations arise as the spiral of time uncoils, and if these situations be handled with similar wisdom, or with similar folly, they may be expected to produce roughly similar results. That, however, seems to me to be only a small part of the matter. More specifically would I claim for students of history that their study – if properly conducted – can strip the mind of illusions, leading them from heady abstraction back to men and women in their infinite diversity – warning them, by reference to actuality, against this or that ideology which oversimplifies the past under a single formula or promises the millenium the day after tomorrow.

Quarry the granite rock with razors, or moor the vessel with a thread of silk, then you may hope with such keen and delicate instruments as human knowledge and human reason to contend against those giants, the passions and the pride of men.

Newman's great lectures on the 'Idea of a University' were not, however, addressed specifically to historians, and let us hope that these stand in less need of the caution that the myth of perpetual and inevitable human progress finds little support from an examination of the past. Human nature is surely revealed to students of history not as a variable but as a constant; for they have seen men at all times capable of virtue, and equally capable, in all periods, of every extreme of folly, cruelty and vice. The most that seems to occur by way of alteration is that, within restricted periods, manners and customs change for better or for worse; but there is no guaranteed permanence in such fluctations, nor any assurance that they will endure. It may perhaps be suggested in this respect that the besetting temptation of the historian might by cynicism;

his ultimate peril, despair. But this need not be so. The scope for improvement within restricted periods, and subject to recognized hazards, is always large. It is a sceptical wisdom that historical studies should inculcate, not cynicism. Older writers were wont to speak of history as a 'school of virtue'. Nor were they wrong. The historian may even claim a modest share in rescuing the Sermon on the Mount from the blood-stained handling it habitually receives from the friends of humanity. More safely can it be concluded that the impulse to endeavour need not be weakened by a sense of historic reality.

Further than this, I would suggest that historical studies can also conduce to social stability by setting a nation on its guard against the transitory lure of the temporary phase. Such studies may even impart a belief that social growth, like growth in nature, should, in a healthy organism, be so gradual as to be almost unperceived; that times change and customs with them; that to deny such flux would be folly; but that a new era should enter like a thief in the night, and, like a sunset fading, a dead epoch should pass away. Exaggeration would here be easy, but it may at least be permissible to doubt the logic which would specifically deny to those who have studied antiquity the right to speak about the present. Nor would it be easy to deny that a nation is the better for being possessed of a vivid consciousness of its living past.

This social consciousness is, however, of slow growth, and in relation to my theme today it is of secondary significance. Earlier in this lecture I suggested that historical writing is at its best always the response to a private curiosity. And now I similarly assert that the greatest reward for readers and students of history is an intimate personal enlightenment. The frontiers of time are as enticing as those of space, and to be vitally aware of the fact is to be highly privileged. Such realization, if it be permanently won, will impart a special quality to every judgement, and lend a special savour to each perception. Thus (to give only one example) it may for an Englishman serve to endow a familiar countryside with an ever-freshening significance. A place-name here that suggests a racial admixture pregnant with future consequence; and there a roadstead peopled with little ships. Perhaps the sudden twist at Fountains from the medieval vista to the formal garden where Stanhope might have walked; or Dundrennan Abbey, populous in solitude, hard by the Solway whence Queen Mary sailed. These are, however, but random examples of the marriage between time and the hour, but they may serve to illustrate my general point. The veil between the past and the present hangs stiff, but it is sometimes translucent, and through it there penetrates the reflection of a life which is intangible, but not alien, to the informed spectator. For him, if he be eager and attuned, there may even be moments of surprised and unforgettable revelation when the seamless robe itself for an instant appears displayed, and as still unriven. Such moments are, of course, exceptional and rare. None the less, I emphasize my conclusion. It is no small thing if a man can be brought to feel himself as one with the past, and as no stranger to the future. And some such intimate and intensely personal conviction may well be Clio's greatest gift.

II

The Development of English Medieval
Scholarship between 1660 and 1730

Though the subject of this paper is over-large, its purpose was begotten of
piety, not presumption. If, therefore, I lack the confidence which pertains
to discovery, I am not for that reason without my apology; and I aspire to
the hope that the Fellows of this Society may deem it a seemly relaxation to
pause from their labours for the space of an hour in order to reflect
gratefully upon some of their forerunners in learning. Between 1660 and
1730 English medieval scholarship advanced to a notable achievement,
and the names of the chief men who contributed thereto are almost
household words to all modern students to medieval England. But the
history of that pregnant movement of research has still to be written and
few of us would claim that we had made full use of the work of our
predecessors. Consequently, since the distant converse of dwarfs with
giants conduces to humility, it may be salutary to recall once more this
great adventure of English erudition, and profitable, also, with an eye to
the present, to speculate upon the cause and character of its astonishing
success. The praise of famous men has earned an ancient commendation
and even a cork may sustain a draught of fishes.

I am well aware that the selection of these dates is to some extent
arbitrary, and that, in particular, the widespread study of medieval
England was no novelty at the time of the Restoration. The seventeenth
century was throughout marked by the strangely consistent appeal
which the majority of its opposed leaders made to medieval precedent, and
no fundamental break in the assiduous cultivation of English medieval antiquities is to be discerned between the days of Laurence Nowell and those
of Thomas Madox. Robert Bruce Cotton and Robert Harley were in one
sense partners in a common enterprise, and the links which connect
Spelman with Wake, Ussher with Stillingfleet, and even Selden with Hale
are not such as can be broken by any facile dichotomy. Twysden looked
back to Savile and forward to Hearne, whilst Hickes, nourishing the

rising genius of Wanley, paid reverence not only to Junius and Marshall but also to Joscelin and Lisle. Hearne and Tanner both laboured to enlarge the work of Leland, and Gibson remodelled the *Britannia* of Camden in a manner which had been desired by Thomas Browne.[1] The work of the earlier scholars in this procession of learning was thus continuously developed by their successors, and it was a corporate effort sustained for the space of nearly a hundred and fifty years which was brought at last to its close by Hearne's editions and Wanley's catalogues, by the *Fœdera* of Rymer and by the *Concilia* of 1737.

Nevertheless, the Restoration began an epoch in English scholarship as surely as it marked a change in English politics, and the seventy years which followed witnessed a positive achievement in medieval learning which was distinct alike by reason of its extent and from the unity of its corporate character. It would not be difficult, for example, to defend the opinion that Old English studies have never progressed with greater rapidity than in the years which elapsed between the appearance of Somner's *Dictionary* in 1659 and the death of Wanley in 1726, or that, during this period the scholars, albeit sustaining a great tradition, made to their subject a particular contribution. Characteristic of this endeavour was the development of Anglo-Saxon studies at Oxford where at first Marshall and Hickes laboured at Lincoln to enlarge the work of Junius, and where later, after William Nicolson had become the first official College preceptor in this subject, Edward Thwaites elicited from Queen's that 'profluvium of Saxonists' which (as was said) 'poured forth from the House of Eglesfield'.[2] The activities of these Oxford 'Saxonists' have indeed attracted such attention that scant justice has been done by some later commentators to the Saxon research which at the same time was prosecuted in the University of Matthew Parker. Yet, at Cambridge, Robert Sheringham and Aylett Sammes were both trained, and, at Cambridge also, there was produced in 1722 the magnificent edition of Bede's *Ecclesiastical History* wherein John Smith developed the earlier labours of Wheloc. The energy which at this time transformed the study of the Old English past was not in fact confined to either of the two Universities or even both. It was not as a Fellow of Lincoln College, nor yet as Dean of Worcester, but as a hunted renegade that George Hickes advanced by the sheer force of his dominant personality to be its acknowledged leader, and the scattered research, which he directed to its climax in the monumental *Thesaurus* of 1703–5, was almost national in its scope. When Humphrey Wanley, his pupil, who perhaps taught Hickes as much as he learnt from him, finally left Oxford for London at the beginning of the eighteenth century, it meant that Old English learning was beginning to concentrate in the metropolis, and when, in 1726, Wanley lay dropsical and dying in his London lodging,[3] he could look back on the astonishing progress that Saxon studies had made during his lifetime. Modern criticism has done nothing but emphasize the magnitude of this achievement. The technical excellence of Smith's *Bede* aroused the enthusiasm of Charles Plummer when at last that book was superseded in 1896.[4] The reputation of Hickes probably stands higher today than at any time during the last fifty years. And (to quote Mr Sisam) 'one can seldom look at an Anglo-Saxon manuscript without thinking gratefully of Humphrey Wanley'.[5]

The particular advance in English medieval scholarship that occurred between 1660 and 1730 was thus exhibited in the progress of Saxon studies, and it could be illustrated with equal ease by reference to the research which was at the same time devoted to the problems of later medieval history. The Norman Conquest, for example, remained the object of an especial attention, and retained its fascination alike for political propagandists and for objective historians.[6] After the Restoration, as before, it was still considered, even in some erudite quarters, to be more decent to speak of the Norman 'acquisition' or perhaps of the Norman 'purchase' of England, and the astonishing *Argumentum Anti-Normannicum* of 1682,[7] with its pictorial representations of the social contract made between William and a lady described as 'Britannia his Sacred Queen', was representative of a fairly large class of literature. Then, as now, these events of eleventh-century history generated a strange heat in unlikely bosoms, and they inspired the flow of much flamboyant ink. But, amid the welter of argument, Robert Brady was, despite his own partisanship, making an important contribution to these studies by means of his elaborate and careful use of authorities. Brady's *Introduction to the Old English History*, which in its collected form appeared in 1684, was a notable piece of savage and constructive criticism, and its main function was to insist that the sources must be examined in the light of their meaning to the men who wrote them. Progress could only be assured if the old arguments, illustrated by time-worn extracts, were replaced by a new investigation of the authorities themselves and in particular by a more complete and more accurate presentation of the great chronicles of medieval England.

Thus, during these seventy years, the earlier tradition of Savile and Camden, of Selden, Jennings and Twysden, was itself gradually transformed. Henry Wharton, with the enthusiasm of his shrill and perverted[8] genius, made here, before his early death in 1695, an indelible mark upon all future study of English ecclesiastical history, and the majority of the monastic annals which were later to be edited with such scholarly care by Luard were investigated and printed between 1684 and 1691 by William Fulman and Thomas Gale. At the same time, men such as Joseph Sparke[9] at Peterborough and Thomas Rud[10] at Durham were devoting themselves to the chronicles of the particular sees they served. It was, in short, an age

of assiduous editing carried on in many diverse quarters, and, despite
occasional backslidings towards inaccuracy and undue haste, a steady
advance was maintained, until at last in the long series of chronicles
issued by Thomas Hearne during his tempestuous career a more faithful
reproduction of the manuscript texts was offered to the public than had ever
been achieved before. Hearn's credulities have been sufficiently mocked,
and his criticism was often beyond defence. But the meticulous care of his
transcription was such that it was made a reproach to him by his enemies:

> One Rule – [it was noted] he generally speaking closely observed
> was always to follow his Authors religiously. Their Mistakes by this
> means were punctually copied and sacredly preserved – *Sic MS* he has
> noted perhaps in the Margin to shew that he was not ignorant of the
> Error in the Copy—Still amid all these Regulations the Text is generally
> kept *purely corrupt* and scarce a Blunder thro' the whole but what is very
> industriously preserved.[11]

The fault was one for which generations of scholars have had cause to be
grateful, and the sneer illustrates better than could columns of eulogy the
progress that was being made towards a proper presentation of medieval
chronicles.

It is not necessary to reiterate familiar names in order to illustrate the
manner in which research of a special character and directed towards
particular ends was at this time widely pursued in England under the
influence of outstanding scholars. This was not a movement confined
to a few specialists or to a fortunate constellation of pre-eminent men.
The strength of English medieval scholarship in this period derived from
the fact that it was the common concern of an ever-increasing number of
English squires, of lawyers and particularly of doctors, of clergymen
scattered up and down the rectories and vicarages of England. The
assiduous cultivation of local history at this time was a further mark of
this pervading interest, and the correspondence of William Nicolson and
Samuel Gale, the diaries of such as Ralph Thoresby and Abraham de la
Pryme, demonstrate its ramifications. Dugdale's *Warwickshire* and
Thoroton's *Nottinghamshire* were the two great county histories of the
age, but they stand out from amid an extensive production. Sir Robert
Atkyns in Gloucestershire, Sir Henry Chauncy in Hertfordshire, Robert
Wright in Rutland, and White Kennett at Ambrosden were representative
of a large company whose abilities were not always equal to their zeal; and
the earlier example of Dodsworth in the north, and of Somner in the
south-east was followed during this period with varying degrees of
success by men like Torre and Nathaniel Johnston on the one hand and by
writers such as John Harris and the Batteleys on the other. Roger Gale's
anonymous folio of 1722 on the Honour of Richmond was for all its

defects a notable example of the pervading antiquarian enthusiasm which was thus being profitably diverted into the channels of local investigation.

The variety of this production came from its being made by many and devoted hands. Its value depended to a large extent upon its originality. Books such as the *Baronage* of Dugdale carried with them their own especial faults, but they are so often criticised as if they were written yesterday that it is sometimes easy to forget that the research behind them was pioneer work. It would not be difficult to illustrate at length the new departures in medieval investigation which were made by the scholars of this age. The first Englishman, for example, to demonstrate the importance of originals rather than cartulary copies for the technical study of the feudal charter was probably Thomas Madox, and the first competent presentation of a Middle English text was possibly Hearne's edition of Robert of Gloucester.[12] The originality of these men needs little emphasis, but it may be permissible to recall attention to two specific comments upon the use of medieval material, the one made in 1684 by Robert Brady and the other in 1711 by Thomas Madox.

> The *Records* I have used [said Brady] are Faithfully Cited, and like wise the *Historians*, who are such as lived in the *Times* when the *Things I Vouch them for, were acted*—whose *Writings* in very many things do agree with the *Publick Records* as to the *Matter* and *Time* though not as to the *Form* and *Composition*; and this I Affirm from my own Collating and Comparing of them.[13]

And here is Madox:

> Great regard is indeed to be had to the Annals or history contained in Registers of Churches; and in the Manuscript collections of Ancient Writers; particularly in relation to things done in their Own life-time, or lying within their personal knowledg. But no doubt the Publick Records of the Crown and Kingdom are the most important and the most authentick of All. And these are the Foundation which sustain the whole Fabrick of this History. A Foundation solid and unshaken.[14]

Inasmuch as the twentieth century has been marked by a greater insistence upon the especial value of record sources for the study of English medieval history, these men may surely claim an astonishing modernity.

It is perhaps a reproach to us that pioneer work of this originality has not been more uniformly followed up, for our deficiencies in this matter become apparent if we merely reflect that the only edition of *Hemming's Cartulary* is still that of 1723, or that very little of the third book of the *Liber Eliensis* has ever been printed apart from the long extracts which are to be found in *Anglica Sacra*. It would certainly tax the energies of a committee working for a generation to supersede the *Exchequer* of Madox or

Wanley's catalogue of 1705, but there is still very much to be done
in the re-editing of texts whose importance was first discovered for us by
the labours of men working more than two centuries ago. Sometimes
time has made this task impossible, since disasters like the great fire which
ravaged the Cottonian library in 1731 have on occasion given a unique
value to the editions made before that date. Stubbs showed us how much
our knowledge of one of the chief sources of the chronicle ascribed to
Benedict of Peterborough derives from a fortunate transcript made by
Wanley and used by Hearne;[15] and it is for modern 'Saxonists' to state
what their study has gained from the fact that the Maldon Poem was
printed as an appendix to Hearne's edition of John of Glastonbury.[16] Our
restricted knowledge of the lost manuscript of Asser owes something to
the edition made by Francis Wise in 1722,[17] and John Smith's great
edition of Bede's *Ecclesiastical History* incidentally preserved in an Appendix
a valuable series of West Mercian Old English charters whose originals
have since been lost.[18] Such examples taken from among many indicate
afresh the claim of these scholars upon our gratitude and upon our
study.

Not the least valuable result which would ensue if this whole movement
in scholarship was submitted to the detailed investigation it deserves
would be the revelation of material hidden in unexpected places. It is not
surprising that Brady's work should contain much information concerning
Domesday which is still not easily obtainable elsewhere, or that considerable later discussion upon the origin of the jury might have been avoided
by a reference to Hickes's *Dissertatio Epistolaris*.[19] It is, however, perhaps
something of a shock to find a remarkably good text of Ine's laws in an
Appendix to that strange essay on the Phœnician contribution to English
history which Aylett Sammes published in 1676 under the title of *Britannia
Antiqua Illustrata*; and a superficial investigator into the development of
the English baronage might well be excused if he omitted in his search
Humphrey Hody's contribution to the Convocation Controversy.[20] We
are all aware how much the study of English feudalism has owed to
Spelman's essay on *Feuds and Tenures by Knight Service* which Edmund
Gibson edited among the baronet's posthumous papers in 1698, but others
among our predecessors in feudal study are perhaps less assiduously
cultivated. Fabian Philips, for example, was something of an eccentric.
More royalist than the king, he was particularly offended by the abolition
of feudal tenures after the Restoration. He wrote voluminously on the
subject and his work here is of quite exceptional interest in that it concerned the antiquity of institutions in the maintenance of which he was
himself directly involved. The quaint titles of his very lengthy tracts –
Tenenda non Tollenda or *Ligeancia Lugens*, for instance – concealed a mass of
antiquarian learning; and this culminating folio on the *Established Government*

of England, which was published in 1687 when its author was eighty-two years old, is a mine of information. The critical ability of Fabian Phillips was mediocre, and his literary style was repulsive.[21] But he combined in himself qualifications which have perhaps never co-existed in any other writer on English feudalism. He discussed feudal institutions as an antiquary in the age of Burnet, but he discussed them also in something of the spirit of Glanvill or of Bracton.

Such haphazard examples of erudite activity are of themselves sufficient to emphasise afresh the wide range and the special quality of the research which marked the age. To this movement of inquiry, men of all parties and of all temperaments contributed. Non-jurors such as Sancroft and Collier shared here the interests of Whig ecclesiastics like Kennett and Hoddy, and the Middle Ages became the concern of men as divided in their opinions as were Prynne and Lloyd, Atterbury and Nicolson. The detailed achievements of the long succession of English scholars who devoted their lives to the study of medieval England between the time of Dugdale and that of Wake are not to be appraised in the course of a single paper or indeed of a single book. But it is permissible to inquire what were the general conditions which made possible such an astounding efflorescence in English medieval studies.

There can be little doubt that, after the Restoration as before, the main spur to medieval research in England came from the conviction that the burning questions which divided contemporary society could best be settled by means of an exhaustive examination of precedent. In the past, the circumstances of the Reformation had produced a marriage between ecclesiastical polemic and antiquarian zeal, and the constitutional debate had sent politicians and lawyers questing into the past. By the latter half of the seventeenth century such ardours had to some extent been sublimated, but ecclesiastical controversy and political argument still survived as the most potent sources of historical research. Thus George Hickes considered that Old English studies were especially to be commended in that they would supply an answer to 'that never-ending question: Where was your Church before Luther?'[22] and the turning point in Matthew Hale's book on the Common Law was his discussion of the Norman Conquest. Fortescue Aland in 1714 eloquently defended historical studies as conducing to constitutional and ecclesiastical stability,[23] and the valuable research of such as Atwood and Petyt, of George Harbin and Hilkiah Bedford was directed to similar propagandist ends. The same motives are also clearly to be discerned in the ecclesiastical scholarship of the early eighteenth century. The Convocation Controversy was in many respects undoubtedly dull. But the heats which it stimulated were directly responsible for Wake's *State of the Church*, and thus for the subsequent production of the *Concilia* of 1734.[24] A dominant characteristic of English medieval

B

scholarship during the seventy years which followed the Restoration –
perhaps even the chief reason for its remarkable progress – was the
close inter-relation between historical research and the problems of
contemporary life. This association was capable of inspiring an immense
energy in men who held that in their study of medieval England they
were probing questions that concerned their personal honour or even their
personal salvation.

It might not even, perhaps, be too fanciful to discern a further cause for
this productivity in the fact that the motives which inspired these scholars
were particularly congenial to the race from which they sprang. The
search for wisdom in precedent flourished as if naturally among a people
whom foreign observers at a later date have praised especially for its
reliance upon tradition rather than upon those wide general theories
which claim universal validity.[25] Similarly, though Halifax might liken the
pleasures of research to those of 'wrestling with a fine woman',[26] the
close relation made by the scholars between inquiry and conduct has ever
been more characteristic of what John Stow described as 'the searching and
unsatisfied spirits of the English'.[27] Certainly, no explanation of the scholarly achievement of this age can ignore the crusading ardour of the men
who made it. Some explanation of that astonishing production may be
found in the mere contemplation of Prynne bending his earmarked head
over his interminable pamphlets.[28] The dedicated energy of Hickes informed his wonderful 'Preface to Ottley' as surely as it moved him to go to
console his friends on the scaffold.[29] And the force of Thwaites appeared
not only in his labours on Boethius but also on the occasion when he
watched the amputation of his leg 'without distortion or ho', and rammed
his fingers 'like spickets' into his own spurting arteries.[30] The positive
contributions which these men made to learning were extremely personal,
and while the correspondence of the time shows how much of their
achievement was due to collaboration, their work was in each outstanding
case lit by an inward individual fire. Herein, also, they were fit products of
the nation which they taught.[31]

The absence of any organisation of study in this period tempts speculation how far a great movement of scholarship is dependent upon the
regimentation of research. During these seventy years the Universities, for
example, gave little official lead in these matters. The Spelman lectureship
at Cambridge was unique of its type, and it lapsed; the Camden Chair at
Oxford, despite the tendency of the lectures of Degory Wheare, its first
occupant,[32] soon became devoted almost exclusively to ancient history;
and the Regius Chairs of History and Modern Languages, established in
1724 at the instigation of Edmund Gibson, were originally designed to
serve a political purpose and did not, during this period, serve to stimulate
medieval research.[33] Similarly, the Society of Antiquaries was in abeyance

during most of this period, and its revival in the early years of the eighteenth century by Wanley, Talman, Bagford and their friends was not fully to produce its beneficial results until a later generation. Towards the end of this period there were beginning to spring up local societies of which the *Gentleman's Society* of Spalding[34] was the chief, and also associations such as Antiquity Hall at Oxford or the Zodiac Club of St John's College, Cambridge. But these, though interesting in themselves, were mainly important as foreshadowing a later type of activity. Generally speaking, it may be said that the greatest movement which English medieval scholarship has ever seen took place without any great assistance from Professors, and without any substantial aid from official organization. It derived from a widespread consciousness of the interest and the importance of the subject capable of stimulating unparalleled industry in remarkable individuals.

These conditions prevailed throughout the seventeenth century. But, after the Restoration, a new incentive to good historical production came in a modification of the motives and in an improvement of the technique of the earlier scholars. An increased specialization began to appear which was itself a mark of progress towards more modern conditions. The indiscriminate riot of erudition, characteristic of the earlier work, gave place to investigations which by their very limitation were more efficient and English medievalists like Dugdale and Brady began to submit themselves to a narrower discipline.[35] As history gradually came to be regarded as a distinct branch of learning, a greater objectivity appeared in its investigation. The close connection between antiquarian scholarship and current controversy had undoubtedly stimulated production, but it was apt to make history the handmaid of faction. This danger also was fairly met after the Restoration. The scientific interests of the age reacted upon medieval inquiries, and though it is impossible to particularize shortly about a general tendency, its scope may be perceived by a comparison of the spirit which animated the work of Wanley and Hickes, or by a perusal of that wonderful preface wherein Madox, at the outset of his greatest work, expressed for all future students of medieval England the aims which should animate their criticism of medieval sources.[36] Unflagging energy derived from a sense of the significant in medieval studies conditioned the work of these men as it had that of their predecessors, but their unique performance was due to the fact that this fervour was now being generally disciplined by specialization and purified by a fresh objectivity.

The enterprise of these scholars was moreover continuously fertilized by the consistent support which it received from educated England. It is unnecessary to illustrate, and easy to ridicule, the vagaries of private patronage, but it must be noted that, during the seventy years which followed the Restoration, English medievalists had little reason to complain of the manner in which their work was received. William Elstob lamented 'evil days, cold patrons and neglected efforts',[37] and the reek of Rymer's garret[38] was a reproach to his generation. But these were exceptional cases of particular hardship, and when all due allowance is made for individual misfortunes, it remains true to say that during this period the medieval scholar in England could count on a public sympathetic to his studies. Preferment in the Anglican Church has perhaps never more consistently followed learned achievement, and towards the close of the seventeenth century it might almost have seemed that medieval erudition was among the most certain qualification for the episcopal bench. When the Church was adapting itself to the exigencies of the Revolution settlement, a most influential group of prelates – William Nicolson, Edmund Gibson and White Kennett among their numbers – were recruited from the ranks of distinguished medievalists, and William Wake was ideally qualified to preside over a Church which had long delighted to reward medieval learning. Nor were the laity backward in the encouragement of the study of medieval England. 'It is observed,' wrote Thomas Madox in 1711, 'that the Science of Antiquities hath in this last age been cultivated with more industry and success than in several ages past,' and he gave it as his opinion that the chief explanation of this was the 'encouragement that hath been given to these studies by several persons of eminent learning and superior order in the realm'.[39] The eulogy was justified and it would be easy to multiply examples of the beneficent effects of this discriminating munificence. When Hearne for instance sold his numerous editions of medieval chronicles by subscription at half a guinea a volume he amassed a small fortune in the process;[40] and when Hickes as a political outcast issued at a very high price his huge folios of difficult Latin on the origins of the Teutonic languages, he was able to add to them a list of subscribers (headed by twenty-six peers of the realm) longer and more distinguished than could now be found for a similar work. This is no place to enlarge upon the debt of English literature to the aristocracy in an age justly famous for its patronage. But it deserves emphasis that a work of pure scholarship devoted to a medieval theme probably stood a better chance of a remuneration between 1660 and 1730 than it does today.

During these seventy years conditions in England were thus peculiarly congenial to the propagation of medieval studies. The solemn zeal which had sent the earlier generation on its search through medieval England had not expired, but at the same time the modern ideal of objective research was beginning to be understood. The scholars were personally worthy of their opportunity, and a large public was eager to welcome their work. In the light of these considerations the corporate achievement of the time is perhaps best to be understood. For by the third decade of the eighteenth century conditions were once again beginning to change, and the age of

Enlightenment was not favourable to the acquisition of medieval erudition. The transformation of the temper of the Church could hardly be
better illustrated than by a comparison of the correspondence of Nicolson
with that of Warburton, and the latter prelate who had been bred in the
Church of Gibson and Wake saw fit to castigate those divines who
solaced themselves in 'Monkish Owl Light'.[41] The prejudices of men of
sensibility which had once been subjected to the lively scorn of Elizabeth
Elstob[42] flourished in a society which prided itself on disdaining the past,
and their sentiments were fittingly crystallized in the familiar phrases of
Bolingbroke about the year AD 1500:

> To be ignorant about these ages which precede this æra would be
> shameful. Nay, some indulgence may be had to a temperate curiosity in
> the review of them. But to be learned about them is a ridiculous
> affectation in any man who means to be useful to the present age.[43]

Certainly a 'temperate curiosity' was not the emotion which had driven the
earlier scholars to their enduring achievement, and, equally certainly, this
transformation in English intellectual taste produced a slackening in the
momentum of medieval research. The only considerable contribution to
Old English studies, for example, which was made during the mid-
eighteenth century was Lye's *Dictionary*,[44] the progress of ecclesiastical
research which had marked the Convocation Controversy ceased with its
close;[45] and Hearne for nearly a hundred years found no worthy English
successor as an editor of medieval chronicles[46] Any division between
epochs of learning must admit modifications. The opinions which were
later to prove so deleterious to these studies were freely expressed in
England long before the close of the seventeenth century, and in the years
which followed the death of George I medieval research still found
devoted adherents particulary in respect of local investigations. But, when
all due allowances have been made, it remains hard to escape the conclusion
that medieval scholarship in England underwent during the eighteenth
century not a development but a reaction.

The seventy years subsequent to the Restoration, set as they were
between a period of preparation and one of decline, may probably be
regarded as the golden age of English medieval scholarship. It still needs
to be stated that this achievement was of the highest positive value,
and that it can in no sense be regarded as an antiquated product of bygone
enthusiasm. In their successful application of exact criticism to historical
materials, scholars like Wanley, Tanner and Madox differed from their
best modern successors only in the immensity of their production. They
were, moreover, outstanding members of a very numerous company, and
their lesser contemporaries were worthy of being associated with them.
Much of the erudition, thus laboriously accumulated, has become embedded

in our present knowledge of medieval England. No student of Old English history can ignore his debt to Hickes, and no worthy investigator of ecclesiastical antiquities is likely to forget his obligation to Wake and to Wilkins. The work of Brady and of Phillips lives in our constitutional histories, and if modern editions have largely (though not entirely) supplanted the books of Wharton, Hearne, John Smith and Thomas Gale, their very excellence derives in part from the labours of the earlier scholars. It is seemly to recall these obligations, but there is here little reason for complacency. Our debt to these men is by no means exhausted, and their many and scattered volumes have, I venture to think, never received the full and the respectful attention they deserve. The very limited purpose of this paper will, at all events, have been achieved if I have recalled to your notice the value and the scope of this production, and if I have suggested that this pregnant movement of research ought now once again to be examined in its entirety. The time has perhaps arrived when English medieval scholarship may derive much benefit from a fresh study of its past progress in an age that was uniquely propitious to its growth.

NOTES

1 ''Tis time to observe Occurrences, and let nothing remarkable escape us. The Supinity of elder days hath left so much in silence, or time hath so matyred the Records, that the most industrious Heads do finde no easie work to erect a new *Britannia*.' (*Hydriotaphia*: Preface.)

2 Cf. Firth, *The School of English Language and Literature* (1909).

3 For malicious descriptions of the last months of Wanley's life and of the unfortunate marriage he then contracted, see Hearne, *Coll.*, x, 377, and Portland MSS., Rep. v, p. 638; vii, pp. 439, 442.

4 Cf. Plummer's remarks in his edition of the *Ecclesiastical History* (i, Preface, esp. p. lxxx). Smith apparently used for his Latin text three out of the four best manuscripts known to Plummer. Both he and Plummer were unacquainted with a fifth important manuscript discussed by Dr Lowe in *Eng. Hist. Rev.*, xli, p. 245.

5 Sisam in *Rev. Eng. Studies*, vii, pp. 7–9.

6 In 1613 John Hayward, in the preface to his remarkable *Lives of the Three Norman Kings of England*, had shown himself well aware that a study of the Norman Conquest might readily be made to serve the needs of propaganda. Some more modern scholars have derived yet deeper satisfaction from a conviction that a solution to the problems of eleventh-century history should be sought in the political sentiments of their own time. They have possessed their reward, even as did Sir William Temple when in 1695 he devoted so many pages of his *Introduction to the History of England* to a discussion of the substitution of William for Edgar the Atheling. William Nicolson, who was himself committed to the Revolution settlement, found in this book 'such Reflections as become a Statesman' (*English Historical Library*, ed. 1736, p. 76).

7 Sometimes attributed to William Atwood but more probably the work of Edward Cooke.

8 See the extracts from his Latin autobiography printed by D'Oyly, *Life of Sancroft* (1821), ii, pp. 105–54.

9 Despite his reputed eccentricity of being 'mad a quarter of a year together in every

year' (Hearne, *Coll.*, viii, p. 382), Sparke's *Historiæ Cænobii Burgensis Scriptores Varii* was a notable production. It contains material which is still not to be found elsewhere.

[10] Thomas Rud in collaboration with Thomas Bedford produced in 1732 an edition of Simeon of Durham's *Historia Dunelmensis Ecclesiæ*, which superseded the version which had appeared in Twysden's *Scriptores*. Rud in opposition to opinions previously expressed by Bale and Selden argued in his fine preface for the true attribution of the authorship of the History.

[11] *Impartial Memorials of Thomas Hearne* (1736), pp. 25, 26; cf. *The Times Literary Supplement*, 6 June 1935.

[12] D. N. Smith, *Warton's History of English Poetry*, p. 9.

[13] Brady, *Introduction to the Old English History*, 'Advertisement'.

[14] Madox, *Exchequer* (1711), p. iv.

[15] Stubbs, *Benedict of Peterborough* (Rolls Series), i, pp. xxi–xl. He adds the tribute: 'It seldom falls to an editor to be able to bestow on the labours of his predecessors in the same task the unqualified praise that I can give to this edition.'

[16] *Joannis Glastoniensis Chronica*, ed. Hearne (1726), ii, pp. 570–7; Wülker, *Grundgriss zur Geschichte der Angelsächsischen Litteratur*, pp. 334–8; E. D. Laborde, *Byrhtnoth and Maldon* (1936); E. V. Gordon, *The Battle of Maldon* (1937).

[17] Cf. Stevenson, *Asser's Life of King Alfred*, p. xliii.

[18] Smith, *Historiæ Ecclesiasticæ...Libri Quinque auctore...Bæda* (1722), pp. 764 sqq.

[19] *Thesaurus: Diss. Ep.*, pp. 33–44.

[20] Cf. Stenton, *English Feudalism* (1932), p. 86; Hody, *History of English Councils and Convocations* (1701), pp. 287, 288.

[21] 'His parts,' observed Anthony Wood (*Fasti*, ed. Bliss, ii, col. 5), 'were never advanced when young by academical education.'

[22] Hickes to Bishop of Bristol, 22 May 1714 (Portland MSS., Rep. v, p. 445).

[23] *Difference between an Absolute and Limited Monarchy* (1714), pp. xiv, xv, lxix.

[24] E. F. Jacob, R. Hist. Soc. *Trans.*, 4th Series, vol. xv, pp. 91–131.

[25] 'The instinct of every Englishman,' remarked Emerson in 1856, 'is to search for a precedent'; 'the taste of this people is conservative'; 'the stability of England is the security of the modern world'. (*English Traits,* ed. 1883, pp. 109, 137, 167.) Price Collier, another foreign observer, arrived at the same conclusions in 1902 (*England and the English*, pp. 253, 363): 'The Englishman,' he remarks, 'looks back for his standard and makes precedent serve as his guide.' 'They are the last race of all to be fuddled and disturbed by new religions, new theories of government, new solutions of the problem of existence.'

[26] Halifax, *Works*, ed. Raleigh, p. 249.

[27] Quoted by Firth in *Sir Walter Raleigh's History of the World*. See his *Essays*, ed. Davies (1938), p. 36.

[28] Cf. Aubrey's *Life of Prynne*.

[29] E. C. to Robert Harley, 29 January 1691: 'Mr Ashton was executed at Tyburn. – He would not permit the Ordinary to pray with him but desired Sir Francis Child to let him have the divine that went along with him to perform the last ghostly offices, which was permitted. They say it was Divine Hicks and after him came little Cook of Islington, both non-jurats, and so he went into the other world.' (Portland MSS., Rep. iii, p. 458.)

[30] Brome to Charlett, quoted in Nichols' *Literary Anecdotes*, iv, pp. 148, 149.

[31] Brunetière, for example, specifically contrasts the highly individual character of English literary expression with the 'social' tendency of the French. (*Essays*, trans. D. N. Smith, esp. p. 52.)

[32] Wheare, *Method of Reading Histories*, ed. 1698.

[33] Cf. N. Sykes, *Edmund Gibson*, pp. 95–105.

[34] Cf. Nichols, *Literary Anecdotes*, vi, pp. 1 sqq.

[35] Cf. Powicke, *Sir Henry Spelman and the Concilia*, esp. pp. 7, 8; Douglas, 'William Dugdale the Grand Plagiary' in *History*, xx, pp. 194, 195.

[36] Madox, *Exchequer* (1711), Preface and esp. pp. iii, iv.

[37] Cf. M. A. Richardson, *Reprints of Rare Tracts* (1843–8), vol. ii.

[38] For a graphic description see J. Caulfield, *Portraits, Memoirs and Characters of Remarkable Persons from the Revolution to the Death of George II*, i, pp. 51, 52; Hardy, *Syllabus of Documents in Rymer's Fœdera*, i, pp. xxiv, xxv.

[39] Madox, *Exchequer* (1711), p. i.

[40] 'Life of Hearne', p. 33, in *Lives of Leland Hearne and Wood* (1772).

[41] Figgis, 'William Warburton' in *Typical English Churchmen from Parker to Maurice*.

[42] Prefaces to *Rudiments of Grammar* (1715) and *English Saxon Homily* (1709). Cf. *The Times Literary Supplement*, 28 September 1933.

[43] Bolingbroke, *Study of History* (Sixth Letter) in *Works* (1754), ii, p. 360.

[44] D. N. Smith, *Warton's History of English Poetry*, p. 8.

[45] Stubbs, *Seventeen Lectures* (1900), p. 281.

[46] Specifically noted by Pinkerton in *Gentleman's Magazine* (1788) in connection with the project sponsored by Gibbon for new editions of the chronicles of England. Cf. Gibbon, *Address Recommending Mr Pinkerton* (*Misc. Works*, iii, p. 571).

III

John Richard Green

When, fifty years ago this month, John Richard Green died from consumption at the age of forty-six, a competent observer remarked that had he lived he would have been the greatest historian since Gibbon. The author of the *Holy Roman Empire* considered that he might not unreasonably be adjudged as nearly the equal of Macaulay; and Bishop Stubbs, with a rare enthusiasm, asserted that 'there was no department of our national records which he had not studied and (I think I may say) mastered'. Green's own opinion of his work was much more modest. 'Do you know what they will say of me?' he asked, and gave the answer: 'He died learning.' And now after the lapse of half a century, during which the standards of historical writing have been transformed, posterity has perhaps found time to revise all these verdicts and to pronounce a different judgement upon the most popular and perhaps the most influential historian of the latter half of the nineteenth century.

The place of John Richard Green in English history and literature depends upon one book. It is as the author of the *Short History of the English People* that he impressed his personality upon his contemporaries, and it is through that book that he has exercised his immense posthumous influence. Posterity, speaking generally, has cared but little for his other work. The dust lies thick upon his contributions to the *Saturday*, and the charm of those historical articles brilliantly written as an undergraduate at Oxford and lovingly collected after his death is not such as to win immortality. His larger *History of England* does not enhance his reputation. It adds nothing to its predecessor and it cannot take the place of works based upon original research. Even his later and more detailed books on the *Making of England* and the *Conquest of England* have not stood the test of time. But the triumphant career of the *Short History* has never been checked. Its instantaneous success was comparable among historical books only to the work of Macaulay. Within a year, 32,000 copies of the work had been sold; and by 1909 it had been translated into French, German, Italian,

Russian, Japanese and Chinese. Today it is still the most widely read
single-volume history of England. Green's quite special place among the
historians of England does not depend upon reviews or upon antiquated
works of research. It is due to a single masterpiece.

But when a modern critic takes up this historical text-book which,
unlike its fellows, has thus miraculously escaped the melancholy oblivion
of schoolroom shelves, he is at first at a loss to account for its immediate
success and its far-reaching influence. It bears the superficial appearance
not only of a mere students' manual, but of a manual written unmistakably
at a particular period to give expression to transitory and often erroneous
ideas. And yet this is the book which has enjoyed the initial popularity of
a successful novel and the long life of a monument of research. Nor does
a preliminary perusal of its contents dispel the feeling of perplexity. The
defects in the book were indeed immediately apparent to Green's contemporaries, and time has done little to lessen them. Here can certainly be
heard the echo of moribund enthusiasms; and the political ideas of fifty
years ago seem to resound strangely from a half-forgotten world. 'This is a
history not of English kings or English conquests but of the English
people.' True; but what partisanship this may serve to introduce and
what an ephemeral indignation! The people may be idealized as an entity
far removed from any historical fact, and at least we may be sure in
advance that in any dispute between rulers and ruled, Green will defend
the latter. He cannot, for example, appreciate the economic difficulties of
the Government at the time of the Peasant Revolt; and, almost in the
manner of a seventeenth-century pamphleteer, he attacks the policy of the
Crown during the Stuart epoch. He is even unfair to England in his
account of the rebellion of her American colonies. As a result of the same
predisposition, he finds it very hard to say anything good of royalty.
Nothing is for him 'more revolting' and yet nothing is 'more characteristic' of Elizabeth 'than her shameless mendacity'. For James I we have
'gabble and rodomontade', 'want of personal dignity', 'pedantry' and
'contemptible cowardice'. George III 'had a smaller mind than any other
English king before him save James II', and his reign contained (an
astonishing hyperbole) 'the shame of the darkest hour of English history',
for which, indeed, the king must be held to be directly responsible. Even
Alfred can be quaintly cited as an enemy of democracy, while Henry I was
'jealously aloof', and Henry II 'built up by Patience and policy and craft a
dominion alien to the deepest sympathies of his age'. Every one of these
judgements could now be confidently disputed. Their presence in the
Short History unmistakably 'dates' a book which nevertheless continues to
exercise its immense influence both over professed historians and over the
general English public. Since Green wrote, we have learnt the great debt
which England owes to her kings. We have been taught that Henry I and

Henry II were great constructive statesmen. It has been shown how Parliament took its beginnings largely from the development by the Stuart kings and cannot be judged solely by the opinions of their enemies; and the publication of the letters of George III has done something to rehabilitate a monarch who at least was honest according to his lights. Even among Green's contemporaries there were men at work whose calmer judgement might have saved him from many exaggerations and misstatements. Green knew Stubbs and borrowed largely from him, but neglected to profit by his caution in describing medieval development. He praised Gardiner, but failed to appreciate his insight and sympathy into the motives of both sides in the Civil War, and so turned the historian of the Stuarts into a bitter critic. Lecky was already at work giving a more charitable and more accurate account of the policy of England in respect of her American colonies. In all these important matters the work of Green was clearly inferior in judgement and in accuracy to that of his contemporaries. How then are we to account for the remarkable fact that for every reader of Stubbs or of Lecky today there are at least ten readers of Green?

A book dealing with the entire history of England was bound to contain some errors of detail. But it is difficult to accept the judgement of Stubbs, who contended that Green's mistakes were always on unimportant matters and that they never affected either 'the essence of the picture' or the 'force of the argument'. No modern critic can fail to note how Green's account of early English history is coloured by two theories, both unhistorical and both derived from the prejudices of the age in which he lived. He was doubtless entitled to range himself among the Teutonists, but we can hardly escape the conclusion that, following Kemble, he imitated rather the vices than the virtues of that great historian. It can at all events be little short of amazing today that an historical writer professing to sum up the whole growth of the English people could pass over in two pages both the Celtic background to the history of this island and also those four centuries during which the majesty of Rome made its indelible mark upon England and gave to us the Latin tradition of civilization for an inheritance. No historian could now see the origins of the English people solely in the actions of our forefathers in Sleswick, that 'older England', 'the far-off fatherland by the Northern sea'. And even more unhistorical was Green's assumption of a primitive and an idyllic democracy as the origin of the English constitution. He went further than Stubbs here, and took what was least valuable from the teaching of his master. Green's picture of primitive society in England as consisting of communities of freemen all equal in status and with equal shares of land, legislating for themselves in democratic committees which in the last resort could elect and depose their kings, is one which can be defended on the grounds neither of history nor of probability. And yet it affected the whole structure of this influential book. It accounts for the dispro- portionate length of the Anglo-Saxon section. It explains Green's failure adequately to appreciate the fundamental nature of the Scandinavian settlements of the ninth century. It leads to a distortion of Norman history; and it accounts for the fallacy which runs through the later chapters of the *Short History* that popular representation has always been in England the essence of constitutional growth. Green's story of English origins is based, in short, upon a legend. The nineteenth century crowds in upon the sixth, and Simon de Montfort in the thirteenth speaks with the voice of Gladstone. The same legend appears elsewhere in the book so as to make whole paragraphs seem today strange and antiquated. And yet the *Short History of the English People* survives as part of the canon of English historical literature. Almost as truly as when it was written it may be said to be the one really great single-volume history of England. That is the paradox of John Richard Green.

The attempt to resolve this paradox may be of value if only for the reason that modern historians have much to learn from Green's achieve- ment. It is easy to say that the success of the *Short History* depended upon the graceful and easy style in which it was composed. But this would be altogether too facile an explanation, and an apologia on these lines might well do damage to its subject. It is true that Green took much trouble to make his book popular, but he was quite conscious of the dangers latent in the attempt. He criticized himself for 'slurring over the uninteresting parts', and in his preface he defends his method, though it had been adopted 'at the risk of sacrificing much that was interesting'. Nevertheless, it would be quite unjust to charge him with the parentage of that un- worthy progeny of historical romances and *chroniques scandaleuses* which has now become a permanent feature of commercial literature. Green's work was in the highest degree serious and sincere, even though he had a tendency to dramatize every event of which he wrote. This quality indeed appeared in his conversation, which, many of his friends declared, was even more remarkable than his written work. In talk 'he could not tell an anecdote or repeat a conversation without unconsciously putting into people's mouths better phrases than they would have themselves em- ployed and giving a finer point to the moral which the incident expressed'. Verbal accuracy might suffer, but what he thought was the inner truth would come out the more fully.

Here is to be found at once the strength and the weakness of Green's historical method, and the style in which the *Short History* was written could by no means of itself account for the permanent influence of the book. 'All through the earlier sections,' he wrote, 'I see the indelible mark of the essayist'; and a generation which has grown somewhat cautious of superlatives may occasionally here experience satiety from a monotony of the picturesque. Nevertheless, Green was at least acutely conscious of the marriage between history and literature. 'I learnt my trade as I wrote,' he remarked; and his numerous redrafts of the book made him at one time almost the despair of his publishers. Men have thanked God for the makers of dictionaries. But does not Green's work even today provide a salutary warning to the writers of monographs? To parade a concentrated learning, to please a few expert critics and to scare the public away from history, these can never be the true aims of historiography. The modern historical specialist may permit himself a supercilious smile at the recollection of the *Short History* selling vigorously from the railway bookstalls of the 'seventies, but the joke is by no means wholly at the expense of Green.

The prime cause of Green's popularity and influence was his originality and it is the measure of his achievement that we are now in danger of forgetting this. He reconstructed in a single volume the development of a nation, taking cognizance not only of the political but also of the social, the cultural and the religious aspects of its life. His whole method was startlingly novel when he wrote; and it may be remarked that no one has since accomplished on the same scale the same task for this or, indeed, for any other nation. When Green found it necessary to remark: 'As you see in my own Wee Book, I think moral and intellectual facts as much facts for the historian as military facts,' he uttered what has now become a truism. The doctrine was of course not new, but Green was the first resolutely to apply it to the general history of a great nation. And it was exactly on this ground that he had to meet his opponents. Here even his friend Freeman was vehemently opposed to him, and in other quarters the criticism was bitter. By discarding the old regnal divisions of English history, Green laid himself open to violent attack; and it was then a novel, and to many an unwarrantable, method which 'devoted more space to Chaucer than to Cressy, to Caxton than to the petty strife of Yorkist and Lancastrian, to the Poor Law of Elizabeth than to her victory at Cadiz, to the Methodist revival than to the escape of the Young Pretender'. That such a view of English development has now become commonplace is due to Green more than to any other one man. As a living intellectual theme pervaded this book which was sold everywhere, so did general English historical studies begin to take on a new orientation. Just as Dante had seen a continuity in history whereby the long pathway of the Roman genius became merged into Christendom, so now did the same effort at a philosophic continuity appear for the first time in a popular history of England. The tramplings of armies and the fall of thrones could no longer justify the historical terms of oblivion and rebirth, and even in popular history the historian could no longer indulge

without misgiving in that 'snobbery' by which every triumphant party
was held to have possessed the juster cause. Green was in this sense an
original figure among English historians; and if, and when, his book is
superseded it will be by a work which owes more to Green than to any of
his critics.

It is in the light of such considerations that the deeper meaning of
Green's success can be understood and his real greatness appraised. It is a
curious fact that no better criticism of Green could be found than in
Croce's well-known work on history; and by no standards would Green
receive so favourable a judgement as by those of the Italian philosopher.
The twentieth-century theorist could be made the champion of the nineteenth-century historian. All history, we are now taught, if it be not a
dead chronicle of unrelated facts, must be the expression of some philosophy. It must be 'contemporary' in the sense that, just as every historian
must select, so also he must select according to a definite plan that can
only be constructed from the writer's own philosophic system. History
is not merely the past; it is the perception of the past. And the 'brute fact'
does not exist for the historian until he has perceived it in relation to some
process of development or degeneration, or until he has related it to some
chain of causation. Green was perfectly conscious of this notion of true
history. Indeed, he emphasizes it in phrases which serve as an odd
commentary on Croce's latest book. He writes to Freeman:

> I give English history in the only way in which it is intelligible to me.
> . . . There is such a just aversion to philosophies of history on account
> of the nonsense which has passed under that name, that it is quite
> likely people may turn away from a story which strives to put facts on a
> philosophic basis and to make events the outcome of social and re-
> ligious currents of thought.

This was a notable saying when it was written, and it may be well compared
with Meinecke's twentieth-century plea:

> Historical inquiry must elevate itself to freer movement and contact
> with the great forces of political life and culture without renouncing
> the precious tradition of its method, and it must plunge into philosophy
> and politics without experiencing injury in its end and essence, for thus
> alone can it develop its intimate essence and be both universal and
> national.

Green's work was an attempt to translate into historical terms the philo-
sophy of a passionately strenuous life; and herein lies its real importance.
Mrs Green was quite right when she asserted that the story of the *Short
History* is the biography of its author. In it we can see the intellectual

independence which in its earlier growth manifested itself at Oxford when (in Green's own words) the 'little restless animal in black, covetous of applause – sharp, sarcastic, bustling, pressing to the front', revolted against the set curriculum of 'Schools' and refused to take honours. Similarly, the general trend of the *Short History* is to be seen already when Green, dependent upon a curacy at Hoxton, gave away to his poor parishioners his hardly earned and much-needed stipend and subsisted upon articles written rapidly during the night after his day's work was done. Cannot the leading characteristics of this oddly passionate text-book be discovered even in that fine face which today peers out strangely from conventionalized portraits? The square chin bespeaks determined originality; the eyes radiate an understanding of suffering and of the struggles of the less fortunate; the whole suggests the keen and penetrating gaze of the pilot, of one who could gaze into a nation's past with sympathy or face a black personal future without dismay. And Green was a man whose strong convictions could only express themselves in historical work. History was the ruling passion of his life. It coloured the whole of his youth at Oxford, and it persisted, until the last picture that we have of him is his dictating his last book on his death-bed and almost with his dying breath. At thirty-two the 'poor curate' was at the crisis of his life – without settled income, without hope of advancement, with as yet no solid literary work accomplished, in the grip of a deadly disease which might at any moment cut short his career – yet this was the man who at this time could confidently say: 'I shall never be content until I have superseded Hume, and I believe that I shall supersede him.' He did. And his achievement was directly due to the fact that his work was a living whole constructed according to a plan derived from his own philosophy. His permanent influence is due to the method and the character rather than to the matter of his book.

But if history to be alive must be the expression of a contemporary philosophy, it must be controlled by its own subject matter. History is not merely the expression of opinion any more than it is merely the art of telling a story. It is also an attempt to rediscover truths hitherto unappreciated. The painter cannot himself work without technique, and the historian (who is not absolutely an artist) must undergo the discipline of research. The selection which is the basis of his work must be capable of justification in the record of the past. Otherwise his work will become a party pamphlet or a tendentious tract. This was in fact the danger to Green, and it accounts for the striking defects in what was such a great achievement. The strange fallacies which mar a book which has never lost its beneficial influence are all due to the fact that, here, a quality essential to great historical writing is not sufficiently under control. Green certainly never achieved that completely historical standpoint

attained, for example, by Stubbs or Maitland, neither of whose pro-
nounced opinions could be guessed from their historical work. But, on
the whole, Green succeeded in overcoming most of the difficulties inherent in his great design, and his passionate love of England and of her
past was alone sufficient to save him from disaster. He was not himself
averse from pure research and was widely read in the available authorities.
If he was no discoverer in the narrower sense, no man has ever been more
conscious of the way in which the present is the direct outcome of the
development of the past. 'All his work was real and original work,'
remarked Stubbs, 'and few people except those who knew him well would
see under the charming ease and vivacity of his style the sustained industry
of the laborious student.' No one at any rate has ever been more conscious
of the historical map of England, of the appearance of her cities at various
periods, or of time's alterations to the spectacle of her countryside. And
no modern reader can peruse the description of Green's visit to Ebbsfleet
and deny to him on the one hand an imagination which was purely
historical, and on the other a critical faculty which could hold it in check.

'Be not like the empiric ant which merely collects nor like the cobweb-
weaving theorists who do but spin webs from their own intestines; but
imitate the bees which both collect and fashion.' After the lapse of four
centuries this continues to be the ideal of the historian. And, with all his
faults, Green approached it. He steered successfully between the opposed
extremes of a romancer writing picturesquely for profit and the barren
compiler whose massed and contradictory authorities produce a stalemate
of suspended judgement. He was the child of his age and he shared its
prejudices. But he did not write history the less well because he loved
England like Morris or reverenced liberty like Mill. Green had an original
contribution to make to English literature and thought, and this could
only be stated by him in historical terms. For the first time he wrote the
history of the people of a great nation as if it was a record of organic
growth. The English people whom Green loved and served was for him
the product of forces which had operated through remote centuries.

After Green, English history became, for the mass of English students,
something different from a dead record of the fall of forgotten dynasties
and the clash of superseded factions; it was transformed into a story which
was almost personal since it concerned the inherent life of a still living
community in whose vitality both he and his readers shared. As the
brilliant and original expression of this vital continuity linking the present
indissolubly with the past, the *Short History* added to historical scholarship
a work which has something of the unity of a biography and something of
the majesty of an epic. Herein lies the secret of Green's influence, and this
was the achievement of a brief life which itself almost approached the
heroic. In contemplating it we can turn without great difficulty from

Victorian England to find Lord Berners presenting a very different historian to the English people:

> What condygne graces and thankes ought men to gyve to the writers of historyes, who with their great labours, have done so moche profyte to the humayne life. . . . Albeit that mortall folke are marveylously separated, both by lande and water, and right wonderously sytuate; yet are they and their actes (done peradventure by the space of a thousande yere) compact togyder by th' histographier, as it were the dedes of one selfe cyte, and in one mannes lyfe.

England's introduction to Froissart: her tribute to the memory of Green.

IV

Marc Bloch: A Master-Historian

In 1939 there appeared the first volume of a great book by a notable French medievalist. Its title was *La Societé féodale*, and fellow scholars of Marc Bloch in England will recall the emotion with which they received its sequel, in 1940, as from 'an author on active service'. The earlier books of Marc Bloch had led them to believe that this would be a work of major importance, and they confidently expected that it would be followed by other studies of equal importance. Only one of these hopes was to be fulfilled. The work which had been delivered into their hands was in truth to become, in the words of Professor Postan, 'the standard international treatise on feudalism'. But Marc Bloch, himself, was soon to enter the last and most distinguished phase in his career. In 1940 this middle-aged scholar who had fought for France with honour in the First World War joined the Resistance: in 1941 he was captured and subjected to torture: and on 16 June 1944 he was led with others into a field near Lyons and shot. He fell with the cry 'Vive la France'. He was then fifty-eight years of age.

His influence on medieval scholarship has been profound, and it is remarkable therefore that his last major work of erudition, so large in scope and so fundamental in content, has never until now been translated into English. The appearance of *Feudal Society* is thus wholly to be welcomed, and Mr L. A. Manyon deserves our gratitude.[1] His translation is not impeccable, but it is competent and adequate, and it may serve to introduce to a wider English public a seminal scholar and remarkable man.

This is certainly to be desired. For Bloch never addressed his work solely to professional historians, and it was his aim to relate history not only to cognate studies but also to those problems of contemporary life with which he was himself so closely concerned. A distinguished American medievalist has rightly called attention to Bloch's 'conviction of the unity of all history, and of the living connection between past and present'. And it is noteworthy how many of the questions discussed with detailed learning in *Feudal Society* appear as topics in *Strange Defeat*, that moving fragment of autobiography which was written in the months before his death and published after his murder.

The general character of the present book may help to account for the influence of Marc Bloch, which otherwise might be difficult to explain. Bloch was not the greatest French historian of his generation, nor does his prose always possess that limpid lucidity which is peculiarly characteristic of the best French scholarship. None the less he is of the same company as Fustel de Coulanges, who was one of his predecessors at Strasbourg, or of Ferdinand Lot and Joseph Bédier who were among his colleagues at Paris.

He had the ability to paint on a wide canvas without ever losing his mastery of detail: he could draw illuminating analogies from past and present events; and he could lay bare the essentials of his subject without indulging in 'those paper wars in which scholars have sometimes engaged', he remarks, 'not historians, is my concern,' and for this reason the integrated bibliography which he added to his text was not the least interesting part of his book. This has, fortunately, been reproduced, 'History,' almost intact, in the present volume, and it is nearly as valuable as when it first appeared. The same praise cannot, however, be accorded to the short supplement which has apparently been added by the translator, for this includes at least three items which are incorrectly cited, including one magisterial book by Bloch himself.

Feudal Society is as important for its method as for its content. 'Feudalism' is a term of many meanings, and Bloch gave it the widest possible connotation, recalling wittily that present officers of the Légion d'Honneur are required by its constitution 'to combat . . . any enterprise tending to re-establish the feudal *régime*'. And what were the marks of that regime in his historical setting?

> A subject peasantry; widespread use of the service tenement (particularly the fief) in place of salary . . .; the supremacy of a class of specialized warriors; ties of obedience and protection which bind man to man, and, within the warrior class, assume the distinctive form called vassalage; fragmentation of authority – leading inevitably to disorder; and in the midst of all this the survival of other forms of association, family and State – such seem to be the fundamental features of European feudalism.

Though a slightly different emphasis might now be given to some of the terms – notably the date at which salaried service became important – the summary, after twenty years, could today hardly be bettered. But even this statement did not comprise the full scope of this inquiry. The ideas, and the ideals, of men must also be examined to analyse and to explain a social organization and its unifying principles. 'Like all the phenomena revealed by that science of eternal change which is history, the social structure thus characterized certainly bore the peculiar stamp of an age and an environment.'

This wide treatment of the subject has a special relevance to English feudal studies which have in the main been concentrated more exclusively upon the military and legal aspects of feudalism. Since the days of Round, the origins of English feudalism have been sought predominantly in those contracts which William the Conqueror made with his magnates whereby these, in return for their lands, were required to come to the service of the king with a specified number of trained and fully equipped mounted knights. This military organization, it is said, ignored Old English precedent, and, in this sense, it has been concluded that 'it is hardly possible to speak of any trend towards feudalism in England before 1066'. Moreover, much of the later development of English public law and constitutional growth is found to have depended upon these arrangements, and the manifold obligations they entailed. These too may, thus, in their turn, be referred back to the events which followed the Norman Conquest – events which gave a new aristocracy to England, but which had no corresponding effect on the life or the condition of the English peasantry.

The special value of this approach (thus inadequately summarized) to the particular problems of English medieval history need not be emphasized. Certainly, Bloch gave full prominence to such ideas in his own book, a large section of which describes the origin and character of vassalage with a wealth of erudition. On the other hand, in his view, the fief was only one element, though an important one, in feudal organization; and to concentrate too exclusively on the military and aristocratic features of feudal society would be, for him, to oversimplify its nature. Only by means of a far wider inquiry did he hope to elucidate the social structure of western Europe between, say, 850 and 1250, and to account for its distinctive features. There was, of course, within this epoch the division marked by the middle of the eleventh century when economic change, and the growth of settled administration, prepared the way for the twelfth-century renaissance and the great medieval monarchies. But the same broad lines of development can be traced throughout, and the framework of institutions then established 'can in the last resort be understood only through the knowledge of the whole human environment'.

In keeping with these ideas, this great treatise falls naturally into two parts. The first describes the social background which began to form when western Europe was, so to speak, in a state of siege, vexed with the attacks of Muslims, Hungarians or Northmen. Then were evolved those bonds of interdependence between men which, more than anything else,

gave to feudal society its special character, when aristocracies organized
for war, and sustained by a servile peasantry, seemed essential to the
defence of Europe. The other section of the work concentrates more
particularly on the development of social classes until at last the resuscitation of central authority, economic progress and the rise of the bourgeoisie
begin to presage the end of feudal society.

The value of such an extended inquiry depended of course on the manner
in which it was conducted, and the merit of this book derives in the first
instance from the massive scholarship upon which it is based. Bloch's
command of his material is always impressive, and his generalizations
were securely founded upon a meticulous examination of the available
evidence. His conclusions on points of detail were naturally not invariably
correct, and (to take a specific example) his re-dating of the first life of
Edward the Confessor was probably wrong. But, in general, he is admirably critical, and when he found finality impossible he was scrupulous to
proclaim uncertainties as dubious. His theories, in short, were formidably
buttressed by fact, and he lived up to his own precept that 'those who
teach history should be continually concerned with the task of seeking
the solid and the concrete behind the empty and the abstract'.

Equally remarkable was the range of his investigations, and his constant
endeavour to utilize new types of evidence. It is a truism that the materials
of the historian are multitudinous, and are not confined to written records.
But Bloch was particularly successful in his search for additional testimony. Some eight years before the appearance of *Feudal Society*, he had
published what some would regard as his greatest book: *Les caractères
originaux de l'histoire rurale française*, wherein place-names, aerial surveys,
ancient implements and folk-lore are all profitably called in to assist the
elucidation of the relevant documents. The result was perhaps the most
illuminating exposition that exists of the realities of French peasant life
in the Middle Ages. Soil and topography, techniques of cultivation and
forms of settlement were for Bloch among the essential sources of exact
history, and they were particularly important in describing an age in
which agriculture was the basic occupation of men.

Bloch's interests were strongly directed towards the material bases of
historical development. His Chair was that of Economic History, and the
review which he conducted with Lucien Febyre – the *Annales d'histoire
économique et sociale* – became a principal forum for the discussion of such
topics. His own personal concerns led him also in the same direction.
Bloch was keenly interested in the industrial problems of his own age, and
not aloof from its political controversies. It deserves emphasis, therefore,
how resolutely he refused to restrict himself, in his interpretation of the
past, to the observation of economic phenomena.

And if man is not to be treated merely as an economic animal, so also is he not to be regarded solely as a rational being. The institutions he creates, the social structures he builds, cannot be explained without reference to 'modes of feeling and thought'. Thus the method of *Feudal Society* has to be related (in Bloch's earlier work) not only to his fundamental studies of the French peasantry but also to his equally remarkable *Rois thaumaturges* – a fascinating investigation of the supernatural character attributed to the royal power, particularly in France and England. And this treatise in its turn has exercised a wide influence which is to be discerned, for instance, in the more recent studies of E. H. Kantorowicz. It was entirely characteristic of Bloch to remark:

> There are two categories of Frenchmen who will never grasp the significance of French history: those who refuse to be thrilled with the Consecration of our Kings at Rheims, and those who can read unmoved the account of the Festival of Federation.

Bloch's sympathies were not to be circumscribed, nor was his intellectual curiosity to be restricted. A Jew by birth, he confessed that he had 'never professed any creed whether Hebrew or Christian', yet he would not depict feudal Europe without due regard for the religion which informed it. Passionately French in his patriotism and in his culture, his work never bore any trace of provincialism. And the sincere integrity of his scholarship was matched by his pervading reverence for justice. The austere morality which pervades his work was perhaps in part derived from an ancestor who fought in the Revolutionary Wars, and almost the last words he wrote were taken from Montesquieu: 'A State founded on the People needs a mainspring; and that mainspring is Virtue.'

All these preoccupations find expression in *Feudal Society*. The peasant appears in company with the knight, the manor alongside the fief, and throughout there is displayed the formative undercurrent of emotions and ideas. The worker is questioned in the field, the scholar in his study, the poet with his theme. There is the 'folk memory' which he finds expressed, for instance, in the *Song of Roland*; there is the religious background with its hopes and haunting terrors; there are the foundations of law, chivalry and the rules of aristocratic conduct.

It is not to be suggested that the more immediate sources of information have been thereby neglected, for the basis of the work remains the feodaries and cartularies, the law books and surveys of the age. But here it is not only military service, not only tenures and dependencies, not only legal obligations, and the modes of military action, that are so thoroughly examined, but also the motives which underlay their establishment. The Bayeux Tapestry, here so carefully considered, was not made in order to provide historians with evidence for the techniques of medieval mounted warfare; charters were compiled in answer to a present need, and not to supply later commentators with testimony about the development of contracts. The precise nature of vassalage must be elucidated, but we must also ask 'what it was in the actions and hearts of men that constituted the real strength of vassalage as a social cement'.

A book thus planned and executed may be held to present a fuller and more authentic picture of European society in the feudal age than can be supplied by any treatise restricted to a more limited conception of feudalism. But perhaps the greatest quality of *Feudal Society*, and that which has ensured its enduring influence, is that, like all the greatest works of historical scholarship, it is unmistakably lit from an inward individual fire and stamped from first to last with the author's own vivid personality. For that reason, the erudition displayed, which is both detailed and profound, is here illumined by human warmth and sympathy, and as a result it is paradoxically true that while *Feudal Society*, always intensely readable, remains the best first introduction for any student to the subject with which it deals, it serves, for the specialist, as an inevitable starting-point for further research. The scholarship and the life of Marc Bloch were both of heroic texture. Together they have placed him unassailably among the masters.

NOTE

[1] Marc Bloch, *Feudal Society*. Translated by L. A. Manyon (Routledge and Kegal Paul).

V

The Norman Conquest and
British Historians

My purpose in this lecture is to consider a great and familiar event in British history; to illustrate how it has been regarded at various times by British historians; and to show how their conclusions were influenced not only by their own studies, but also by the circumstances in which they wrote. Such an investigation[1] is perhaps unusual, but I should like to claim for it a dual interest. It should concern students of medieval history as perhaps indicating profitable lines for future research, and it should also raise certain other related questions. How far in the light of the story I am about to tell can history be regarded as a dispassionate science? Have improvements in the technique of discovery always produced increased understanding? Can a people at any time be judged to some extent by the manner in which it regards its own past? Does a nation usually get the historians it deserves?

The Norman Conquest has now engaged the constant attention of British historians, and inspired the voluminous production of English men of letters for more than four hundred years. A great turning-point in our history has perhaps naturally provoked a mass of erudition which is staggering in its weight and bulk; but it is more surprising that a political crisis of the eleventh century should have led generations of statesmen and lawyers, pamphleteers and scribblers into a war of words about a subject which might well have been deemed to lie outside their interest. Here surely is a most curious phenomenon of British scholarship. And the end is not yet. Today, although the Norman Conquest has been assiduously discussed for over four centuries, few periods in our history remain more controverted. That, in fact, is the sad and salutary paradox which I wish to pose to you this afternoon, and if possible to explain and resolve.

The modern literature of the Norman Conquest covers almost the whole span of English prose. Already in 1530 John Rastell gave the matter some attention in his *Pastyme and Peoples*,[2] and with the opening of the seventeenth century men of all sorts and conditions began zealously to discuss the history of eleventh-century England. In 1613 John Hayward produced what may be called the first text-book on the subject,[3] and shortly afterwards two very great scholars directed their energies to its investigation. In 1623 John Selden published his memorable edition of Eadmer's *Historia Novorum*,[4] and six years later Sir Henry Spelman inaugurated the study of Anglo-Norman feudalism with his great essay on *Feuds and Tenures by Knight Service*.[5] A like concern with the legal antiquities of the eleventh century was shown after the Restoration by Dr Robert Brady,[6] Physician in Ordinary to Charles II; and Matthew Hale, Chief Justice of the King's Bench, devoted to the same theme no less than forty pages of his remarkable *History of the Common Law*.[7] Similarly, when in 1695 Sir William Temple issued his *Introduction to the History of England*, it was found that five-sixths of that book were concerned with the Norman Conquest, and during the eighteenth century Abraham Farley devoted forty years of his industrious life to produce in 1783 what is still the standard edition of Domesday Book.[8] Such erudition was not easy to master or imitate, but many rushed in where they might have feared to tread, and almost all the controversies of that disputatious age were adorned and disfigured by references to Anglo-Norman history. Writers like Fabian Phillipps[9] and William Prynne[10] found here plenty of material for scholarly dispute, and at the same time the story of the Conquest, duly coloured, was made available to the general reading public. Sir Roger de Coverley,[11] who placed the history of Sir Richard Baker[12] conveniently in his hall window, could read therein comfortably about the adventures of William the Conqueror, and the subject, differently embroidered, was later treated in the standard Whig histories of Echard and Tyrrell.

Before the middle of the eighteenth century the literature of the Norman Conquest had already grown to a vast size, and to explain this productive zeal it would be necessary to refer to the special temper of an age which combined a fervent partiotism with a respect for tradition. It is well to remember that all the controversies which vexed England during that epoch of Civil War and Revolution were debated by reference to precedent, whilst the exuberant nationalism of the period coloured all its embattled disputes. The result was curious. On the one hand this immediate purpose gave the spur to a scholarly production of enduring value. But on the other hand the history of eleventh-century England became so denaturalized that even today it is hard to penetrate to the realities of eleventh-century history save through a haze of heated polemical vapour. The fathers had eaten sour grapes and the children's teeth were set on edge.

The nationalistic interpretation of the Norman Conquest which was later to find notable expressions in the work of Thierry[13] took from the start two contrasted forms. Some moved by the personal glory of the Norman kings found in their achievements the beginnings of British greatness. John Hayward in 1613 dedicated his book on the Conqueror and Henry I to the sons of James VI because (as he said) 'the persons of whom it treateth are those most worthy ancestors of yours who laid the foundations of this English Empire'.[14] For other reasons, Sir William Temple dilated on 'the happy circumstances of this famous Conquest',[15] and the comforting thought was powerfully reinforced by aristocratic prejudice. To assert descent from one who had fought for William at Hastings came very early to be almost a matter of course in any noble family. Elizabethan heralds – notably Gilbert Dethick – were at hand to supply the necessary evidence, and the claims did not cease to multiply. The Victorian poet might prefer kind hearts to coronets, but many of his contemporaries seem to have been eager to distil into their veins a synthetic mixture of Norman blood.[16] Although the names of less than forty of King William's followers at Hastings can be vouched by express testimony,[17] and although direct descent in the male line from any one of these would be very hard to establish, 'to have come over with the Conqueror' is a boast not entirely unknown today. Nor can this apparently harmelss foible be wholly ignored by the historian. 'The ludicrous side of pedigree-making,' wrote that fine scholar, George Burnett, Lyon King of Arms, 'must not blind us to the graver consequences connected with it.'[18] It has certainly since the Elizabethan age cast a deceptive and illusory light on Anglo-Norman scholarship.

In such manner has the Norman Conquest been treated as a matter for patriotic pride. But the same preoccupation with nationalism led to an equally strained interpretation in the contrary sense. By many early writers the Norman Conquest was represented as a national tragedy and even as a national disaster. The note of regret which is strikingly absent in Rastell is to be heard already in Camden's *Britannia*,[19] and I have sometimes wondered whether here is the reason why one of the most dramatic episodes in the British story was not used by Shakespeare in his Histories. Be this as it may, when Winston Churchill, father of the first Duke of Marlborough, produced in 1685 his *Divi Britannici*, he paid tribute to those who fought against William as being

> willing to be as they were then made immortal who bravely strove with Destiny to save their country from the calamity of foreign servitude.[20]

This conception, reproduced with endless reiteration during the ensuing generations and consecrated at last by popular novelists,[21] remains as probably the most widely-spread idea respecting the Norman Conquest today.

From the beginning, however, it entailed curious consequences. Propagated at a time when Puritanism was in the ascendant, it supplied the obvious occasion for a moral judgement. A well-known passage in the chronicle of William of Malmesbury[22] thus gave the opportunity to John Milton, who in his *History of Britain*[23] painted this picture of Anglo-Saxon society at the time of its downfall:

> The great men given to Gluttony and dissolute Life, made a prey of the Common People . . . the meaner sort tipling together night and day, spent all they had in Drunkenness, attended with other Vices which effeminate men's minds. Whence it came to pass that carried on with fury and rashness more than any true fortitude or skill of War they gave to William their Conqueror so easie a Conquest.

This view, also, had been frequently reproduced. Sir Francis Palgrave found an explanation of the Norman Conquest in a degeneracy of the Anglo-Saxon character,[24] and at about the same time Thomas Carlyle re-echoed Milton with ringing emphasis. Without the Normans, he cried:

> What had it ever been? A gluttonous race of Jutes and Angles capable of no grand combinations; lumbering about in pot-bellied equanimity; not dreaming of heroic toil and silence and endurance such as leads to the high places of this universe, and the golden mountain tops where dwell the spirits of the dawn.[25]

As applied to the race which in 1066 fought the battles of Fulford and Stamford Bridge, and which some eighty years before gave perfect expression to the heroic spirit in the Maldon Poem, Carlyle's judgement can perhaps best be excused by the fact that it was not original. National disasters have, however, a way of inspiring the rhetoric of political moralists, and, as we have recently observed in France, men discover very readily in such calamities an expiation of national sin.

From regarding the Norman Conquest as a national humiliation, it was but a step to explain it away. At a very early date, therefore, it was in some quarters held to be more decent to speak of the Norman 'acquisition', or even of the Norman 'purchase' of England.[26] A veritable social contract could be postulated between the Conqueror and a lady described as 'Britannia', 'his sacred queen'.[27] This conception, too, has survived from the seventeenth century in a continued effort to regard the period of Norman and Angevin rule in England as a kind of interruption – as an unproductive interlude – in our national story. 'For nearly two centuries after the Norman Conquest,' asserts the writer of a deservedly popular manual, 'there is no history of the English people',[28] and he goes on to liken the rule of the Normans in England to that of the English in India. England, it is elsewhere suggested, as a result of a 'wave of barbarian immigration', then passed under 'foreign kings',[29] but these and all they represented disappeared, at some unspecified date, and the waking life of the nation was then resumed once more. 'A man may end,' wrote G. K. Chesterton, 'by maintaining that the Norman Conquest was a Saxon Conquest.'[30] He was scarcely exaggerating.

By such devious routes did William the Conqueror descend into the arena of seventeenth-century politics, and in so doing he became the especial enemy of the Whigs. If he was justly to be stigmatised as a foreign tyrant, then the lessons of his life must surely be brought home to the discontented subjects of the Stuart kings. The controversies of the Oxford Parliament were thus embellished by a documented diatribe against the first Norman king, which quoted Coke that it was neither 'ingenious or prudent for Englishmen to deprave their birthright', and concluded that 'the true honour of our worthy Saxon ancestors' should be supported.[21] This was in 1681. But soon the Whig historians were faced, as a result of the Revolution of 1688, by a perplexing problem. After all, there was a third William as well as a first, and both came from overseas. Here was food for uncomfortable reflection! 'I propose,' wrote John Toland in 1701

to deduce this argument from William the Norman to this very time . . . to undeceive those (or their adherents) who may think themselves injured by being set aside though they be next of kin.[32]

Thus for two decades after 1688 a certain discomfort appears in these writers, and with some cause. To display the Conqueror as a tyrant destroying ancient liberties, and at the same time to depict him as the prototype of William of Orange, the Great Deliverer, was a task which might well prove daunting. Yet during the latter years of the seventeenth century it was actually attempted – notably in 1695 in the work of Temple and his commentators.[33] But to explain 'what we gained by our loss in this Conquest'[34] proved at last too much for the ingenuity even of the Whig historians, and in 1714 John Fortescue Aland succinctly stated what was henceforth to be orthodox Whig doctrine in this matter.

Should we allow our laws to have an uncertain Original, I fear that some people would of themselves fix their original from William the First and . . . I don't know what ill use the Champions of Absolute monarchy may be inclined to make of such a Concession.[35]

Yet another idea respecting the Norman Conquest was thus at length hatched out of contemporary controversy. It was seemly – it might even be useful – to depict William as a tyrant, but if proper point was to be given to the story, it was necessary to assume the nation which he subdued to have been imbued with Protestant sympathies, and to have been possessed of democratic, or at least of Whig, institutions. What a lesson for posterity, if a people so admirably disposed could be sadly shown to have succumbed in 1066 to the combined forces of Popery and Absolutism! The attempt was made. As early as the time of Elizabeth, Matthew Parker had sponsored a great movement in Anglo-Saxon scholarship in the hope that he might find in the Old English church a prototype of the reformed Establishment over which he was called to preside. 'This is no small satisfaction,' wrote a later scholar in 1709, 'that we reap from Saxon Learning that we see the Agreement of the reformed and the ancient Saxon church.'[36] But for the analogy to be made effective it had to be pressed more particularly on its secular side, and in this manner there was prepared in a long series of books the still familiar picture of Anglo-Saxon society as consisting of communities of freemen legislating for themselves in democratic committees which in the last resort could elect and depose their kings. The wheel had at last turned full circle. William the Conqueror is no longer the founder of British greatness: he has become the subverter of the British constitution. The Anglo-Saxons whom he overthrows are no longer a race of drink-sodden degenerates, but the fit forbears of those who wrought the Glorious Revolution.

The posthumous career of William the Conqueror in English letters is almost as remarkable as his actual career in British history. Nevertheless this long-sustained interest in the Norman Conquest was productive not only of an ebullient polemic, but also of profound erudition, and it will be an object of this lecture to recall attention to this neglected learning. Nor were there wanting some writers who in this matter did strive after objectivity. Thus Sharon Turner, albeit with imperfect equipment, sought to represent the Saxons as they were and not as they ought to have been,[37] and John Lingard, in writing his admirable account of the Norman Conquest, avowedly in the first instance applied himself only to original authorities in the expressed hope that he might thereby be enabled to avoid copying the mistakes of others.[38] Such conscious attempts at detachment were, however, rare,[39] and public opinion was slow to change. In general, it is true to say that William the Conqueror, who in the time of the Stuarts became a combative figure in English party politics, continued to remain so in the middle of the nineteenth century.

Then Edward Freeman came.

Between 1867 and 1879 Edward Augustus Freeman produced in five large octavo volumes each containing over seven hundred pages the most elaborate history of the Norman Conquest which has ever been compiled. A disciple of Dr Arnold, he was himself a product of the nineteenth-century revival of historical studies, and with a clear-cut conception of history he brought to his task rare qualities of mind and character. He had tireless energy, a fine sense of historical topography,[40] and a knowledge of the narrative sources of Anglo-Saxon history which has rarely been equalled. Thus equipped, he set out to tell the story of the Norman Conquest down to the ultimate detail, and it is little wonder that he produced a remarkable book. The fact needs emphasis. As a detailed narrative of the Norman Conquest, Freeman's book has never been superseded, and it is those best versed in the history of eleventh-century England who are most conscious of its value.

Nevertheless, it may be doubted whether any work of comparable importance in English historical literature has ever been more easy to criticize than Freeman's *Norman Conquest*. It was in Green's phrase 'far too rhetorical and diffuse',[41] and yet despite its excessive length, it concentrated too exclusively upon strictly political events. Nor was the treatment of the authorities itself comprehensive, so that a generation which has been taught to value the record sources of history, and which pays perhaps even an excessive reverence to material which has not yet been printed, is inevitably sceptical of an historian who neglected records, who misinterpreted Domesday Book, and who positively boasted his contempt for manuscripts.[42] Freeman was, in fact, more erudite than critical, and even the narrative sources which were the sure foundation of his work were sometimes by him mishandled. Generally, as J. R. Green remarked,[43] he tended to be unjust to the Norman writers, but otherwise he often gives the impression of giving equal credence to all his authorities and of blending together their contradictory accounts into an unreal synthesis. In this way his account of the crisis of 1051–2 is, for instance, incomprehensibly confused.[44] It must, moreover, be added that, having made up his mind, he could show a most obstinate bias towards his sources, selecting only those which could best illustrate his point of view. His famous battle-picture of Hastings was itself vitiated by being so largely derived from the *Roman de Rou* of Wace.[45]

Freeman's *Norman Conquest* was, in short, magisterial without being definitive, and the book which might have been expected to induce a calmer temper into Anglo-Norman studies had paradoxically precisely the opposite effect. The reasons for this were personal as well as public. Besides being a sincere historian, Freeman was also a brutal controversialist, and he was at the same time himself unduly sensitive to criticism.[46] Such a man should not present himself as a target to his enemies. This Freeman did. His critics thereupon advanced to the attack with an outraged acerbity, and his friends replied by defending him where he was

least defensible.[47] The prolonged controversy[48] which ensued was conducted by both sides with an astonishing lack of generosity,[49] and it is
now chiefly memorable as having provoked the constructive criticism of
John Horace Round. Round was to influence Anglo-Norman scholarship
for a generation, but it is none the less permissible to deplore the manner
in which his fine erudition was here utilized to give point to a personal
attack. Concerned without restraint to demolish the scholarly reputation
of his chief opponent, he was so far successful as unduly to diminish
Freeman's posthumous fame. The man who had dealt out small justice
and less courtesy to Froude thus himself received scant justice from
posterity. It is unfortunate, however, that today most undergraduates
should know of Freeman only through the writings of his embittered
critics. It would be still more unfortunate if he were to be finally judged
by means of some facile caricature[50] made of one who can justly be
claimed as an Eminent Victorian – that is to say, a distinguished man in a
most distinguished age.

There is little doubt, however, that as the historian of the Norman
Conquest, Freeman developed many of the worst elements of the tradition
he inherited. He, too, like his predecessors, treated the eleventh-century
struggle almost as a matter of present politics and judged it accordingly. A
militant Teutonist, he declared that he would gladly have fought against
William at Hastings, and he specifically described William's opponents as
the 'patriotic leaders' of the 'national party'.[51] In one respect, indeed, he
carried these preoccupations a stage further. Many previous writers had
compiled as history a political polemic against the Conqueror, but usually
they had done this not in the interests of Godwin and Harold, Earls of
Wessex, but in those of Edgar Atheling.[52] For Sir William Temple,
Harold was 'perfidious and insolent';[53] for Matthew Hale a 'usurper';[54]
William's title, observed Blackstone, was 'altogether as good as Harold's'.[55]
In his glorification of Godwin and Harold, Freeman certainly had some
predecessors, and in particular he had read a popular novel by Lord
Lytton.[56] But it was left to Freeman authoritatively to present to the
British public Godwin and Harold, Earls of Wessex, as the champions of
English nationalism, as the enemies of priestcraft, and most strangely of
all, as among the friends of Parliamentary government.[57]

Freeman's approach to his subject was in essentials not different from
that of his predecessors; and as an historian of the Norman Conquest he
belongs to an earlier tradition. Since his day, therefore, Anglo-Norman
scholarship has been marked not so much by a development of his ideas as
by a reaction from them. Modern research has tended to destroy at last the
old notion which he popularized that the Norman Conquest was a
national struggle, and it has questioned the very existence in 1066 of an
English nation in the modern sense of the term. There are, it is true,

certain remarks in the Anglo-Saxon chronicles which indicate the occasional appearance of sentiments common to all England at this time,[58] but these found little expression in the politics of the period. England under Edward the Confessor showed small disposition to unite against the Normans; her political history was dominated by the rivalries of great earldoms; and her social structure was marked above all by the differences which continued to distinguish the several provinces of the late Old English state.[59] Godwin throughout his career acted primarily in the interests of his family, and Harold less than any of his immediate predecessors can be regarded as a national king. William the Conqueror on his side never had to face the resistance of a united England. He overcame separately a number of provinces, and in so doing he had a considerable measure of English support. Great English prelates such as Aldred of York and Wulfstan of Worcester showed little hostility to William's rule in England, and when the king in 1068 went to the West to suppress the Exeter rising there were already English soldiers in his army.[60]

The revulsion against a nationalistic treatment of the Norman Conquest has been caused, moreover, not only by a more detached investigation of political events, but also by the impact upon English historical scholarship of a new range of studies. In the same year which saw the completion of Freeman's *Norman Conquest* there appeared in Denmark the first of the four volumes of Steenstrup's *Normannerne*. It was the beginning of a movement of research which had as its object a new assessment of the Scandinavian contribution to European growth in the Middle Ages. Stubbs saw at once that this might have a considerable bearing on English historical studies,[61] but the Oxford school seem to have been strangely reluctant to recognize the importance of what were described as 'lucubrations' in 'an unknown tongue'.[62] Nevertheless, Scandinavian studies continued progressively to affect the interpretation of English history with consequences to be seen particularly in the agrarian and social investigations associated with the names of Maitland and Vinogradoff. Finally Professor Stenton in his *Danelaw Charters* and in his *Danes in England*, brought this Scandinavian learning into direct relation with English history, and his conclusions have more recently been reinforced by the systematic investigation of English place-names.[63]

A result of this work has been to place the history of England during the eleventh century in a new perspective. It is now realized that the consequences of earlier Scandinavian settlements in this country endured until the Norman Conquest. The Anglo-Saxon annals of the reign of Edward the Confessor show how constant was the threat that a Scandinavian dynasty might be restored in England, and there can be little doubt that such a restoration would have been welcomed through large areas of the country. When in 1070 men from a raiding Danish fleet took refuge in north

c

Lincolnshire, they joined naturally in the festivals of the countryside,[64] and Domesday Book reveals clearly that in 1086 the region formerly comprised in the Danelaw still retained many features characteristic of Scandinavia. It was therefore entirely in keeping with earlier history, and with its results, that the great crisis of 1066 should have been marked not only by the advent of William from Normandy, but also by a great Scandinavian invasion led by Harold Hardraada, King of Norway. The political significance of the Norman Conquest can no longer be sought in a struggle between 'English' and 'Normans'. It must be found in a triangular contest between a Norman Duke, a Norwegian King and a West Saxon Earl, as a result of which it would be determined whether for the remainder of the Middle Ages the development of England would be linked up with the Scandinavian north or with Latin Europe.

If the political interpretation of the Norman Conquest has thus been altered by modern scholarship, even more drastic has been the change in the assessment of its social consequences. In 1891 and 1892 John Horace Round, in two notable articles which were subsequently reprinted in his *Feudal England*,[65] contended that English feudalism was, in its essential military arrangements, a creation of the Normans in England. The Anglo-Norman knight was henceforth to be distinguished sharply, both as to status and obligations, from the Anglo-Saxon thegn, and the feudal organization to which he belonged owed little or nothing to Anglo-Saxon precedent.[66] Such a theory ran counter to what was then accepted teaching, for it was then strange doctrine to derive English feudalism not from the Saxon past, but from arrangements made by the Conqueror after his coming to England.[67] It was Round's achievement to emphasize the revolutionary importance of the contracts made between the Conqueror and his tenants-in-chief, whereby the latter in return for their land performed military service to the king with a specified number of knights; and it was in 1891 no less startling to suggest that the number of knights actually enfeoffed with land was determined by the tenant-in-chief at his pleasure, and bore no fixed relation either to the amount of service he owed or to the extent of the land he held.

Round's theory of knight-service is now the property of Macaulay's schoolboy, and he stated it with such combative emphasis that it is now always, and properly, associated with his name. But to the historian of English scholarship it is interesting to observe that the revolutionary doctrine which Round propounded in 1891 had been clearly stated in both its parts before the death of Charles I.[68] Henry Spelman, for instance, had been well aware that the feudal consequences of the Norman Conquest were cataclysmatic. 'Touching tenures in capite,' he remarked, 'I think I may boldly assert that there were none in England in the Saxons' time.'[69] Even the second and more original part of Round's theory had been neatly summed up in a more obscure tract of Sir Robert Bruce Cotton, which in 1657 was published among his posthumous papers:

> To supply his occasions of men money or provisions the Conqueror ordered that all those that enjoyed any fruit of his Conquest should hold their lands proportionably by so many knights fees of the Crown, *and admitted them to infeoff their followers with such part as they pleased of their own portions*.[70]

In explaining the feudal results of the Conquest, Round was in fact restating a theory which in its most essential implications had been held by scholars early in the seventeenth century, but which had been overlaid by a long tradition of misconception.

As a consequence, judgement on a considerable portion of British constitutional history has been affected. It is hardly unfair to suggest that Freeman and many of his contemporaries strove to introduce into Saxon England the beginnings of Parliamentary democracy. 'We must recognize,' he writes, 'the spirit which dictated the Petition of Right as the same which gathered all England round the banners of the returning Godwin, and remember that the "good old cause" is truly that for which Harold died on the field, and Waltheof on the scaffold.'[71] We are asked to note of Godwin that 'his eloquent tongue could not always *command a majority* in the Witan',[72] and to contemplate 'the fluctuations of success and defeat which he underwent in the great deliberative assembly'. 'We shall have to pass over several centuries,' concludes Freeman, 'before we come to another chief whose influence so clearly rests to so great a degree on his power of swaying great assemblies of men, or the personal affection or personal awe with which he learned to inspire the Legislature of the country.'[73] We shall indeed: for here in the eleventh century has been placed something very like a Victorian Parliament, and the phrases which describe Godwin, Earl of Wessex, could be applied without qualification and with greater truth to William Ewart Gladstone.

It has been a task of modern students of English feudalism not only to criticize the essential anachronism of such descriptions, but also and particularly to insist that at the Conquest there was a radical break in constitutional continuity. After the Conquest they would suggest the Witan was replaced by an assembly formed according to radically different principles – a feudal *curia* consisting essentially of the King's tenants-in-chief, and it was out of this *curia* that Parliament eventually grew. Nor were the Commons – 'the assembled people of England' – in any sense a part of this *curia* until the thirteenth century, and their first appearance therein is in the capacity of petitioners. Such a conception of Parliamentary growth popularized by Professor Pollard[74] and G. B. Adams[75] has now become a common-place. But it, too, for all its modernity, had been stated in a more distant past. When in 1694 Robert Brady produced his *Introduction to the History of England*, he had been careful to observe that before the thirteenth century:

> the Body of the Commons of England or Freemen collectively taken had not any share or votes in making of laws for the Government of the Kingdom unless they were represented by tenants in capite.[76]

This view would have shocked most Victorian historians, but it would hardly be disputed today.

Its final corollary is, however, being more slowly accepted. It is now generally recognized that the Norman *Curia Regis* was a feudal body formed to assist the King in the government of his realm, and that no part of its functions was to act as a constitutional check on the royal power. Nevertheless, the old Whig notion of Anglo-Norman history as a perpetual struggle between Legislature and Executive dies hard. Even Round was sometimes inclined to view the Norman aristocracy mainly as supplying elements of resistance to the Crown. But in truth the Norman magnates who surrounded William had no constitutional right, and can have felt little personal desire, to limit the Conqueror's power. Round's own fundamental researches, and the intensive study of private charters more recently undertaken by Professor Stenton,[77] have revealed how much the feudal settlement of England owed to the activities of the great Norman families. There was always, it is true, a danger of rebellions such as those which occurred in 1075 and 1102, and the disputed succession which ensued after 1135 provoked a disastrous civil war. But it was none the less essential to the survival of this small Norman aristocracy that it should cooperate in large measure with the Norman kings in the governance of England, and it is misleading to interpret the history of Norman England in the light of the constitutional crisis of the seventeenth century. All political systems when they are operative tend to exhibit a certain balance or tension which is very real, but the dominant theme of Anglo-Norman history is probably to be found not so much in an opposition between 'Crown' and 'Baronage', as in the reorganisation of England upon a feudal plan by a very able group of men with the King at their head.

It was largely owing to this cooperation that the Norman Conquest affected so vitally the future growth of the British constitution. So thorough, however, had been the recognition of the benefits conferred upon England by Anglo-Norman administration that this appreciation has even tended in some quarters to obscure the high qualities of the vernacular civilization which almost perished at the Conquest. As early as 1830 a Danish scholar, Grunvig, roundly declared:

> The creation of the modern civilized world . . . will never be understood without a familiar acquaintance with those Anglo-Saxons of whom it

has hitherto been held that no gentleman could wish to be introduced to them . . . From the beginning of the eighth century to the end of the eleventh [England] appears . . . to have been the most truly civilized country on the globe.[78]

Such sentiments (whatever their value) found little support in England during the ensuing decades, and even the Teutonism of the dominant Oxford historical school did not inspire its most prominent members to attempt any close investigations of Anglo-Saxon literature. The most recent movement of Anglo-Saxon linguistic studies has, however, led some of its foremost exponents to echo Grunvig's complaint that historians now pay too much attention to what the Normans created and too little to what they destroyed. Here, suggests Professor Chadwick, is 'the great defect of our historical education' – that the early history of this country has come down to us 'mainly through a Norman French tradition'.[79]

No one who has examined the Whig interpretations of the Norman Conquest dominant in this country for over two hundred years will be inclined to think that these were marked by any notable French bias, but it is still necessary to insist that an appreciation of what the Norman accomplished in England need involve no disparagement of the Anglo-Saxon achievement. In agriculture, in the local courts of shire and hundred, in the connection of these with the monarchy, in a long legislative tradition, and in many other ways the work of the older order was to survive into the new age. Moreover, although there can be little doubt that England was politically decadent in 1066, this decadence had not as yet seriously affected the civilization which the Saxons had produced but which they could no longer defend. The real weakness of Freeman's treatment of the Norman Conquest was in no sense that he over-praised Anglo-Saxon culture, but rather that he championed the Old English state for the least admirable of its features. But Round, owing to his own imperfect acquaintance with that culture,[80] never brought this criticism home to his chief opponent, and as a consequence the controversy tended to miss the chief point at issue. As Sisam has demonstrated,[81] England in the eleventh century was continuing to produce with great energy a vernacular literature not to be paralleled in contemporary Europe.

This literary output was by the Norman Conquest brought to an untimely end, and perhaps for that reason students of Saxon literature have often found it difficult to approach the events of the eleventh century with critical detachment. 'Thanks be to God,' exclaimed William Lisle in 1623, 'that he that conquered the land could not so conquer the language,'[82] and although his successors in linguistic study seem sometimes to disagree about the manner in which our language was transmitted to us, they seldom fail to share Lisle's pious gratitude for this limitation of the Norman Conquest. It would, however, be unfortunate if today a notable advance in a related field of studies were allowed to revive the special forms of nationalistic anachronism which have for so long disfigured Anglo-Norman historical scholarship.[83] Perhaps the two greatest achievements of medieval England were Anglo-Saxon vernacular culture and Anglo-Norman executive administration. I plead that now it should surely be possible to do justice to both without distorting the critical decades which divided them.

The extent to which recent studies in Old English have affected the interpretation of the Norman Conquest can be seen in the work of its greatest living historian. In 1908 Professor Stenton published his *William the Conqueror*) in 1943 he issued his definitive study of *Anglo-Saxon England*, wherein by carrying the story down to 1086 he included the best short account of the Norman Conquest which has ever been written. No one of the numerous company who have benefited, and who will continue to benefit, by both these remarkable books can fail to observe in the latter a greater emphasis on the value and persistence of Anglo-Saxon tradition. In 1943 Professor Stenton concluded:

> The Normans who entered into the English inheritance were a harsh and violent race. They were the closest of all western peoples to the barbarian strain in the continental order. They had produced little in art or learning and nothing in literature that could be set beside the work of Englishmen. But politically they were the masters of their world.[84]

The judgement is perhaps harsh. But it may well prove decisive.

If in the future it is modified to any appreciable degree, this will probably come about from an increasing knowledge of Norman history. Far less is known of pre-Conquest Normandy than of pre-Conquest England, and the result has been doubly unfortunate. Some scholars, faced by this lack of available information, have been eager hastily to deny to a province about which so little is known any formative influence on English growth. Others, less cautious, have sometimes been tempted to derive from pre-Conquest Normandy institutions and ideals whose operation has hitherto only been watched in English documents of a later date. As W. H. Stevenson wrote in 1896:

> The great tendency to ascribe to the pre-Conquest Normans the organization of later times and to exaggerate their civilization would be checked if it were more generally realized how exceedingly slight is the information that has come down to us as to their legal, fiscal, military and other organizations.[85]

The complaint in 1896 was probably justified, and even today, after the more recent work of Haskins,[86] it can be defended.

Nevertheless, it would be rash to endorse the opinion now widely current that this lack of information about the early history of Normandy is due to lack of material for its study. The history of Normandy in the earlier half of the eleventh century is illustrated by a contemporary chronicler of good standing, and by numerous narratives of a later date, one of which is of very high quality. It is illustrated also by a series of charters comparable in character, and when the relative size of the Kingdom and the Duchy is considered, comparable even in number, with the magnificent series of *diplomata* which have been made to illuminate the last century of Anglo-Saxon history. It deserves considerable emphasis that there are extant and in print not less than nineteen charters of Duke Richard II covering the period 1006–26; that for the period 1027–35 there are likewise available nearly as many charters of Duke Robert I; and that numerous similar documents exist for the Norman reign of William the Conqueror. A large number of private charters relating to Norman history between 1000 and 1066 have also been published. Such is the printed material. It is certain, moreover, that in the *archives* of Normandy, and particularly in those of Seine Inférieure, there remain happily unscathed large stores of still unprinted documents. It is premature to assert that all this evidence could not be used to elucidate the quality of the Norman influence on England. If little is known of the Normans before the Normans invaded England, it should not be assumed that this lack of knowledge is inevitable.

The comparative ignorance which prevails respecting early Norman history may be caused not so much by paucity of evidence as by the fact that this material has not as yet been adequately studied. The investigation of Norman antiquities conducted in the seventeenth century by André Duchesne and J. F. Pommeraye inspired no such company of successors as did in England the work of their contemporaries Spelman and Dugdale. The study of Norman history has until recently in France often been left in the hands of local investigators, sometimes of limited competence,[87] whilst in England this same study has usually been undertaken not for its own sake, but in a perfunctory manner as a prelude to the serious examination of some specifically English problem. As a result, much of the Norman material still remains, in point of criticism, in much the same condition as was the contemporary English evidence in the middle of the eighteenth century. Thus even the ducal charters have never been made the object of systematic collection such as in England was undertaken by Kemble, and these instruments which often explain each other are mainly to be found obscurely scattered in many various publications that are not easily accessible even to French students. Before it can be utilized, the vast bulk of this valuable material, both printed and unprinted, will need to be subjected to a far more searching criticism than it has as yet received. Points of chronology, authenticity, and especially of topography, which in English texts of similar date and comparable importance have usually received competent investigation, in the Norman documents very often still await elucidation.

Here, then, it may be suggested is an important field of research, which has up to now been only very imperfectly explored. He who should attempt its investigation will undoubtedly find himself faced by many intractable problems such as are usually associated with pioneer work. But if the guides are not very numerous, some of them are unusually distinguished. The labours of Stapleton and Round in England, of Haskins in America, of Gerville, Le Prévost and Charles de Beaurépaire in France have, for instance, prepared much of the ground, and there is clearly room here for close cooperation between English and French historians. Most important of all is the fortunate fact that one of the greatest medievalists of modern France devoted so much of his tireless energy to investigating the antiquities of his native province.[88] If the story of the 'Rise of Normandy' should ever be told, its telling will owe more to Leopold Delisle than to any other single man. And that chapter of still unwritten history will contribute directly to a better understanding of the Norman Conquest of England.

To survey a long movement of controversial scholarship in the course of a single lecture is in truth a hazardous undertaking, but I hope you will not think it has been presumptuous or wholly profitless. It may even have suggested to you certain general reflections. The Norman Conquest, by being so long an issue almost of contemporary politics, was studied with consistent zeal which would otherwise have been lacking, but as a consequence this eleventh-century crisis has been strangely and erroneously presented in terms of modern nationalism, of Whig theory, or Protestant fervour, and nineteenth-century liberalism. The shadow of polemic has hung heavily over these studies, and we are even now only tardily escaping from the consequent anachronisms. Today, indeed, it is even possible that the very effort at detachment may subject us to a new danger. The careful display of erudition which so often characterizes the modern monograph is wasted if the theme be insignificant, and if its treatment is such as to quench interest. Certainly, the subject I have ventured to offer to you this afternoon should induce in us a respect for our predecessors. The work of Brady and Farley, for example, is still of immediate value; modern feudalists have still much to learn from Spelman; latter-day Saxonists still debate with similar sentiments the problems which once so profitably engaged the attention of Lisle and Wanley; and when the history of pre-Conquest Normandy comes to be written, its basis will be the work of Delisle. Here, then, as I should like very diffidently to suggest, are obligations which it would become us more frequently to acknowledge, and here is an inheritance which it behoves us more assiduously to use. The vast literature of the Norman Conquest has placed at our disposal an accumulated erudition. For this very reason, that literature is not to be regarded merely as a curiosity of the past. It is a legacy to the present. It is an inspiration to the future. The modern student of medieval Britain is in very truth compassed about with a great cloud of witnesses, and our knowledge of the early history of our country may today be very substantially increased by paying reverent attention to the scholars of former centuries who laboured to teach us all.

NOTES

[1] I wish to thank Professor F. M. Stenton and Professor V. H. Galbraith for their kindness in criticizing this lecture. It would be a poor return for their generosity if I were to imply that they would necessarily have been in agreement with all the opinions here expressed. For these I must hold myself responsible.

[2] Ed. 1811, pp. 137, 138.

[3] *The Lives of the III Normans, Kings of England, written by I.H.* The matter was also discussed in the *Breviary of the History of England*, printed in 1693, and attributed, wrongly as it seems (cf. Hearne, *Collections*, x, 198), to Sir Walter Ralegh.

[4] The 'Notae et Spicilegium' are of particular value.

[5] Printed posthumously in *Reliquiae Spelmannianae*, edited by Edmund Gibson in 1698.

[6] For him and his work see Douglas, *English Scholars* (1939), pp. 154–60.

[7] Ed. 1739, pp. 70 *sqq.*

[8] Cf. P. C. Webb, *A Short Account of Domesday with a View to its Publication* (1756); H. Ellis, *Introduction to Domesday*, (1833), i, p. 360.

[9] In particular, *The Established Government of England vindicated from all Popular and Republican Principles and Mistakes* (1687). This rare book is repulsive in style, but valuable in matter.

[10] See list of publications given in Wood, *Athenae Oxonienses*, ed. Bliss, iii, cols. 854–877.

[11] See *Spectator*, no. 269.

[12] *Chronicle of the Kings of England*, first published in 1643.

[13] *Conquête d'Angleterre* (1825).

[14] 'Epistle Dedicatorie.'

[15] *Introduction to the History of England* (1695), pp. 313 *sqq.*

[16] On this matter see the twelve volumes of the *Ancestor* (1902–5).

[17] Cf. Douglas, 'Companions of the Conqueror', in *History*, xxviii, pp. 129 *sqq.*

[18] See *Popular Genealogists; or the Art of Pedigree Making*, published anonymously in 1865.

[19] Ed. 1772, i, p. 114.

[20] p. 187.

[21] *e.g.* Kingsley, *Hereward the Wake* (1866); C. Macfarlane, *Camp of Refuge* (1887).

[22] *Gesta Regum*, ed. Stubbs (1889), ii, p. 305.

[23] Ed. 1695, pp. 356, 357.

[24] Cf. *Collected Works*, iii, p. 332. 'I am reading Palgrave,' wrote Stubbs, apparently with reference to this passage, 'and am sorry to say I do not believe in him' (*Letters*, p. 105).

25 *Frederick the Great*, i, p. 415, quoted by Stubbs, *Constitutional History*, (ed. 1891), i, p. 236.

26 Cf. Spelman, *Glossarium Archaiologicum*, in voce 'Conquestum' ([ed. 1664], p. 145).

27 *Argumentum Anti-Normannicum* (1682).

28 A. F. Pollard, *The History of England* (Home University Library), pp. 31–3.

29 Green, *Short History*. Cf. also *History* (1937), xxii, p. 13.

30 *Orthodoxy* (1909), p. 126.

31 *Argumentum Anti-Normannicum* (1682), p. cliii.

32 *Anglia Libera* (1701), p. 110.

33 *Introduction to the History of England* (1695), especially pp. 302–17. The ingenuity of this most plausible piece of special pleading challenges admiration, and it was perhaps natural for Bishop William Nicolson, who did so much to stabilize the Revolution settlement in the North, to observe (see *English Historical Library* [ed. 1736], p. 76) that 'he makes such Reflections as become a Statesman and a Person so conversant in the Management of publick Affairs'.

34 Temple, *op. cit.*, p. 313. He adds, not without reason: 'it seems a contradiction'.

35 *The Difference between an Absolute and Limited Monarchy* (1714), p. xv.

36 E. Elstob, *English-Saxon Homily* (1709), p. xiv. The political implications of this in relation to the Norman Conquest are stressed by Lord Lyttleton in his *History . . . of Henry II* ([ed. 1767], i, pp. 10 *sqq*.). Lingard (*History of England*, [ed. 1835], ii, p. 8, note) protested effectively against this notion. 'I am aware,' he wrote, 'that this account is very different from that which is generally given in which Stigand appears to act the part of a patriot, and the success of William is attributed to the influence of the Bishops unwilling to offend the Pope.'

37 *History of the Anglo-Saxons* (1799–1805), esp. vols iii and iv.

38 See the fine passage in his preface (*History of England.* [ed. 1835], i, p. iv). Compare also M. Haile and E. Bonney, *Life and Letters of John Lingard* (n.d.), p. 138.

39 It was, however, with some exaggeration that J. R. Green (cf. *History*, xxviii, p. 88) described Roscoe's *William the Conqueror* (1846) as 'the most worthless biography in the English language'.

40 His *Sketches of a Tour in Normandy and Maine,* published posthumously in 1897, is a wholly admirable commentary on Anglo-Norman history.

41 Green to Dawkins, 2 February 1869 (*Letters,* p. 226).

42 See *Quarterly Review* (June 1892), p. 29.

43 Green to Freeman, 19 August 1868 (*Letters,* p. 197).

44 Cf. B. Wilkinson (*Bulletin of the John Rylands Library*, xxii, pp. 368–87).

45 Cf. Round, *Feudal England*, pp. 322 *sqq*.; Douglas in *History*, xxviii, pp. 131, 132.

46 According to his friend Canon Venables, 'he sometimes manifested an intolerance which was not always kept within the bounds of courtesy, and was painful to his victims and distressing to others'. For an effective protest against his controversial methods see H. Paul, *Life of Froude* (1905), pp. 147–98.

47 Cf. Round, *Feudal England*, pp. 322 *sqq*., etc.

48 The extent of this controversy can be judged by the long bibliography given in *Sussex Archaeological Collections*, vol. xliii. The discourtesy of the disputants can only be judged after a perusal of what they wrote.

49 Was it really necessary to print a savage attack (*Quarterly Review*, June 1892) upon Freeman within three months of Freeman's death? Round seems subsequently to have stated that he wrote this at some previous time (cf. Memoir by W. Page in Round, *Family Origins*, 1930, p. xxvi), but if so, the Editor of the *Quarterly* would appear to have taken his responsibilities lightly.

50 Lytton Strachey, *Portraits in Miniature* (1931), pp. 199–203.

⁵¹ Freeman, *Norman Conquest*, vol. ii *passim*; G. P. Gooch, *History and Historians in the Nineteenth Century* (1913), p. 348.

⁵² *The Hereditary Right of the Crown of England Asserted* (1713), a non-juring publication, defends William as 'the only person capable of defeating the Designs of Harold' (p. 29), and this view is strongly reflected in Hume's *History of England*.

⁵³ *Introduction to the History of England* (1695), p. 105.

⁵⁴ *History of the Common Law* (ed. 1739), p. 89.

⁵⁵ *Commentaries on the Laws of England* (ed. 1785), p. 89.

⁵⁶ He refers specifically to Lytton's *Harold* in *Norman Conquest* (ed. 1870), ii, p. 35.

⁵⁷ It should be noted how much more balanced is Green's estimate of these Earls of Wessex in his *Conquest of England* (1883). Mandell Creighton remarked, 'Freeman's worship of them is ridiculous. They were clearly ruffians' (Creighton to Mrs J. R. Green, 31 December 1883, printed in *Life and Letters of Mandell Creighton* [1904], i, p. 264).

⁵⁸ *A. S. Chron.* 'C' and 'D', s.a. 1052; and cf. R. W. Chambers, 'Continuity of English Prose' (*Early English Text Soc.*, vol. 183).

⁵⁹ See Stenton, *Types of Manorial Structure in the Northern Danelaw* (1910); Douglas, *Social Structure of Medieval East Anglia* (1927). Research has abundantly confirmed Green's acute comment to Freeman in 1869: 'What I am certain of is that up to the Norman Conquest these provincial divisions and provincial feelings played a far more important part than you historians have given them credit for' (*Letters of J. R. Green*, p. 220).

⁶⁰ *Orderic. Vitalis*, ed. Le Prévost, ii, p. 180.

⁶¹ Stubbs to Mrs J. R. Green, 29 March 1883: 'There are clearly rising controversies (Steenstrup, etc.) on some of these Danish questions' (*Letters of William Stubbs*, p. 194).

⁶² Stubbs to Macmillan, 9 January 1883 (*Ibid.*, pp. 189, 190).

⁶³ For a summary of the historical implications of the work of the English Place-Name Society on this question, see Stenton in *R. Hist. Soc. Trans.*, 4th Series, xxiv, pp. 1–24.

⁶⁴ *Orderic. Vitalis*, ed. Le Prévost, ii, p. 194.

⁶⁵ pp. 225–317.

⁶⁶ For subsequent criticisms of Round's theory, see Stenton, *English Feudalism* (1932), and in particular Chap. IV. Modifications of the doctrine now current are suggested in Douglas, *Feudal Documents* (1932), pp. xcv–c, and in *Domesday Monachorum* (1944), pp. 59–63.

⁶⁷ Freeman voiced opinions which would not have been gainsaid by Gneist or Stubbs when he observed (*Norman Conquest*, ed. 1876, v, p. 372): 'There is no ground for thinking that William directly or systematically introduced any new kind of tenure into the holding of English lands.' For parallel passages in the writings of other contemporary historians, see Round, *Feudal England*, pp. 261, 262.

⁶⁸ It must be emphasized that Round himself paid proper tribute to 'old views of the subject', but it may perhaps be doubted whether he fully realized the extent to which he had been anticipated by seventeenth-century writers. The name neither of Henry Spelman nor of Robert Bruce Cotton is to be found in the index to *Feudal England*.

⁶⁹ *Reliquiae Spelmannianae* (ed. Gibson, 1698), p. 10.

⁷⁰ *Cottoni Posthuma* (ed. 1672), p. 14 (my italics).

⁷¹ See *Life and Letters of E. A. Freeman*, i, p. 125.

⁷² Freeman, *Norman Conquest* (1870), ii, p. 35 (my italics).

⁷³ *Ibid.* He here quotes Lytton with approval: 'when the chronicler praises the gift of speech, he unconsciously proves the existence of constitutional freedom'. This makes strange reading today.

⁷⁴ e.g. *Evolution of Parliament* (1920).

[75] *e.g. Origin of the English Constitution* (1920).

[76] *Introduction to the Old English History* (1694), Preface.

[77] Notably in his *Documents illustrative of the Social and Economic History of the Danelaw* (1920), and most particularly in his *English Feudalism* (1932).

[78] See R. W. Chambers, *Exeter Book of Old English Poetry*, pp. 4–5.

[79] *The Study of Anglo-Saxon* (1941), p. 27.

[80] Round complained of Freeman's 'almost frantic prejudice' (*Peerage and Family History* [1901], p. 7), but the man who could refer (*Feudal England*, p. 318) to the 'arid entries in our jejune national chronicle' can hardly have approached with critical detachment the magnificent account given by the Anglo-Saxon chronicles of the reign of Edward the Confessor.

[81] *Review of English Studies*, vii, p. 7; viii, p. 51; x, p. 1.

[82] *Saxon Treatise* (1623), Preface.

[83] The militant nationalism which coloured the remarks of Professor Chambers about the Norman Conquest (see *Early Engl. Text Soc.*, vol. 183) is probably in this sense to be regretted, and the same attitude towards the Conquest may be detected even in Professor Chadwick's *Study of Anglo-Saxon*, particularly at pp. 25–7.

[84] *Anglo-Saxon England* (1943), p. 678.

[85] *English Historical Review*, xi, p. 733.

[86] In particular, *Norman Institutions* (1918). This is a notable book, but it is probably too soon to state (cf. Stenton, *English Feudalism*, p. 11) that 'unless discoveries of which there seems little prospect are still to be made, it is unlikely that future work on early Norman society will do more than supplement the outline which Professor Haskins has laid down'.

[87] As notable exceptions to this tendency must be mentioned the productions of the Chair of Norman History established in the University of Caen. Historical scholarship is indebted to its distinguished holders, such as Professor Contamine and the late Professor Prentout.

[88] Cf. P. Lacombe, *Bibliographie des Travaux de M. Leopold Delisle* (1902). The fine appreciation of Delisle by R. L. Poole is to be found in vol. v of the *Transactions of the British Academy* (1911). It was written by one of the very few men among Delisle's contemporaries who, as a medieval scholar, can be claimed to have ranked among his peers.

VI

Medieval Paris

There are men who in their time seem so to bestride their generation as almost to stand outside it. So also is it with cities which likewise possess their own inherent life. Yet in the one case as in the other, it is often the pre-eminent which best represents the generality, and no town has ever better reflected the civilization of which it formed a part than did medieval Paris. Its early growth was intimately connected with that of the medieval social order; the transformations which later came upon it exhibited the changes which were in due course to disrupt the medieval world; and in the resplendent interval of its medieval maturity, Paris between 1150 and 1300 took its place, as of right, as the most characteristic city of western Europe. It was, in this sense, the heir after a long interval of Antonine Rome. It was also in some respects the heir of that newer Rome on the banks of the Bosphorus which had helped to preserve the legacy of Mediterranean culture for the benefit of western men. In so far as the cultural achievement of the Middle Ages was based upon a classical tradition modified by the teaching of the Church, to this extent may medieval Paris be said to have represented that civilization at the climax of its development.

If, therefore, medieval Paris is best to be surveyed as it was in the thirteenth century, it was none the less the product of a long growth which itself accurately reflected some seven hundred years of European history. Certainly, no visitor to Paris in the time of St Louis could fail to be conscious of an intimate blend therein between the past and the present. At his first impression, for instance, he would have perceived the town to be dominated by the Christian Cathedral of Notre-Dame set on the island of the *Cité*, which is the heart of Paris and which had been the seat of the first Roman administration. To the south, on the hill of Sainte-Geneviève – which is even now the Latin Quarter – he would have found the most famous University of Europe, and there he would have discovered men concerned above all with questions of divinity, but speaking

77

Latin as the language of learning, and studying Aristotle as a guide to Christian theology. In such ways were the ancient sources of medieval civilization displayed in thirteenth-century Paris, and its very streets might have served yet further to impress the traveller with the continuity of western culture. It was a Roman road (now the Rue Saint-Jacques) which could lead him from the Christian cathedral through the academic home of secular and ecclesiastical learning. It was likewise a Roman road (now represented in the Rue Saint-Martin) which could take him from the same essential starting-point northward through the merchant quarter of the Halles. Even today there is perhaps no spot in all northern Europe better suited than the *Parvis* in front of Notre-Dame to impress the modern observer with that subtle medieval achievement whereby the long pathway of the Latin genius was merged almost imperceptibly into the *Via Sacra* of the Cross.

Yet during the twelfth and thirteenth centuries Paris might also have been regarded as a new city pregnant with the impulses of a new life. Our visitor would have found established there the greatest of the new monarchies which were giving secular order to Europe, a monarchy which had its first home in the *Cité*, and which had but recently created the fortress of the Louvre outside the walls. The merchants of the Halles would have told him of new privileges recently won, and new economic ventures recently undertaken. Passing to the Left Bank, he would have met a multitudinous student body which had but lately been set all afire with a new curiosity. A fine wind of hopeful endeavour was in fact already blowing through the narrow alleys of this thirteenth-century city whose stench impelled Philip Augustus to his plan of paving the Paris streets. Men were living adventurously in the present, although so conscious of the past, and the urgent quality of their immediate enterprise was plentifully exhibited in their town. Most clearly of all was it to be discerned in the new ecclesiastical architecture that was everywhere arising. Massive Romanesque arches, redolent with age, could still be seen in the abbey of Saint-Germain-des-Prés, but it was a fresh 'Gothic' impulse that was now giving expression to the most lively inspiration of the age. Notre-Dame was still in this sense new, but newer still was the lovely shrine which Louis IX had just erected. The Sainte-Chapele remains today almost as it was when it was completed in 1258 after three years' labour, and it typifies the resurgent energy of medieval Paris at the height of its constructive endeavour.

This city was at once intensely individual and widely representative, and if today every instructed traveller can find in Paris a cosmopolitan as well as a French town, and is conscious that here the two qualities are in harmony, that is due in large measure to a legacy from the Middle Ages. The golden age of medieval Paris lasted for little more than a century, but it enshrined, between 1150 and 1300, very much of the European past, and it held much of the European future in its keeping. So active, however, was its own contemporary life that this may be studied for itself: in the men who then dominated the city, in the buildings they erected, and in the labours they undertook. This was the Paris of Philip Augustus and Louis the Saint, the greatest of the medieval kings of France. This was also the Paris of the great churches, of the earliest Halles, of the first Louvre, and of the first walls. This was, finally, the Paris of Abelard and the rising university. Nor is the bare recital of these famous names itself without significance to an explanation of the greatness of medieval Paris, or of its influence upon Europe. Medieval Paris was royal; it was ecclesiastical; it was (though to a lesser extent) mercantile; and it was above all the centre of European learning. By combining together these essential characteristics Paris became in the thirteenth century a unique city, and only thus was she then enabled to mirror the civilization of the age.

It was the royal house of Capet which was primarily responsible for the rise of medieval Paris, but the kings of that dynasty none the less here built upon foundations which were already old. The importance of the site of Paris was in fact clearly indicated by geography. The three islands in the Seine, chief of which is the present *Cité*, commanded the most important reach of the greatest waterway of northern France, and dominated the plain that controlled the confluence of the Seine with the Oise and Marne, the one leading to Picardy and the other making an avenue from the east. With their strong sense of actuality, the Romans had, therefore, recognized the importance of this site, making *Lutetia* (as it was then called) the centre of a road system. They erected a temple on the *Cité* and also administrative buildings, whilst on the hill to the south, which they termed *Mons Lucotitius*, an urban settlement grew up. There was a forum near the present Luxembourg gardens and an amphitheatre where now runs the Rue Monge. With the breakdown of the Roman administration, however, this flourishing settlement slowly declined; and continuity was, here as elsewhere, only maintained through the permanence of the ecclesiastical organization which inherited so much of the Roman political system. St Denis, bishop of Paris in the fourth century, had his successors, and it was these men and their followers who were enabled, albeit with difficulty, to preserve the Parisian identity. From the fifth century to the eighth the chief persons in the history of Paris are thus the saints who were in due course to give their names to Parisian churches: Marcellus and Germanus the bishops, and Geneviève, from Mont Valérien. All else save the Church was in decay. The Roman buildings crumbled; over the baths and edifices of *Mons Lucotitius* vegetation spread; the *Cité* remained intact but deserted; and no secular ruler came to revive the splendour of the Roman past. Paris was but one – and not the most important – of the seats of Merovingian government; Charlemagne looked rather to Rome and Aachen; and his successors in Gaul reigned not from Paris but from Laon. Not until the last quarter of the ninth century did the fundamental importance of medieval Paris begin to be foreshadowed in connection with a new dynasty.

Western civilization was in greater danger between 850 and 950 than ever it was in the sixth century, and it was in the work of preserving this civilization in its darkest hour that Paris emerged into the European consciousness as in a true sense a capital of the west. The wave of Scandinavian expansion which formed Normandy, and transformed England, all but submerged western Christendom under a pagan tide. That it did not do so was due largely to the work of the West Saxon monarchy in England, and also to the achievement of a family of magnates in northern France whose home was by the Seine, and who took the title of Counts of Paris. The successful defence of Paris against the pagan 'Northmen' between 885 and 887 was one of the turning-points in the history of Europe, and neither the city nor its secular rulers ever lost the prestige which they then won. Later when a successor of these early Counts of Paris, by name Hugh Capet, in 987 established a new royalty in France he centred this in his own town by the Seine. From henceforth every advance in Capetian power was reflected in the city, and it was from these beginnings that the royal Paris of the Middle Ages arose.

It is well to observe, however, how much these early Capetians had here to do. The ancient town which Hugh Capet chose for his royal seat had shrunk to scarcely more than the *Cité* with some few buildings on each of the adjoining banks of the river. Grass grew where the Roman forum had stood on *Mons Lucotitius*, and there were till marshes between the river and Saint-Paul. Around the central settlement there was thus the desolation of ancient decay, but farther out (though still by modern standards very close) there remained the great monasteries which during the long centuries of decline had stood like rocks in a receding tide: Saint-Germain-des-Prés and Saint-Germain-l'Auxerrois faced each other across the river; Sainte-Geneviève was on the southern hill; Saint-Marcel stood near the modern boulevard of that name; and towards the north there was Saint-Merry near the present Halles. These great churches, all situated in what is now the midst of Paris, had in the past been each the centre of a small hamlet, and at the beginning of the eleventh century these hamlets still remained distinct from the central Paris of the *Cité*. The first growth of medieval Paris under royal tutelage was, so to speak, to enclose them. Slowly did the new monarchy grow under the first four Capetian kings (987–1108): equally slow was the concurrent growth of their capital. Nor were the two movements ever unconnected. There is an account of Philip

Augustus at a later date sitting in the palace that had been built on Roman foundations at the western extremity of the *Cité*; he is described as gazing at the turbid waters of the river and brooding over the town which lay around him; and that picture is symptomatic of the origins and early growth of medieval Paris.

Thus did the eleventh century come and pass, and before its close there was everywhere the stirring of a new life. The Normans set out on their triumphant career of conquest. The Crusades were about to start. Hildebrand at Rome was presiding over an ecclesiastical revival. The 'Twelfth-Century Renaissance' was at hand. In all this Paris and its kings shared, and all this likewise they helped to promote. In the early twelfth century there were in Paris, at one and the same time, Abelard representing the revival of learning, and Suger, the great minister, developing the royal government. If they ever met they would have had much to say to each other about their related, though distinct, interests, and about the city in which they dwelt. For Paris was responding to such stimulus more rapidly than ever before. It is reported to have doubled its size during the reign of Louis VI (1108–38). The 'suburb' of Saint-Merry was already absorbed, and there were now scattered dwellings where stands today the Church of Saint-Eustache. Eager students were beginning to move southward from the *Cité* into the Latin Quarter. The *Mons Lucotitius* had become the famous 'Mount' of Sainte-Geneviève. Paris was still small but it contained within itself all the germs of a great expansion. Already, too, it had become the special home of most of what was most productive in medieval civilization.

With Philip Augustus, who succeeded in 1180, the profitable results of this close connection between the Capetians and their capital reached their climax. This king became, more truly than any of his predecessors, king of 'France', and his reign was marked, as if inevitably, by something of a transformation of the royal city. He began to pave the streets with stone, and he built the first walls, so that medieval Paris was for the first time circumscribed and can be watched as an entity. The walls of Philip Augustus have only survived in fragments but their course was reconstructed by the careful scholarship of M. Halphen, and they are worth contemplating in that they girdled what had become the most important city of transalpine Europe. Perhaps, however, it is the smallness of the area which they marked out which may be of most surprise to the modern observer. For the Paris thus walled by its great king did not stretch so far as the Louvre on the west, or east beyond the present Rue Saint-Paul. The northern circuit of the walls did not extend beyond the streets north of Saint-Eustache, and the southern circuit which started on the east at the Quai de la Tournelle did not go farther than to include the site of the modern Pantheon, and then swept back along the line of the Rue des Fossés-Saint-Jacques, past the present École de Médecine, to regain the river at a spot near the present Institut de France. In this restricted area so much of primary importance to Europe was already enclosed! Not until the middle of the fourteenth century were the northern ramparts of Paris to be constructed along the line now made familiar by the Grands Boulevards.

The Paris of Philip Augustus and Louis the Saint was, however, far larger than any town which had previously existed on this site, and it possessed a unity which it had not exhibited since Roman times. Of ancient lineage it had, moreover, been so transformed that physically it must then have appeared white and new. For this was not only the capital of a rising monarchy, it was also an ecclesiastical capital whose importance was reflected in the number and character of its churches. To this phase in the history of Paris must for instance be assigned the familiar outline of Notre-Dame which in its present form was begun by Maurice de Sully, bishop of Paris from 1160 to 1196, and continued by his successors until its virtual completion in 1235. What was later to be added, was, so to speak, in the nature of an elaboration of a design which had been conceived and brought to perfection during the most brilliant years in the history of medieval Paris. Elsewhere, too, similar, if smaller, churches were arising, sometimes freshly built, though more often created by an adaptation of older Romanesque edifices. By the middle of the thirteenth century Paris was in fact studded with churches, some old and some new, but all giving an impression of recent construction, and all testifying to the ecclesiastical influence which pulsated through the royal city.

The Church had preserved the continuous life of Paris through the Dark Ages. The kings of the house of Capet gave it a new life. But neither the Church nor the Monarchy could of themselves have provided for Paris its unique position in the medieval social order. Alone among the great capital cities of medieval Europe, Paris possessed a university, and the University of Paris was in turn to serve as the prototype of nearly all the universities of northern Europe. Moreover, although the University of Paris was at different times to be styled 'the eldest daughter of the King of France', and also 'the first school of the Church', it possessed always its own inherent life. It sprang in some sense from the two chief forces which combined to make Paris great, but it derived from Paris it gave to that city as much as it received. Like Paris itself, of which during the Middle Ages it was the mind, and in part the soul, this university was a force of European significance. Perhaps more than any other institution in the West it reflected the special quality of medieval culture. The *University* as an instrument of learning was, it should be remembered, a creation of the Middle Ages. The University of Paris was the greatest of all the European universities and is the parent of many of them. Its uprising in the city of Louis the Saint was, therefore, an event of European importance, and one which of itself would have made medieval Paris the worthy representative of a golden age in European culture.

The beginning of the University of Paris – and indeed the prime cause of its activity – must be found in that great stirring of the European mind which is often termed 'The Twelfth-Century Renaissance' – a revival which in its manifold products must be reckoned as one of the most important factors in the growth of western civilization. The pervasive manifestations of this movement could be watched in many directions. It was marked, for instance, by a revival of legal studies which in due course were to find their special home in Bologna. It was marked also by the fine humanistic learning which spread over the west from centres such as Chartres. It found expression, again, in the new developments in ecclesiastical architecture which were characteristic of that age. Best of all perhaps might it be detected in the spread among humble people of an ever-extending curiosity. There has been much sentimental eulogy about the wandering scholars of this period, but it is none the less a phenomenon of great significance to the historian of European culture that at this time the roads of western Europe became alive with the figures of men and boys constantly travelling, eager to learn, to inquire, to argue, and to teach. They moved from place to place to sit at the feet of the master of their choice. They were often shabby, frequently disrespectful, sometimes unworthy of their high profession. But they formed, so to speak, the seed-bed from which sprang the flowering scholarship of the age. And where they came, and where they most settled, there were to arise the great universities of medieval Europe.

That Paris was to become the chief of such centres is now a commonplace of knowledge. But at the beginning of the twelfth century there was as yet little to indicate that such a development would take place. There were, however, in Paris at that time schools established at the monasteries of Sainte-Geneviève, Saint-Victor, and Saint-Germain-des-Prés, and at the Cathedral of Notre-Dame; and these, though not specifically distinguished, were made to serve as the basis of the new movement. One of the great educational changes of the period was to be a transference of general teaching from the monks to the secular clergy, so that in one sense the rise to predominance within Paris of the cathedral school of Notre-Dame might be regarded as the first movement towards the later formation of the university. But by itself this would have meant little, for as yet even the school of Notre-Dame had not begun to rival the more notable schools established elsewhere, as at Chartres and Rheims. It was, in short, not through any administrative action but owing to an astonishing wave of popular enthusiasm that the schools of Paris rose to leadership in Europe. The University of Paris was not to be created. It grew. And the beginning of its growth is to be dated from the coming to the *Cité* of one of the most famous teachers of his age. It was from the presence of Abelard in Paris in the middle of the twelfth century, from the disputes he stimulated, and above all from the crowds of pupils he attracted that the University of Paris took its origin, in spirit, if not in form.

To estimate the place of Abelard in the history of European thought is no part of the purpose of this essay, but he is certainly to be regarded as one of the makers of medieval Paris. For it was he who first gave to the Capetian capital its position as a centre of European learning. As an exponent of a new Nominalism he brought into opposition against himself many of the most notable scholars of the age, and the debates between them attracted an ever-increasing audience. The neighbourhood of Notre-Dame began to swarm with an ardent, tumultuous and disrespectful student body, and Abelard's own conflicts with the ecclesiastical authorities led him and his followers to desire a position of greater independence from the officials of the cathedral. The abbot of Sainte-Geneviève on the Mount was thought by some to offer a suitable counterpoise to these, and partly for this reason Abelard migrated for a time from the *Cité*, and his followers began to establish themselves in what has ever since been known as the Latin Quarter – a district which has from that time remained unique in the world. This community, which was rapidly becoming self-conscious, was still, however, completely unorganized, and not until after Abelard's stormy and unhappy life did any university exist in Paris in the modern sense of the term. The intellectual and social ferment which had been engendered, can, none the less, be regarded as the true mainspring of the University of Paris which at a later date was to achieve a distinct and independent existence.

The evolution by the University of Paris of a constitution proper to itself is, none the less, itself of considerable interest, because it concerns the formal establishment of what has ever since been regarded as the best medium for the higher education of Europe, and because university organization everywhere still tends to reproduce with suitable modifications the forms which were first crystallized in Paris during the twelfth and thirteenth centuries. The original schools at Paris were (like those of Chartres and elsewhere) under the control of the bishop's chancellor, and as has been seen it was from these schools that the university grew. The chancellor therefore always remained an extremely important figure in the government of the university. But the beginnings of a more distinct type of organization can be seen in the development of a guild of teaching masters which was gradually to become self-conscious and to vindicate its right to a considerable measure of independence. A charter of Philip Augustus suggests that this Guild was already of importance in 1170, but for a long time after this the Masters' Guild had still to struggle for its autonomy against the bishop and his chancellor. The claim of the teaching masters could in fact best be watched in relation to what was called 'Inception' – that is to say the ceremony through which the Masters of Paris insisted that a newcomer should pass before he was admitted to their fellowship. And so far were they successful in this that before the end of the twelfth century, two things had become necessary before a man was permitted to teach in Paris: firstly he must have obtained the permission of the bishop's chancellor, and secondly he must have been made free of the Masters' Guild by the ceremony of 'Inception'. And the authority of the Guild became predominant when after a long struggle it was recognized that the chancellor's licence must be given gratuitously to anyone who had formally been made a member of the Masters' Guild. Soon, too, the corporate character of this Guild was to be more formally recognized when it was allowed to plead by means of a proctor, to elect common officers, and to use a common seal. By these steps medieval Paris was brought to give to the world the idea of the university as a learned corporation possessed of its own independence and informed with its own individual life.

The Guild of Masters was thus in Paris the core of the nascent university, but in respect of the control of teaching it had to contend with a formidable rival. From the first the two great Orders of Friars had been closely connected with the learned movement in medieval Paris. In 1221 the Dominicans established themselves by the banks of the Seine, and speedily developed what has been described as a separate and exclusive school of orthodox theology. Within the next few years the Franciscans followed, and even before the death of St Francis the learned Franciscan, Alexander of Hales, was lecturing on the Mount. From this time forward, throughout the Middle Ages, many of the greatest scholars in the university were to be friars, and a mention of even a few of their names would indicate the magnitude of their achievement. Bonaventura the theologian, and Roger Bacon the scientist, were both Franciscans, whilst in the work of the Dominican Thomas Aquinas, who likewise studied and taught on the Mount, the medieval theological system achieved its formal perfection. Such men, and many more like them, gave to the University of Paris a distinction it would never otherwise have possessed, but the coming of the friars none the less created a difficult institutional problem. The friars wished to occupy University Chairs without submitting to the discipline of the Masters' Guild, whilst the Guild strove to exclude them altogether from the university. After a long struggle, which culminated between 1251 and 1257, a compromise was reached. The Guild was compelled to recognize the claims of Mendicant teachers of theology, though the Masters of Arts managed to exclude them from their faculty. On the other hand the friars undertook to observe the oath of teaching masters and to abide by the university statutes.

As a result of these conflicts, the medieval University of Paris perfected its organization – an organization which was to be followed in whole or in part by nearly all the universities of northern Europe, and to give us the academic terms with which we are familiar today. For by the end of the thirteenth century the Masters' Guild had itself become elaborately organized. It was divided into four 'faculties' – Theology; Law; Medicine; and Arts. And the Faculty of Arts was divided into four 'Nations': France; Normandy; Picardy; and England. The faculties other than Arts were each presided over by a 'Dean'; and each of the 'Nations' in the Faculty of Arts by a 'Proctor'. The whole Guild was under the rule of its 'Rector'.

This organization, with its elaborate regulations as to membership and duties, on the whole worked well since it provided at least one of the most vital necessities of university life: the free interchange of thought among an independent and qualified professoriate. But it carried within it certain defects which needed remedy. In the first place it made no pecuniary provision for teaching, since there were no salaries, and since every doctor, master, or professor (the terms in the thirteenth century were almost synonymous) had the right to teach for whatever fees he could extract from such students as he could persuade to come to his lectures. Secondly, the Guild of Masters tended to be out of touch with the student body as a whole, which was frequently undisciplined and could itself provide no assistance to its poorer members. It was largely to meet these two needs that a college system early came into existence in medieval Paris. The colleges were at first only unofficial lodging-houses for students, but they later came to be officially recognized, and became more and more a part of the university organization, making themselves responsible both for the teaching and for the good conduct of those they housed. The earliest of these Paris colleges was a small house for poor students set up in the *Cité* in 1180 and known as the Collège des Dix-Huit, but during the next century more important colleges were established on the Mount. It was in 1257 that the Collège de la Sorbonne was founded, and some twenty-five years later the Collège d'Harcourt. Even more lavish in their early endowments were the Collège du Cardinal Lemoine, and the Collège de Navarre founded respectively in 1301 and 1304. Many of these medieval colleges were to have a long and distinguished history, and that of the Sorbonne was finally to give its name to the University of Paris itself. They have left abundant traces in the street names of the Latin Quarter today.

The developing form of the University of Paris supplied the whole of north-western Europe with a pattern of academic organization. Thus before the twelfth century had closed, Oxford had started its career as a university modelled upon Paris, and during the thirteenth century the movement spread through the west. Its amazingly rapid growth is not, however, to be explained solely, or even chiefly, by reference either to administrative skill or to lavish endowments. The beginnings of the movement in Paris derived directly from an awakened curiosity stimulated by the presence of great teachers filled with ardour, and from the enthusiasm of a multitudinous student body eager to learn. It was this tradition carried out without interruption from the time of Abelard which gave to medieval Paris an undisputed hegemony in the republic of European learning. To write the history of the University of Paris would in fact necessitate a survey of almost the whole of medieval scholarship. Law might find a special home in Bologna. Some of the older humane studies characteristic of twelfth-century Chartres may have been lost. But philosophy and theology, and later law also and medicine, were prosecuted at Paris to an extent unparalleled elsewhere. Between 1150 and 1350 there was hardly a single notable scholar in western Europe who did not at some time in his career either study or teach in Paris. To such an extent did the pervasive influence of the Parisian university inform the mind of western Europe in the Middle Ages.

The great masters in the University of Paris during this period were not only notable scholars themselves: they were also great teachers developing the older educational system of the *Trivium* and *Quadrivium* to impart an instruction to their pupils which might stand comparison with that of any age. And the student body which surrounded them was equally remarkable. Constantly changing, it can seldom during the thirteenth century have numbered less than six thousand persons at any one time. And it was cosmopolitan in character. The teachers at Paris were not invariably or even usually Frenchmen, and their pupils came from all over Europe. They thus gave to the Parisian population a special quality. They were, moreover, the future clerics in an ecumenical Church, and having been welcomed on the banks of the Seine, they carried the influence of Paris throughout the west. It was not only through the medium of professed scholars, but also at the hands of popes and prelates, that the teaching learnt at Paris became the affair of all Europe. Indeed, it is doubtful whether the independence of the University of Paris could ever have been achieved apart from the support given to the Masters' Guild by popes such as Innocent III, who could recall the years of their youth spent on the Mount. The teachers and students of Paris in the thirteenth century were conscious of forming an intellectual *élite*: a scholarly leaven in European society.

It is hardly surprising, therefore, that the dominance exercised by this cosmopolitan society should have conferred a unique prestige on the city in which it was established. There seem indeed to have been hardly any limits to the respect and affection which Paris could excite in those who had passed through its university. 'Paris!' exclaimed one of these – 'Paris! Queen among cities! Moon among stars! On that island Philosophy has her ancient seat, who with Study her sole comrade, holds the eternal citadel of light!' 'Happy city!' declared another, 'where the students are so numerous that their multitude almost surpasses that of the lay inhabitants!' No scholar could feel a foreigner in Paris, remarked John of Salisbury, the great English humanist of the twelfth century; and in the fourteenth century, Richard of Bury, bishop of Durham, could still enlarge on the 'mighty stream of pleasure which made glad his heart' whenever he had leisure to revisit the city. Such declarations are constant, and their significance to the position occupied by Paris in the medieval world can well be seen in the contemporary description given by a thirteenth-century chronicler:

> In that time letters flourished in Paris. Never before at any time, or in any part of the world, whether in Athens or Egypt, had there been such a multitude of students. The reason for this must be sought not only in the beauty of Paris itself, but also in the special privileges which King Philip and his father before him had conferred upon the scholars. In this great city the study of the trivium and the quadrivium, of canon and civil law, as also of medicine, was held in high esteem. But the crowd pressed with a special zeal around the professorial Chairs where Holy Scripture was taught or where problems of theology were resolved.

Such sentiments are not to be dismissed as empty phrases. They are among the important factors of history. Certainly, they go far to explain the special function discharged by medieval Paris in the history of Europe. Christian in its scholarship, ecumenical in its interests and membership, the University of Paris in the thirteenth century reflected all that was best and most characteristic in the culture of the age.

Medieval Paris achieved its pre-eminence in Europe as a royal city, and as the home of the greatest university in western Christendom. It thus owed its position to political and cultural causes, and no view of the historical process which is based upon an exclusively economic interpretation of the past will suffice to explain the importance of Paris in the medieval world, or the influence it then exercised over the minds and imaginations of European men. Its commercial development was also notable, but always secondary in significance, for medieval Paris developed no 'heavy industries', and if its crafts were distinguished they were not peculiar to itself. The Parisian bourgeoisie, vigorous and active as it was, had its counterpart in most of the great cities of the west. Nevertheless, no sketch of medieval Paris, even as it reflected to a special degree the civilization of the age, can omit to mention, however briefly, the merchants and traders who served this great capital, who met the needs of the court and the aristocracy gathered in it, and who ministered to the crowd of scholars who lived and wrangled on the Mount. For the city, which had acquired such prestige, steadily grew in size. By the middle of the fourteenth century it had come to comprise a population of not less than 150,000 persons. Even the latest walls to the north, running along the line of the Grands Boulevards, were now insufficient to contain it.

This population needed to be fed and clothed. In its midst therefore were a multitude engaged in retail trade, and within it great mercantile houses arose. The small traders of medieval Paris have formed an attractive subject for detailed study, and they are worthy of it. Among them were the dealers in meat, fish, and wine, and of a wider importance the *marchands à l'eau* developing the ancient river trade, and carrying their enterprise up and down the Seine from Burgundy to Rouen. The drapers and merchants in cloth already famous in the thirteenth century formed early connections with the wool merchants in England, and with the cloth manufacturers of the Flemish towns. The mercers, who were among the richest of the Paris merchants, dealt not only in ordinary apparel, but also in silks from the Levant and in furs from the north. All these had their place in the teeming mercantile life of medieval Paris, and luxury trades also developed and in their turn administered to the arts. Gold and silver ornaments were made and the decoration of manuscripts played such a large part in Parisian commerce that Dante was constrained to give it a special mention in his *Divine Comedy*. Banking in its turn developed, attracting to Paris the Lombard manipulators of the money market, and a large Jewish community which had its first home in the *Cité*, but which later moved, under compulsion, to the *Rive Droite*. Here in truth was the reproduction on a large scale of the economic life of any great medieval town.

Typical also was the organization of that life. The thirteenth century was the golden age of the craft guilds, and those of Paris were notable and distinguished. All the familiar features of that system were developed, for each craft in Paris as elsewhere had its separate organization which fostered the welfare of its members, regulated its production, and supervised its relations with the world outside. These guilds controlled their several crafts, forbidding participation in them to those who were not members of the guild, insisting on a high standard of professional competence by means of the apprenticeship system, regulating wages, and to a certain extent attempting also to regulate prices. Such a system of corporations was in fact characteristic of the age of St Louis, and only after his time did it begin everywhere to break down, with the rise of a new class of capitalist traders who obtained an ever-increasing control of industry, and with the consequent creation of a proletariat of workers who could themselves never hope to become masters. There was, of course, in this tendency towards oligarchy nothing that was peculiar to Paris, but it helps to explain why the municipal history of Paris in the later Middle Ages was to be a stormy one. For a more perfect social equilibrium among the trading classes in Paris it is necessary to turn rather to the condition of the earlier thirteenth century. Never after that time was there the same balance between a large body of independent craftsmen organized in their guilds, and on the other hand a smaller body of wealthier merchants whose activities stretched throughout Europe and beyond. Such an harmony could hardly be expected to endure when trade became less local in its scope. But so long as it lasted it provided a life of self-respect for a large class of small traders, while at the same time it gave to the wealthier members of the mercantile community a political opportunity to impart a sense of communal self-consciousness to the city they aspired to rule.

The special interest attaching to the Parisian bourgeoisie at this period derived, however, not so much from its share in an economic activity that was common to western Europe, but rather from its close association with the monarchy. Paris was the royal town, and as the power of the Capets grew, so also did the importance of the citizens of the capital. From the first, there can be seen a connection between the two interests. Very early royal charters protected the 'Lendit Fair' on the road to Saint-Denis, and established the Halles on the site that the modern building now occupies. Soon, too, an even more remarkable association was to be disclosed. In 1190, when the king was about to depart on the Crusade, among those whom he appointed as regents during his absence were six burgesses of Paris who were entrusted with the custody of the royal seal, and given a key to the royal treasure in the Temple. Subsequently (after the king's return), the names of Parisian burgesses are frequently to be found as witnesses to the royal charters, and when in 1226 the young Louis IX entered Paris against some opposition, he put himself under the protection of a guard of the citizens. From this time, indeed, dates the notion that the citizens of Paris had their own special part to play in the government of France. This claim was to be voiced again and again in French history, and to find its most spectacular expression through the mouth of Danton during the French Revolution.

The primary factor in promoting the greatness of Paris during the period of its finest medieval achievement was, in fact, the close harmony which then prevailed among the dominant forces which were there displayed in exceptional strength. The four cardinal institutions which contributed to the making of this city – the Monarchy, the Church, the University, the Bourgeoisie – seemed here for a brief period to be able to cooperate with a wholly remarkable felicity. Philip Augustus may have constructed his fortress of the Louvre outside his walls in order to be able if necessary to dominate the city, but he never needed to use the stronghold for this purpose, and he is to be remembered rather as the friend of the citizens, the first paver of the Paris streets, and the first man to girdle the capital with ramparts. Similarly, both he, and his greater son, consistently stood friends to the rising university; and the debt was repaid with affection and support as when men out of all countries sallied forth from the Mount in 1213 to acclaim the king on his return from Bouvines, victor over his conquered enemies. In its turn, the influence of the Church impregnated every Parisian activity at this time. The Church fostered the craft guilds which were religious as well as trading organizations. It supported from Rome the Masters' Guild in the university. It inspired the scholarship and art of the town and it gave a special sanction to the Monarchy. Thus were the multifarious activities of this city united in relation to a common purpose. Could the spirit of medieval Paris in its golden age be better discerned in the university where theology was the Queen of Sciences, or in the Sainte-Chapelle which St Louis, as king, constructed as a casket of stone to receive the Crown of Thorns?

The Church, Secular Government, and the University – *Sacerdotium, Imperium, Studium* – these, according to a medieval writer, were the three powers which guarded the health of Christendom, and it was precisely these three which by their combined action on a single favoured city made medieval Paris the capital of European civilization. When these powers weakened in their influence, and ceased in this place to work in harmony, the unique position of Paris in the medieval world at once began to be less assured. Set like a jewel in Parisian history, is, therefore, the brief period which elapsed between the accession of Philip Augustus in 1180 and the death of Louis IX in 1270. Afterwards, there was to be much notable achievement but never again such confident equilibrium. It is not to be forgotten that the fourteenth century in Paris began with the mysterious scandal of the Templars, or that the suppression of this ecclesiastical Order was effected by a French king by means of the most savage brutality. It was a grandson of St Louis who brought the papacy to humiliation at Anagni, and during the same century the activities of Parisian citizens were usually associated with revolt or disorder. The harmonious balance of cultural forces which in the early thirteenth century had made Paris so representative of medieval civilization was itself coming to an end.

Each of the dominant powers within the medieval social order seemed now to be entering upon a period of strain, and the results were speedily to be seen within Paris. The French monarchy was never stronger than under Philippe IV, but it was already displaying a tyrannical lack of moderation. Soon the disasters of the Hundred Years War would fall upon it, and the long Valois tragedy would begin, with calamitous results for Paris. The University of Paris grew in size during the fourteenth century, but its pristine vigour waned, and the philosophical studies which were its pride, though never without importance, seemed often to be degenerating into a war of words. The bourgeoisie increased in wealth, but became more sundered between rich and poor. Étienne Marcel might rouse for a time a municipal patriotism which found expression in the first Hôtel de Ville, but he brought violence to Paris, and he died murdered; and when at the beginning of the fifteenth century the early democratic movement of the 'Cabochins' gave Paris for a time into the hands of the butchers, tripe-sellers, and skinners of the Halles, the atrocities of their rule shocked the conscience even of a brutal age. Finally, the Church, whose influence was pervasive through every institution in medieval Paris, itself entered upon an epoch of difficulty. It continued of course to produce great scholars and great saints; and notable artists were still devoted to its service. But in the increasing ornamentation of the Parisian buildings, and in the growing subtleties of Scholastic theology may perhaps be detected the curse of cleverness which is the symptom of fatigue. The papacy underwent its schism. There were scandals and revolts.

It is, of course, misleading to compare the dominant figures of one century with the lesser men of another, and it is easy to overemphasize a general tendency to which there were plentiful exceptions. But concentrating the gaze more exclusively upon Paris, it is difficult not to make the contrast between the king whom Joinville praised, and the men whom Villon knew. Nor (if the comparison be held unfair) would it be difficult to press it elsewhere. Between 1350 and 1450 Paris suffered many disasters which were not of her making, but within the city itself there were none the less signs of an inherent *malaise* that was exhibited alike in the growing isolation of the rich, in the breakdown of secular order, and in the degeneration of learning from a hard discipline into a soft diversion. Even in the more strictly political sphere something of the same transformation might be watched. Paris shared to the full in the French misfortunes during the Hundred Years War, but perhaps she reacted to them with less than the former vigour which had once for three hard years held the *Cité* against the pagans. Henry V from England might ride in triumph out of a flaming countryside to pass down the ancient Rue Saint-Martin, pausing only to kiss the relics which were successively offered for his veneration, but, in the full waning of the Middle Ages, it was not the men of Paris, but a girl from Lorraine, who saved France.

The golden age of medieval Paris had passed. Men were beginning to listen to new voices – voices which came from over the Alps and which would soon be heard with especial clarity in Medicean Florence and Borgian Rome. They spoke of a *rennaissance* very different from that of the twelfth century, though perhaps no greater. Soon in Paris would be seen in Louis XI a king spinning over Europe a web of other texture than that woven by Louis the Saint, and in the boisterous scorn of Rabelais would in due course be found the solvent of former enthusiasms which had at last grown cold. Yet the earlier achievement was none the less to endure, and it left its abiding mark upon Europe. Medieval Paris may be seen today in many edifices, and more particularly in adapted buildings which still stand on the sites originally chosen for them in the twelfth century. It survives also in the tradition of secular government there propounded, and sometimes put into practice, by the greatest of the French kings. Most particularly does it survive in the spirit which still broods over the university hill of Sainte-Geneviève. These things are all a legacy from the Middle Ages, but separately they represent only part of the inheritance. Medieval Paris represented Europe by being itself, and it bequeathed to the future its own intense personality. It was the microcosm of western Christendom which ever since has been a reality, though often, as today, in mortal danger. And for that reason, no one conscious of being part of western civilization, has, since the Middle Ages, ever been able to enter Paris wholly as a stranger. He comes conscious of a fundamental debt, and confident of recapturing an ancient inspiration. Even as a man in age may revisit a lover of his youth, or an exile after long wandering return to a second home.

VII

The Rise of Normandy

The history of Normandy before the Norman Conquest possesses a special interest for English historians, and a man who ventures today on its investigation, while fully conscious of his own temerity, may at least take comfort that so many distinguished scholars have emphasized the importance of his task. The labours of Stapleton, of J. H. Round and of Professor Powicke in this country, of C. H. Haskins in America, of Le Prévost, Charles de Beaurepaire and Ferdinand Lot in France (to name no others) have illuminated the historic function of medieval Normandy, and all students of Norman history are proud to claim Léopold Delisle for their especial master. But only a fraction of the work of these scholars was devoted to the formative period of Norman growth before 1066, and no integration of their researches has yet been made.[1] Doubtless the time has not yet arrived when such a synthesis is possible, and certainly the purpose of this lecture is to indicate problems rather than to attempt their solution. Nevertheless, the theme invites attention. Far less is known about pre-Conquest Normandy than about pre-Conquest England, and the unfortunate consequences of this gap in our knowledge were properly indicated by W. H. Stevenson.[2] The long debate about the Norman contribution to English growth can now no longer be profitably sustained unless a new attempt be made to examine for its own sake the story of the rise of Normandy.[3]

In one respect at least the way has been prepared for a new advance in this study, for in recent years some of the sources of early Norman history have been subjected to a fresh criticism that has resulted in a re-appraisal of their value. Thus the panegyric of the Norman dukes composed in the early years of the eleventh century by Dudo, canon of St Quentin, has been so discredited that Norman history in its first phase must now be explored with but scant reference to the book which was for so long considered indispensable to its study.[4] Consequently, although the narrative of William of Jumièges which begins to be contemporary in the

95

reign of Robert I has in the edition of Jean Marx[5] been separated from its later accretions, much less reliance than formerly can today be placed on the Norman chronicles as a source of early Norman history. Any future reconstruction of that history must therefore depend in large measure upon the evidence of the Norman charters. In the long series of these instruments is in truth to be found a precious historical source which has not yet attracted the attention it deserves. A critical edition of the charters of the early dukes has become an urgent need of Norman scholarship.

It is probably not an accident that no instrument of Rollo or of William Longsword is known to exist, for a diploma[6] alleged to have been given by Duke Richard II to St Ouen when recording earlier gifts to that abbey states that such benefactions were then made without written sanction; and another charter of Richard II, this time for Jumièges, adds that it was rare even for his father to record his gifts.[7] Both the surviving charters of Duke Richard I, in fact, date from the latter part of his reign and seem to be exceptional instruments.[8] But with the reign of Richard II ducal charters were issued much more frequently. Not less than eighteen charters of this duke[9] covering the period 1006–26 are extant and in print: one in favour of his wife Judith; ten to churches within Normandy; and seven to churches outside the province. The series continues with the so-called *Donatio Adelae* of Richard III;[10] and during this short reign Robert I issued not less than thirteen charters to eight ecclesiastical foundations.[11] It is possible that research in the *archives* of Normandy, and particularly in those of Seine-Inférieure, would bring to light other charters of Richard II and Robert I, but judged even by the documents now available, this material is copious. Much of it, however, still awaits analysis. A few of these instruments have been admirably edited in such editions as that made by Monsieur Lot of the muniments of Saint Wandrille; others are scattered in local histories of varying merit; whilst some still remain in the printed versions prepared in the seventeenth century. The full value of these important texts will therefore not appear until they have all been critically re-edited. But, already, by bringing them together in a single collection, it may be possible to pass a provisional judgement upon some of them, to identify many of the persons and places to which they refer, and to employ them to throw a new light upon some of the cardinal problems of early Norman growth.

The starting-point in the development of medieval Normandy was the intrusion of a Scandinavian population into a province of Gaul. But while scholars are agreed that during the ninth and tenth centuries Normandy was subjected to a long process of colonization from the northern lands, the density of the Scandinavian settlements then formed has remained a matter of some dispute. The latest study of Norman place-names, for example, has been held to indicate a marked contrast in this respect between Normandy and the English Danelaw, suggesting that, in the former province, Scandinavian colonization was 'essentially aristocratic' – 'a process in which the settlement of large groups of peasant warriors was to say the least exceptional'.[12] The historical evidence supporting this conclusion is, however, less clear. All accounts emphasize the depopulation of the lower Seine basin towards the close of the ninth century; and the statement of an Anglo-Saxon chronicler that after Halfdan's conquest of Northumbria his followers 'began to plough and provide for themselves', may in some sense be paralleled by Dudo's remark that after the establishment of Rollo 'the land that had lain waste was put to tillage'.[13] Moreover, the agrarian revolt[14] which broke out in Normandy in the early years of Duke Richard II was so remarkable both for its date and in its organization that it might be tempting to explain it by the survival among the peasantry of traditions of freedom comparable to those which the Scandinavian peasantry of the Danelaw retained until the time of Domesday.

Such general considerations, whatever their worth, only become interesting when they can be particularly reinforced. Dudo's allusion to allocations of land *funiculo* and *sorte*[15] is vague, but it not improbably refers to Scandinavian systems of land-sharing, and a clerk newly arrived from the Vermandois can hardly have derived such phrases from his imagination. Consequently, considerable significance must attach to a passage in a charter given by Robert I to Rouen cathedral in which the duke restored to the church 'in villa quae Oilliacus vocatur xxxiii partes quae vulgo masloth dicuntur'.[16] Oilliacus may be identified as either Ouilly-le-Tesson or Ouilly-le-Basset, both in the Hiémois,[17] and a variant reading describes the *partes* within Ouilly as *Mansloht*. Now the word *manlot* occurs in a tenth-century Nottinghamshire charter, in an eleventh-century survey of lands in Norfolk, in two twelfth-century Lincolnshire charters, and in an East Anglian extent of the thirteenth century, and in all these cases it has been held to indicate the survival of land-sharing arrangements consequent upon the Scandinavian settlements in those districts.[18] Its appearance in a Norman charter belonging to the second quarter of the eleventh century is thus of interest. The thirty-three shares assigned as *manlots* in the village of Ouilly cannot have been large holdings, and while it would certainly be very rash to generalize from a single text,[19] its language may reasonably be held to suggest that in one place at least in Normandy some of the 'rank and file' of the Scandinavian army may have settled down, as in England, to till the soil.

Probably, however, the extent of Viking colonization varied in Normandy from district to district. Latin-Scandinavian hybrids are very common in Norman place-names, and, where they occur, they are considered to point to a state of society in which immigrants from the North formed a

D

minority of the population.[20] Full allowance must certainly be made for
local divergencies, and the miscellaneous character of the settlement
is apparent in the early history of the province. The warfare which
ravaged Normandy during the earlier half of the tenth century was often
waged between men who bore Scandinavian names. Much, for instance, is
obscure about that 'Harold' who supported 'Bernard the Dane' against
Louis d'Outre-Mer, but he appears to have been the leader of a Viking
colony in the Bessin; and if the story of Turmod and Sihtric as told by
the chroniclers of Rheims contains legendary elements, there is good
reason to believe that the one was a Viking settled in Normandy while the
other was a recent pagan arrival from overseas.[21] The new dynasty
which had established itself in Rouen had to fight for its supremacy
against rivals of Scandinavian race, and the dichotomy between Upper and
Lower Normandy long endured. In effect, the Scandinavian impact
entailed more lasting results in the western than in the eastern section of the
province. In the second quarter of the tenth century Scandinavian speech
was apparently already exceptional at Rouen while it was still dominant in
Bayeux.[22]

The duration and the miscellaneous character of the Viking colonization
of Normandy make it impossible to speak with any precision about the
parts of Scandinavia from which the new settlers came. The general
course of Scandinavian expansion westward in the ninth century might
perhaps suggest that apart from those invaders who penetrated into the
province from the south by way of the Loire, the bulk of the settlers in
Normandy would be Danes. Certainly the Great Army which occupied
the English Danelaw established in that district a population which was
predominantly Danish,[23] and, equally certainly, the same Great Army
conducted its operations indiscriminately on both sides of the Channel.[24]
In a similar sense, the place-names of Normandy have been held to
indicate a 'strong East Scandinavian element in the Norman settlement'.[25]
Nevertheless, the question should not yet be regarded as finally settled.
The Frankish evidence from the *Lament for William Longsword* when
brought into juxtaposition with the testimony of Ari the Learned, and
with later Scandinavian tradition, indicates that Rollo, the first of the
Norman dukes, was himself of Norwegian stock,[26] and even the place-
name evidence does not seem to be wholly unequivocal.[27] Doubtless, a final
solution to this problem will not be obtained until the place-names in the
earliest Norman charters have been subjected to exhaustive analysis. In the
meantime, however, it has been assumed, and perhaps with justice,
that the bulk of the Viking settlers were Danish but that men from Norway
were intermingled among them in a proportion not yet known.

Some new evidence may, however, be cited as to the manner in which
the Viking dynasty was established in the province. Dudo's account of

Rollo has now been shown to be completely unreliable,[28] and scholars have therefore been constrained to depend upon Flodoard of Rheims as the main source of his career. According to Flodoard, the agreement between Rollo and Charles the Simple (traditionally associated with the village of Saint-Clair-sur-Epte) took place immediately after the defeat of the Viking chief at Chartres on 20 July 911;[29] and, in this, Flodoard is in some measure confirmed by a dated charter of Charles the Simple[30] which indicates that these arrangements had already taken effect before 918. But Flodoard also states (against the testimony of Dudo) that the conquest of Normandy was a gradual process. Rollo, he asserts, entered Normandy not from the sea but from the landward side; his first acquisition, given him in return for his baptism and by the agreement on the Epte, was a territory comprising the neighbourhood of Rouen together with certain districts on the sea coast pertaining to the city. Not until 924, by agreement with King Rudolf, was Rollo's power extended to the Bessin and Maine; and not until 933, that is to say after Rollo's death, were the Cotentin and the Avranchin acquired by William Longsword, his son.[31]

Now, Flodoard was not a contemporary witness of the events he here describes, and he lived some distance away from the region where they occurred. Consequently, it is of crucial importance that his account can in large measure be confirmed by a testimony of early Norman charters. Thus, a charter of Richard II[32] for St Ouen enumerates a number of estates,[33] alleging that these were given to that church by Rollo, and the great majority of these can now be confidently identified as lying within twelve miles of Saint-Clair-sur-Epte, being all situate together in the modern canton of Écos.[34] Similarly, the benefactions alleged to have been made by William Longsword to the same monastery[35] may be discerned in a cluster of adjacent villages lying immediately across the Seine from Écos;[36] and a group of early charters further shows that William's step-son, Count Rodulf, likewise held extensive estates in the same district or its immediate neighbourhood.[37] Again, an agreement made in 1012 between the abbots of Bourgueil and Jumièges[38] reveals that William Longsword, after his marriage with Liutgarde, endowed his wife with large estates in the adjoining neighbourhood of Vernon.[39] Finally, another charter of Richard II, this time for Jumièges,[40] displays this same William Longsword as possessed of a compact block of estates on the banks of the lower Seine in the vicinity of Rouen.[41] In short, the evidence of the charters indicates that the earliest possessions of the ducal house were in the neighbourhood of Rouen, and more particularly in the region formed by the angle of the Seine and the Epte – precisely, that is to say, in the district which, according to the chroniclers of Rheims, was first acquired by Rollo.

The most ancient muniments of Jumièges and St Ouen thus suggest that the original demesne of the Norman dukes was confined to an area bounded by the Epte, the Vire, and the sea, and that it was concentrated in the small district lying on both sides of the Seine between Les Andelys and Vernon, stretching to the west nearly as far as Évreux, and to the east along the Epte towards St Clair. Correspondingly, the charters of Le Mont Saint-Michel indicate the manner in which this demesne was extended. A charter of Richard III[42] restored to that monastery a group of estates which it asserts had originally been granted to the monastery by William Longsword but of which the monastery had subsequently been deprived. These too can now be placed in a number of contiguous villages[43] which, in this case, all lie within a very few miles of Pontorson; and they must surely represent the acquisitions made by the son of Rollo on the Breton frontier during the successful campaigns which according to Flodoard, were carried out in that district in 933.[44] Whether or not this warfare was connected with the alleged rebellion of 'Riulf'[45] which is stated to have occurred in Lower Normandy about this time must remain doubtful, but it is significant that while William of Jumièges asserts that 'Riulf' was finally defeated at a battle just outside Rouen,[46] a charter of Duke Robert I mentions Amfreville-la-Mivoie (some four miles from the city) as being among the places which 'William the Count' gave to Rouen cathedral when 'he returned as victor over his conquered enemies'.[47]

The early history of the Norman dynasty illustrates at once the strength of the Viking traditions which it inherited and the manner in which these were modified after its establishment in Gaul. Rollo remained the Viking after his baptism. In 925, according to Flodoard,[48] 'the Normans of the Seine' broke the treaty and ravaged the territory of Beauvais and Amiens, penetrating as far as Noyon, and in 942, after the murder of William Longsword, the whole of the province was given over to strife between rival Viking hands. During the early years of the reign of Richard I the chief supporter of settled order in the province was thus not the young Duke but Louis d'Outre-Mer, who overthrew the pagan Sihtric in 942 and himself suffered defeat at the hands of Harold in 945.[49] Sixteen years later, a veritable crisis developed when Richard called on Scandinavian support against Lothair, and once again a Viking power established on the Seine was seen to challenge the stability of Gaul by carrying destruction over the Breton march and southwards from Rouen towards Chartres. The terrible Norman war of 961–5[50] reproduced many of the worst conditions of the ninth century, and the settlement which marked its close was a cardinal event in the history of Normandy. The pact made between Richard and Lothair at Gisors in 965[51] was scarcely less important than the similar agreement of 911.

From this time forward the position of the Viking dynasty in Gaul began more rapidly to change, but none the less for more than half a century after the pact of Gisors Normandy continued to receive settlers from the Baltic lands, and the Scandinavian affinities of the province remained strong. Towards the close of the tenth century, Viking raiders of England appear to have received much hospitality and assistance in the Norman ports, and the intervention of Pope John XV in the ensuing dispute between Ethelred and Richard seems to have been inspired by a fear that the ruler of Normandy might once again associate himself with a Viking attack upon western Christendom. The treaty effected at Rouen in March 991[52] in the presence of the papal envoy, the bishop of Sherborne, and two English thegns thus illustrates the equivocal position occupied by the Norman dynasty at the time. Nor was it permanent in its results. Not without cause did Richer of Rheims[53] as late as 996 refer to the ruler of Normandy as *pyratarum dux*. A Norman tradition which has some claims to credence refers to an unsuccessful English attack upon the Cotentin in 1000, and if this in fact occurred it was probably a cutting-out expedition designed to inflict puishment upon a Viking fleet which had recently raided England and which was refitting in Norman harbours.[54] The famous marriage between Ethelred and Emma in 1002 was probably itself not unconnected with these events. It marked a new attempt to cement an alliance between the English king and the Norman duke, and by this means to detach the ruler of the Viking province from further cooperation with the Viking raiders of western Europe.

Doubtless there is in this respect a personal contrast to be drawn between Richard I, who had been brought up in an atmosphere charged with pagan memories from the Viking past, and Richard II, who was later alleged to have transformed his realm into a *patria Christi*.[55] Nevertheless, even Richard II seems in this matter to have earned somewhat easily his traditional title of 'the Good'. Both Burgundian and Flemish annalists noted the special barbarity of his troops in 1005 and 1006, and attributed this to their Viking affinities,[56] and eight years later Richard II actually followed the fell example of his father by summoning pagan allies from Scandinavia to assist him in his wars in Gaul.[57] In 1012–14, during the same months when Sweyn Forkbeard was assaulting England, Olaf and Lacman were ravaging northern Gaul at the invitation of the Norman duke. Laden with booty from the sack of Dol they at length reached Rouen, where Richard received them with honour.[58] The French king was clearly apprehensive that the conditions of the Norman war were again to be repeated, and the assembly of Gaulish notables which he convoked at Coudres was a measure of his concern.[59] The danger was averted when Richard, perhaps by bribery, divested himself of his Viking allies, and the conversion of Olaf may have seemed to blunt the significance of the crisis. Nevertheless, in considering the formation of medieval Normandy, it deserves some emphasis that, within twenty years of the birth of William the Conqueror, a Norman duke welcomed in his capital a pagan army from Scandinavia which had recently spread devastation over a considerable part of north-western France.

It is only in the light of such considerations that can be appreciated the developing relations during this period between the Viking dynasty and the ruling houses of Gaul.[60] The original concession to Rollo had undoubtedly been made under conditions. Charles's own diploma states that the grant had been made *pro tutela regni*,[61] and Flodoard three times speaks apparently of formal commendation.[62] The practical obligations of vassalage were, it is true, often ignored by Rollo and his immediate successors, but the claim undoubtedly remained and sometimes it was acknowledged. The solemn reception of Louis d'Outre-Mer by William Longsword at Rouen in 942[63] was probably a recognition of this relationship and the subsequent murder of the duke was not unconnected with it.[64] The famous story of the abduction of the young Duke Richard[65] cannot be substantiated by reliable evidence, but it may well represent the assertion by an overlord of his undoubted right to bring up the infant son of a defunct vassal at his own court.[66] What, in fact, is most interesting about this vassalage is not the fact that it was always claimed and sometimes admitted, but that during the earlier half of the tenth century it was transferred from one overlord to another, so that the Capets gained what the Carolingians had lost. Robert the Strong was probably sponsor to Rollo at his baptism,[67] and Hugh the Great was regarded as *princeps* over Normandy.[68] As early as 942 groups of Norman notables were commending themselves to Hugh, and during the minority of Richard I he invaded Normandy in their interests and his own.[69] Hugh Capet in his turn concerned himself directly with Norman affairs and in 960 Richard married his sister.[70] It was therefore a part of Hugh's policy to observe during the Norman war a studied neutrality in the struggle between Richard and his Carolingian overlord, and here again the events of 965 would seem to have been of capital importance. Their significance in this respect may indeed be aptly illustrated in two charters of the period. When in 966 Lothair confirmed by charter[71] the restoration of the monastery of Le Mont Saint-Michel, he described the Norman duke as *marchisus* and not, as might have been expected, as *fidelis*, but in 968, when Richard himself bestowed Berneval upon St Denis, he stated as necessary to the validity of his gift the assent of *senioris mei Hugonis Francorum principis*.[72] It is impossible to escape the conclusion that the transference of allegiance had taken place.

The importance of the change was soon to be exemplified. Only twenty-two years separated the pact of Gisors from the coronation of Hugh Capet as king, and although Norman support was not essential to the Capetian triumph it undoubtedly contributed thereto. Just after the coronation of Hugh, Richard took action on his behalf against the Count of Vermandois;[73] and between King Robert I and Duke Richard II the association was yet closer. In 1005 the duke assisted the king in the siege of Auxerre, and in the next year they kept the Feast of the Ascension together at Fécamp.[74] In 1017 Richard was present at the coronation of the young King Henry, marking the occasion with the gift of a silver cup,[75] and in 1023 he acted on behalf of the king in the matter of the succession of the county of Champagne.[76] In January 1024 he once again welcomed the king with honour at Rouen.[77]

In view of subsequent controversies these events deserve record, for there can be little doubt of the quality of the relationship they reveal. Norman chroniclers were later to explain them as indicating an alliance between equals, but the facts seem decisive against such an interpretation. After 965 the allegiance of the ducal dynasty was transferred from the Carolingians to the Capets. After 987 the French king regarded the Norman duke as his vassal and on many occasions Richard II discharged the duties which such vassalage entailed. The relationship so frequently exhibited during his reign was in fact after its close to be a decisive factor in the survival of both the dynasties concerned. In 1031 the young King Henry, flying from the wrath of his mother Constance, took refuge at Rouen and, calling on his Norman vassal for support, was enabled thereby to regain his inheritance.[78] In 1047 it was the intervention of King Henry which alone secured the defeat of the Norman rebels at Val-ès-Dunes. During the nineteen years which separated Val-ès-Dunes from Hastings, Duke William II was enabled to acquire in practice a new independence from his French overlord, but the position he then achieved would never have been attained if between 965 and 1047 Normandy had not become an integral part of the political system of Gaul.

The history of the ducal dynasty might thus in some sense be taken to symbolize the gradual transformation of the Viking province. The character of medieval Normandy was, however, moulded more fundamentally by two other distinct though related developments, the one involving an ecclesiastical revival, and the other the establishment of a new aristocracy. The baptism of Rollo was to prove the most important feature of the arrangements of 911, and his establishment in Rouen associated his fortunes to some extent with those of the ecclesiastical capital of the province. Many of the benefactions he is alleged to have made to the Church in 911 were certainly fictitious, since they concerned estates which at that time were not yet in his possession. But it is likely that some concessions to the Church were extracted from the newly converted Viking, and the record in later charters of his gifts to St Ouen[79] and St Denis[80] may represent the truth. The reputation of his son as a friend to the Church rests, however, upon surer foundations. It seems incredible that the charters of no less than three religous houses – St Ouen, Jumièges, Le Mont Saint-Michel[81] – should ascribe to William Longsword gifts whose location conforms so closely to the political history of the reign unless some at least of those benefactions had been made. The evidence of the charters also lends some support to later legends[82] associating this duke in an especial manner with Jumièges. Certain monks of the original community returned to Jumièges during his reign,[83] and in addition the Duke established in this house twelve monks from the abbey of St Cyprien of Poitou who had been sent to Normandy by his sister the wife of Count William Towhead.[84] It is perhaps indicative of the changing character of the Viking province that when in 932 the monks of Rebais fled from the ravages of the Hungarians, it was to Normandy that they turned, taking refuge at Marcilly near Évreux, where they deposited their relics.[85]

The progress reflected in such events might, however, easily be exaggerated. It deserves the fullest emphasis that the Latinization of Normandy under ecclesiastical influence was accomplished in face of the stubborn resistance of an alien culture. It is not impossible that Rollo renounced Christianity before his death,[86] and it is certain that a pagan reaction swept through the province after the murder of his son in 942.[87] The ecclesiastical development of Normandy was so remarkable that it is easy to misconceive the hazardous nature of its early stages. In the earlier half of the tenth century the flourishing ecclesiastical life which had formerly distinguished the province of Rouen was all but destroyed. The sees had disintegrated and the monasteries were destroyed. The surviving lists of Norman bishops show gaps at this period which are significant, and five successive bishops of Coutances in the tenth century were resident at Rouen.[88] The monastic collapse was even more notable. The houses were desolate, the congregations dispersed. Some maintained a precarious existence by migration, but more often the desolation of the site of a monastery entailed the extinction of the community, and in the third decade of the tenth century it is probable that not a single monastery remained in the Norman land. Such ruin was not rapidly to be repaired, and the political chaos which marked the early years of Richard I was fatal to an ecclesiastical revival. Not until after the treaty of 965 could any effective action be taken, but then its consequences were immediate. The treaty between Lothair and Richard was followed at once by the king's charter confirming Richard's restoration of Le Mont Saint-Michel,[89] and the pact of Gisors may be said to mark an epoch in the growth of the Norman Church even as it marks a period in the development of the Norman State.

The importance of the latter part of the reign of Richard I in the history of the Norman church has perhaps been unduly minimized. The duke's own interest in Le Mont Saint-Michel is well attested, and a detailed schedule of his gifts to St Taurin of Évreux is preserved in both the cartularies of that house.[90] Charters of Richard II, likewise, display his father as a benefactor of St Ouen and Jumièges,[91] and the former monastery apparently experienced a revival about this time. More important, however, were the relations developed during the latter part of the tenth century between Normandy and movements of reform outside the province. In particular, the fortunes of the dispersed congregation of Fontanelles, which took the community first to Boulogne and then in 944 to Ghent, supplied a link between the Viking province and the revival associated with St Gérard de Broigne. For in 961 there departed from Ghent to Normandy a party of monks belonging to this congregation under the leadership of one of Gérard's disciples named Mainard who obtained from Richard I the ancient site of Fontanelles on which to re-establish a monastery to be dedicated to St Wandrille.[92] Mainard's own sojourn at Fontanelles was short, for in 966 Richard transferred him to Le Mont Saint-Michel where he remained for twenty-five years.[93] Throughout he worked in close cooperation with the duke, and his influence was pervasive. His career would repay a closer study.[94] The effects of the Flemish ecclesiastical revival on the English Church in the age of Dunstan and Ethelwold have been well established.[95] Its influence on the contemporary Norman Church is less generally appreciated.

The dominant external influence on the Norman Church before the Norman Conquest was, however, derived not from Flanders but from Cluny, or at least from the movement which, starting at Cluny, achieved new life at centres such as Dijon and its spiritual descendants.[96] The Cluniac ascendancy in Normandy may, moreover, be regarded as characteristic not of the reign of Richard I but of Richard II. It is true that Richard I, after rebuilding the church at Fécamp and establishing thereat a community of secular canons, applied to St Maieul for monks to replace them,[97] but the appeal was unsuccessful, and though Richard I's charter to Fécamp[98] in its present form contains a clause indicative of the Cluniac exemption, this is usually today regarded by scholars as a later interpolation.[99] On the other hand, William of Dijon is known to have arrived in Normandy in 1001,[100] and in 1006 the Cluniac exemption appears unmistakably in two charters given to Fécamp respectively by Duke Richard II and King Robert I.[101] Later this exemption was repeated and extended[102] by Duke Robert I in his charters to Cerisy-la-Forêt[103] and Montivilliers.[104] During this period, in fact, the revival of the Norman Church may be said to have been dominated by Cluniac ideas. At first the centre of the movement was undoubtedly Fécamp, and its most prominent figures William of Dijon and his successor Abbot John. But William's influence,[105] fortified by his personal prestige, permeated through the province. He is alleged to have introduced reforms at St Ouen and Jumièges, and according to Robert of Torigny he also had Le Mont Saint-Michel *sub regimine suo*.[106] His interpretation of the Cluniac life as embodied in the customs of Fruttuaria in Italy[107] was doubtless applied to the monasteries in Normandy which he controlled, and it is noteworthy that, whereas Cluniac monasticism developed in conscious independence of episcopal control, so also was the revival of the Norman Church in the earlier half of the eleventh century not episcopal but monastic.

Only slowly was the Norman episcopate to be re-established, and its members for long continued to be representative not of the reforming movement so much as of the lay aristocracy from which they were drawn. Between 990 and 1054 the archiepiscopal see of Rouen was held by two sons of Norman dukes, and Herbert, who was bishop of Lisieux at least from 1025, was alleged to be *Normannorum ducum propinquus*. After 1015 the bishopric of Bayeux was occupied first by a son of Count Rodulf, and then by Odo, half-brother of the Conqueror, whilst William, bishop of Évreux from 1050 to 1066, was a son of Gérard Flaitel.[108] It would, of course, be wrong to minimize the ability of many of the prelates drawn from this class. Ivo, bishop of Seez from 1035, who was head of the great house of Bellesme,[109] was a notable bishop; Hugh, bishop of Lisieux, son of Count William of Eu, was a prelate of good repute; and Geoffrey Mowbray, bishop of Coutances, despite his secular activities reorganized his diocese and left a great cathedral as his memorial.[110] Nevertheless, these men are to be regarded as outstanding members of a company which sustained an older ecclesiastical tradition and they were out of touch with Leonine policy. Before the appointment of Maurilius as archbishop of Rouen in 1055, it would be hard to find a member of the Norman episcopate as pledged to the reforms, and the Norman bishops who brought the reforms to England had for the most part been trained in Norman monasteries.

It was through the agency of the reformed monasteries that the Norman Church was revived, and the rapid growth of monastic life in Normandy during the earlier half of the eleventh century is in every way remarkable. Before 1030 no Norman monastery was founded except by the ducal house, but afterwards the Norman magnates played a large part in the endowment of new houses. The initial inspiration of this astonishing growth undoubtedly came from outside the province, but Norman monasticism, once re-established, none the less speedily developed within the Cluniac framework its own special features. Thus, although the great abbots of Cluny were always the unflinching opponents of lay control, William of Dijon relied on ducal support scarcely less than Mainard had done before him. The weakness of the Papacy between

May 1003 and 1009 probably explains[111] why the Pope was apparently not consulted about the exeption of Fécamp in 1006, but Benedict was 'an able and vigorous pontiff',[112] and if his bull of 1016 respecting Fécamp is genuine,[113] it is significant that it speaks of that monastery as a ducal church, and is addressed not to the abbot but to the duke. The integration of the Norman monasteries into the feudal structure of the province was the work of the Conqueror and its importance has been properly emphasized by scholars.[114] But the conditions which made this possible had been formed at an earlier date. The part played by previous dukes, by Richard I, and more particularly by Richard II, in the revival of Norman monasticism was not without its influence in promoting that cooperation between the secular and ecclesiastical powers which was so marked a feature of the Norman settlement of England. The revived Norman monasticism of the early eleventh century was not only Cluniac in spirit; it was also ducal in direction. The work of William of Dijon has here some links with that of Lanfranc.

In other ways also did Norman monasticism, while drawing its main inspiration from Cluniac circles, preserve its own special qualities.[115] Its loose organization allowed for wide variations of type. The earlier impetus from Ghent represented in the monastery of St Wandrille was doubtless to some extent preserved in the daughter houses of Préaux and Grestain, whilst elsewhere the personal influence of William of Dijon survived in the monasteries he restored. Perhaps for this reason the ascetic and ritualistic spirit which came later to inform Cluniac practice was much modified in Normandy, and the four great ultramontanes who in turn dominated Norman monasticism – William of Dijon, John of Fécamp, Lanfranc and Anselm – were all men who possessed a devoted interest in the things of the mind. It would, of course, be easy to judge the cultural consequence of Norman monasticism too exclusively by reference to its most distinguished community, and one which was not itself a Cluniac foundation. The outstanding achievement of Le Bec-Hellouin offers at once an explanation and the gauge of the influence of the Norman Church. But its brilliance must not obscure the work performed in other religious houses. From the start, the revived monasticism exercised an educative and a cultural influence which was a cardinal factor in the rise of Normandy.

Scarcely less significant to the formation of medieval Normandy than the new monasticism was the establishment in the province of a new aristocracy, and the evidence which illustrates the history of particular families leaves little doubt as to the period when this new nobility arose. The pedigrees which Robert of Torigny added to the eighth book of William of Jumièges[116] are certainly inaccurate in many of their details, but they indicate that the advancement of the kindred of the Duchess Gunnor was a factor in the rise of many Norman houses, and the charters likewise place the origin of these and other families in or after the reign of Duke Richard II. Thus the family of Tosny might in the twelfth century claim to be descended from an uncle of Rollo,[117] but the earliest member of this house whose existence is warranted by sound testimony is Ralf I of Tosny, who in 1013 or 1014 was entrusted with the defence of Tillières and who was probably the original grantee of Tosny itself.[118] It is seldom, indeed, that a Norman family can be traced back earlier than this, and rare indeed that a territorial appellation can be found descendible in the manner of a surname during the earlier half of the eleventh century. The earliest known ancestor of the family of Montfort-sur-Risle is Thurstan of Bastembourg, who shortly before 1025 gave land at Pont Authou on the Risle, four miles from Montfort; his son, Hugh I of Montfort, perished in private war about 1040; and it was his grandson, Hugh II, who brought the fortunes of the family to England.[119] The father of Gilbert of Auffay who was probably present at Hasting was Richard, who took his name from Hugleville,[120] and Hugh de Grandmesnil, the Domesday tenant, belonged but to the third recorded generation of the house so styled. In western Normandy the house of Saint Sauveur, hereditary *vicomtes* of the Cotentin, may be referred to Néel who witnessed charters about 1020–5.[121] The hereditary *vicomtes* of the Avranchin, later to become Earls of Chester of the first line, can be traced no farther than Thurstan Goz, who appears in the period 1017–25;[122] while the first recorded ancestor of the hereditary *vicomtes* of the Bessin, later Earls of Chester of the second line, is Anschetil, whose earliest attestation may probaly be placed in the years 1015–22.[123] These examples have been selected deliberately from among the most illustrious houses of feudal Normandy. The story which they reveal is clear. The Norman nobility which was to give a new aristocracy to England did not arise before the first quarter of the eleventh century.

The manner in which the great families of medieval Normandy acquired their land can only be sparsely illustrated. The extensive possessions of the ducal house at an early date are only partially defined in the surviving charters, and it is rare that the process can be elucidated whereby the feudal lords of a subsequent period became possessed of some of them. A certain precision may, however, sometimes be achieved. Thus among the estates given by Richard II to his first wife, Judith, was a large block of territory in the Lieuvin.[124] After her death most of this went to the abbey of Bernay, but among the manors not so bestowed were Ferrières-Saint-Hilaire and Chambrais, and these were to form the endowment of a notable family. Walkelin de Ferrières was clearly established at that place before his death in 1040, and Chambrais probably came into the possession of the family about this time.[125] The more famous case of Beaumont is in this respect particularly eloquent. Both Vieilles and Beaumont on the

Risle had likewise belonged to the Duchess Judith, and in due course they passed to the abbey of Bernay, which still held them in 1025.[126] But in or before 1035 Humfrey, styled of Vieilles, obtained them from Ralf *custos* of Bernay, and his son Roger de Beaumont built his castle on the adjoining hill.[127]

There can be no doubt that this new nobility was further enriched by lands which had previously been possessed by the Church. An interesting record,[128] which provides one of the rare illustrations of the diocese of Rouen in the time of Archbishop Hugh I, shows that already in his time lands were being alienated at Douvren and in the neighbourhood of Envermeu. Similarly, when Ralf I of Tosny went to Apulia about 1015, he was already known by his chief possession in Normandy, but Tosny had previously belonged to Rouen cathedral.[129] Duke Richard II was likewise constrained specifically to restore to the abbey of Le Mont Saint-Michel estates which had been taken from the abbey by the first known count of Mortain,[130] and shortly after 1026 the family of Montgomery, which can be traced no farther than this period, acquired from the abbeys of Jumièges and Fécamp lands which a short time before had actually been confirmed to these monasteries by specific ducal grants.[131] Such transactions must clearly be regarded as representative, for knowledge of them depends on the chance survival of texts. It should, moreover, be noted that ecclesiastical alienations naturally figure with undue prominence in the documents, and that the transference of lay lands must have been at least as extensive. Only because the abbey of St Taurin was apparently interested in the property can any conjecture be made as to the manner in which Meules, which seems to have been part of the demesne of Richard the Fearless, passed into the hands of Gilbert of Brionne, the count, to supply at last a territorial name for the first Norman Sheriff of Exeter.[132]

The establishment in Normandy during the earlier half of the eleventh century of many of the families which were later to dominate the feudal province contributed also to the advancement of their dependents. The rise of the Harcourts cannot have been unconnected with the prosperity of the related family of Beaumont.[133] Again, as tenants in England of Richard fitz-Gilbert who succeeded his father, the count, about 1040, can be found men who took their names from Abenon and La Cressonnière, both of which are in the neighbourhood of Orbec, the *caput* of Richard's Norman barony.[134] Similarly, later tenants of the Counts of Eu in Sussex bore names denoting their original provenance at Normanville and Mesnières, in whose neighbourhood the Counts of Eu had an ancient interest.[135] Express testimony that these families arose with the houses that supplied their later feudal overlords is, however, lacking, but occasionally the earlier association can be precisely shown. The connection between Pantulf and Montgomery, which in 1086 was strikingly exhibited in

Shropshire,[136] must be referred to the time of Roger I of Montgomery, who between 1027 and 1035 issued for the abbey of Jumièges a charter which is subscribed with the sign of *Willelmi Pantulf*.[137] Equally significant is the connection between Tosny and Clères. The latter were the feudal under-tenants of the former from shortly before the Conquest until the last quarter of the twelfth century.[138] But the association between the two families can be traced to a yet earlier date. About 1040 two notable acts of violence were committed: Roger I of Tosny was killed by Roger of Beaumont,[139] and shortly afterwards Robert of Beaumont, Roger's brother, was assassinated by Roger I of Clères.[140] In the light of subsequent family history it is hard not to see in the latter act the revenge of a vassal for the murder of his overlord.

These early connections between Norman families are challenging, but it would be wrong to deduce from them a conclusion that during the earlier half of the eleventh century the structure of Norman society had as yet been made to conform with any rigidity to an ordered feudal plan. In the absence of any cataclysm comparable to the Conquest, the introduction of feudal practices was a more gradual processs in the duchy than in the kingdom, and all the evidence suggests that it took place sporadically and by degrees. It would be difficult to define the obligations of a canon of St Quentin who in 1015 was the *fidelis* of a Norman duke,[141] and the status of those *milites* of Arfast, father of Osbern the Steward, who in a deed of 1022–4 are named *cum beneficiis suis*, would be hard to appraise.[142] Nor has any reference to a relief apparently been found earlier than in a charter a few years anterior to the Conquest.[143] Still more rash would it be to assume that in the time of Richard II and Robert I the new aristocracy had in any general sense been made to regard their position as dependent upon ducal grant. The newly established Norman lords in this period set up their own military tenants for their own purposes. They desired to sustain a position which had recently been won by the sword.

There is therefore little indication among them that they held their lands conditionally upon their performing military service for the duke. No ruler able to exact a *servitium debitum* of knights from all his magnates would, like Duke Robert I, have allowed so many of them to depart with their followers to distant lands. The civil war which broke out on the death of Duke Richard II, and the anarchy which debauched Normandy from 1035 to 1047, also contributed to the failure of the ducal dynasty to coordinate the feudal development of the province to serve its own interests, and Duke William II had to crush not less than four revolts between 1047 and 1053.[144] The persistence of private war as a recognized institution in Normandy must, moreover, have encouraged subinfeudation in excess of the requirements of the duke, and it is in itself evidence of the manner in which the feudal oragnization of the province developed gradually at the will of an aristocracy and not suddenly as in England by the administrative policy of a prince. If by 1066 Normandy had become a feudal – and, to some degree, a centralized – state, this was due primarily to the work of Duke William II during the previous fifteen years – and it was one of his greatest achievements. Even so, it is significant that the *servitia debita* remained lighter in the duchy than in the kingdom, and that before the Conquest they were apparently imposed with greater uniformity upon the Church than upon the lay magnates.

The establishment of a new nobility in Normandy was the most significant feature of the reigns of Richard II and Robert I; and its appearance sharply distinguishes the social structure of the province in the eleventh century from what it had been in the tenth. The men who then first arose to greatness were as yet unorganized in any rigid feudal scheme, but together with their successors and their dependents they were to supply the ruling class of feudal Normandy. Knit together by kinship strong in their newly won possessions, they speedily advanced to dominance. They were stained with the worst vices of a violent age, but many of them learnt early that political sagacity which won for them the admiring panegyric of William of Poitiers.[145] Unamenable to control, they yet contrived to cooperate in some measure with their dukes. Secular and rapacious in their habits, they came at last in some degree to foster and to govern the Norman Church. The superabundant virility which was apparent in their private lives brought them to supremacy within their own province and enabled them to carry its influence beyond the sea. They claimed the future for their inheritance, and henceforward the history of Normandy was to be essentially a record of their acts.

The dominant theme in early Norman history is the modification of a Scandinavian inheritance through the consolidation of a dynasty, the revival of a Church and the formation of an aristocracy, and the greatest period of Norman achievement began when these three movements, which were never unrelated, were fused together by a great constructive genius to provide the overmastering energy of a province unique in Christendom. It is no part of my present purpose to attempt any new estimate of the career of William the Conqueror, but the evidence here considered suggests that his achievement would never have been possible apart from the previous development of the province which he ruled. Further study of early Norman charters will doubtless in time illuminate further the details of that growth, but already it appears to fall chronologically into three main divisions, divided roughly by the dates 965 and 1047. Before the pact of Gisors, the Scandinavian affinities of Normandy, though weakening, were still dominant. After the battle of Val-ès-Dunes, the stage was set for the work of the greatest of the Norman dukes. Between 965 and 1047 was, however, the formative period of Norman development, and every fresh study serves further to emphasize the critical importance of the reign of Duke Richard II. If, therefore, this afternoon I have ventured to transport a modern audience to a French province in an obscure age, I am not without my apology. The transformation of the Normandy of Rollo into the state which confronted England in 1066 is one of the most remarkable in history, and it presents to any student of historical causation a problem of the first magnitude. The complexities of Norman history in the tenth and eleventh centuries may doubtless be relegated to esoteric investigation, but the consequences of the rise of Normandy which then occurred are still alive among us today.

NOTES

[1] A partial synthesis is contained in J. C. H. R. Steenstrup, *Normandiets Historie under de syv første hertuger* (1925), but the importance of this interesting book is diminished by the learned author's refusal to take account of the criticism of Norman sources, and particularly of Dudo, which has been made since the publication of his *Normannerne* in 1876–82.

[2] Cf. *Eng. Hist. Rev.*, xi, p. 733.

[3] In connection with this lecture I wish very gratefully to record my debt to the late L. C. Loyd.

[4] 'You may abandon the history of Normandy if you choose,' wrote Palgrave (*Collected Works,* ii, p. 500), 'but if you accept the task you must accept Dudo or let the work alone.' The erudite attempt of Jules Lair, in his edition of Dudo published in 1865, to rehabilitate this chronicler may, however, be said to have failed, despite the support it received from Steenstrup. A comprehensive appraisal of recent criticism of Dudo is contained in H. Prentout, *Étude critique sur Dudon de Saint-Quentin* (1916).

[5] Published by the Société de l'Histoire de Normandie in 1914. See review by C. H. Haskins in *Eng. Hist. Rev.*, xxxi (1916), p. 150.

[6] Printed by F. Pommeraye in his *Histoire de l'abbaye royale de Saint Ouen* (1662), p. 404.

[7] J. J. Vernier, *Chartes de Jumièges* (1916), i, p. 30, no. xii.

[8] One of these (Bouquet, *Rec. Hist. Franc.*, ix, p. 731) was issued in 968 in favour of Saint-Denis, and there is little doubt it was a product of Parisian initiative and Parisian workmanship. The other (J. F. Lemarignier, *Privilèges d'exemption* [1937], p. 291) was issued for Fécamp, apparently in 990, on the occasion of the consecration of the restored church in that place. A record of Richard I's benefactions to Saint-Taurin is printed in T. Bonnin, *Cartulaire de Louviers* (1870), i, p. 1, no. i.

[9] A list of these is given in C. H. Haskins, *Norman Institutions* (1918), p. 59, note 291.

[10] Printed in Achery, *Spicilegium* (1723), iii, col. 390. Cf. R. L. Poole, *Studies in Chronology and History* (1934), p. 17, and H. Hall in *Genealogist*, n.s. xvi, pp. 140–52.

[11] Cf. Haskins, *op. cit.*, pp. 272–4.

[12] F. M. Stenton, 'The Scandinavian Colonies in England and Normandy', R. *Hist. Soc. Trans.*, 4th ser., (1945), xxvii, p. 6.

[13] C. Plummer, *Two Saxon Chronicles* (1892), p. 74; Dudo (ed. Lair), p. 171.

[14] Will. Jum., Bk. v, chap. 2 (ed. Marx, pp. 73, 74). He adds that the revolt was not confined to one district of Normandy but involved the whole province.

[15] Dudo (ed. Lair, pp. 171 and 182).

[16] The charter is printed in Martène and Durand, *Thesaurus novus Anecdotorum* (1717), i, col. 145. Issued by the Duke in conjunction with his uncle, the archbishop of Rouen,

it probably passed at the time of their reconciliation in or about 1030. The clause here to be examined is further discussed in A. Le Prévost, 'Anciennes divisions territoriales de la Normandie' (*Mém. Soc. Antiq. Norm.*, 2nd ser. [1840], i, p. 49). Le Prévost quotes as his sources 'Neustria Christiana', which is an unpublished MS. of A. du Moustier, now in the Bibliothèque Nationale (see E. Frère, *Manuel de la Bibliographie normande* [1858], i, p. 399), and also a cartulary which seems to be that numbered 3255 in H. Stein, *Bibliographie des Cartulaires* (1907), p. 445, a MS. of the thirteenth–fourteenth century in the Municipal Library of Rouen.

¹⁷ *Oilliacus* is in the charter mentioned in connection with *Leisia* and *Bolon*. The former must be Laize-la-ville (Calvados, arr. Caen, cant. Bourguébus): not only was this place in the patronage of Rouen cathedral, but it was in the diocese of Rouen (A. du Caumont, *Statistique monumentale du Calvados* [1846–67], ii, p. 173). The latter is clearly Boulon (arr. Falaise, cant. Bretteville-sur-Laize), three miles from Laize-la-ville. In the Hiémois there are two places called Ouilly: Ouilly-le-Tesson, nine miles south-east of Laize-la-ville; and Ouilly-le-Basset, eleven miles south of Laize-la-ville.

¹⁸ See Douglas, *Social Structure of Medieval East Anglia* (1927), pp. 30 *sqq.*; 'Fragments of an Anglo-Saxon survey from Bury St Edmunds' *Eng. Hist. Rev*, xliii (1928), p. 376; and the authorities there cited.

¹⁹ The possibility must even be considered that these holdings might perhaps not have involved ploughing. In the Middle Ages the vine was cultivated in the neighbourhood of Ouilly-le-Tesson, at Bretteville, and at Ussy, while the wine of Argences some ten miles to the north was, comparatively speaking, famous (L. Delisle, *Class agricole*, [ed. 1903], pp. 439, 440, 442).

²⁰ Stenton, *op. cit.,* p. 11.

²¹ Cf. P. Lauer, *Louis d'Outre-Mer* (1900), pp. 100, 287–92.

²² Dudo (ed. Lair, p. 221); cf. Adémar of Chabannes (ed. J. Chavanon, (1897), p. 148).

²³ F. M. Stenton, *Danes in England* (British Academy, 1927).

²⁴ Cf., for example, *A.S. Chron.* '*A*', *s.q.* 880, 881, with *Mirac. S. Bertin* (Bouquet, *Rec. Hist. Franc.*, ix, p. 118). See also the remarks of Fulk, Archbishop of Rheims, writing in 886 (Bouquet, *op. cit.*, viii, p. 156).

²⁵ Stenton in *R. Hist. Soc. Trans.*, 4th ser., xxvii, p. 9.

²⁶ Douglas, 'Rollo of Normandy', *Eng. Hist. Rev.* (1942), lvii, pp. 418–23.

²⁷ Compare the examples given on pp. 8 and 9 of Professor Stenton's essay quoted above.

²⁸ H. Howorth in *Archaeologia* (1880), xlv, 235–50; A. Bugge in *Historisk Tideskrift* (1912), pp. 160 *sqq.*; Prentout, *op. cit.*, pp. 111 *sqq.*

²⁹ Flodoard, *Annales*, ed. Lauer (1905), p. 16; *Hist. Rem. Eccl.* (Bouquet, *op. cit.*, viii, p. 163), and cf. Douglas, *op. cit.*, pp. 426–9.

³⁰ Bouquet, *Rec. Hist. Franc.*, ix, p. 536.

³¹ *Hist. Rem. Eccl.* (Bouquet, *op. cit.*, viii, p. 163); *Annales* (ed. Lauer, pp. 24, 55).

³² Printed Pommeraye, *Hist. St Ouen* (1662), p. 404.

³³ 'Id est Uuadiniacum cum ecclesia et omnibus appenditiis suis videlicet Torsiacum, Cupim, Furcas, Maisnile quod dicitur Sanctus Remigius cum ecclesia; Debucin custe quintam partem; Bionval cum ecclesia; Milonis maisnile; Rainolt custem; villam quae dicitur Sancta Geneveva cum ecclesia; Falesiam Giuerniacium com ecclesia; . . . Quae omnia atavus Rolphus praenominato loco partim restituit, partim et dedit sed propriis cartulis ad noticiam futurorum minime descripsit.'

³⁴ I suggest the following identifications: Uuadiniacum–Gasny; Cupim–Coupigny; Furcas–Fourges; Maisnile . . . S. Remigius—Bus St Rémy; Bionval–Bionval; Milonis maisnile–Le Mesnil Milon; villam . . . S. Geneveva–Ste-Geneviève-lès-Gasny; Falesiam Giuerniacium–Givernay (which is backed by high limestone cliffs—*falaises*). All these are in the canton of Écos.

[35] 'Huic subnectimus cessioni quae etiam avi nostri Willermi industria simili modo absque cartarum notamine concessit: id est Balliolum cum ecclesia . . .; Regionvillam cum ecclesia; Campum Mainardi; maisnil quod dicitur sancti Audoeni de Colmont; villam quae dicitur sancti Petri cum ecclesia; Turlevillam; Smitvallam; Batheller; ecclesiam in honore sanctae Mariae et terram cum insula quae dicitur Sancti Petri et aliis insulis et aquis usque ad medium Sequanae fluminis et usque ad medium vallis quae est sub castelliolo.'

[36] I suggest the following identifications: Balliolum–St Pierre-de-Bailleul (Eure, arr. Louviers, cant. Gaillon); Regionvillam–Réanville (Eure, arr. Les Andelys, cant. Vernon); villam . . . Sancti Petri—St Pierre de la Garenne (Eure, arr. Louviers, cant. Gaillon). Turlevillam may possibly be Tourneville, about one mile from St Pierre de la Garenne, and Batheller is perhaps Bailly, a hamlet close to Tourneville. The *insula quae dicitur Sancti Petri* is the Île St Pierre which stretches upstream in the Seine from a point opposite Notre-Dame-de-la-Garenne (the *ecclesiam . . . sanctae Mariae* of the charter), and above it are four other islands in a line (*aliis insulis*). Finally, even the 'little castle' comes into the picture, for the lands here in question stretch into the middle of a valley ('ad medium vallis quae est sub castelliolo') dominated by the hill above Gaillon, where there originally existed the remains of a Gallo-Roman fort.

[37] See Douglas, 'Ancestors of William fitz Osbern', *Eng. Hist. Rev.*, lix (1944), 68–70; 'The Earliest Norman Counts', *ibid.* (1946), lxi, pp. 131, 132.

[38] Printed J. J. Vernier, *Chartes de Jumièges*, i, pp. 16–19, from the original. Vernier dates it '13 avril 1012—4 avril 1013', that is to say he reckons the year as beginning at Easter. The Indiction, Epact and Concurrents are all those of 1012, and the statement that the year was bissextile points the same way. Clearly the year began at Christmas and the date is 1012.

[39] The estate in question is described as 'terra in villa que dicitur Longavilla'. This is not, as might be supposed, Longueville near Dieppe. 'On appelait Longueville le territoire qui environnait Vernon,' remarks Delisle (*Classe agricole*, p. 421). 'On l'a quelquefois pris pour le nom d'une paroisse ou d'un village; mais il désigne ordinaire-ment tout un pays, dans lequel se trouvaient compris une partie de Vernon, Saint-Marcel, Saint-Just et Saint Pierre d'Autils.' Delisle cites charter evidence for each of his statements and there is no need to quote evidence in support of the opinions of such an authority. It may, however, be added that in Duke Richard II's charter of 1025 for Jumièges (J. J. Vernier, *op. cit.*, i, p. 37) there is confirmation of this exchange: *In Longavilla dedimus Haltilz*. This identifies the land now in question as lying in Saint-Pierre-d'Autils (Eure, arr. Évreux, cant. Vernon) in the district of Longueville, and the identification is confirmed by the fact that the Abbot of Jumièges presented to the church.

[40] J. J. Vernier, *Chartes de Jumièges*, i, p. 30, no. xii.

[41] Among the places named as having been bestowed by William Longsword are Yainville, Le Trait, Saint-Paul, Duclair and Épinay.

[42] *Cartulaire des Îles Normandes* (Soc. Jersiaise, 1924), p. 5, no. 3.

[43] Moidrey, Curey, Macey, Cormeray, Vergoncey. For these identifications see *Eng. Hist. Rev.*, lxi (1946), p. 144.

[44] Flodoard, *Annales* (ed. Lauer, p. 55).

[45] The name may represent O. Norse *Hraithulfr*, or O. Swed. *Hrithulf*.

[46] Will. Jum., Bk. iii, chap. 2 (ed. Marx, p. 33). This is derived from Dudo (ed. Lair, p. 188).

[47] See Le Prévost, *Mémoires . . . sur Eure* (1862–9), ii, p. 520: 'in eodem comitatu Amfridi villam et Fredisvillam quas Willelmus comes dedit triumphatis hostibus victor rediens.' It is hard to see to what 'Count William' this could refer unless to William Longsword.

[48] *Annales* (ed. Lauer, p. 24).

[49] See P. Lauer, *Louis d'Outre-Mer* (1900), pp. 100, 287–92.

[50] F. Lot, *Les Derniers Carolingiens* (1891), pp. 346–57.

[51] Lot, *op. cit.*, gives the date as 966. I prefer 965 for the reasons given in Prentout, *Étude sur Dudon*, App. iv, pp. 447–51.

[52] See F. M. Stenton, *Anglo-Saxon England* (1943), pp. 370–1.

[53] Ed. Waitz (1877), p. 180.

[54] The story is found only in William of Jumièges (Bk. v, chap. 4, ed. Marx, pp. 76–7), and has therefore been treated with a proper scepticism. (Cf. E. A. Freeman, *Norman Conquest*, i (1870), 632; F. M. Stenton, *op. cit.*, p. 374, apparently suspends judgement.) It should be noted, however, that *A.S. Chron.* 'E' (*s.a.* 1000, 1001) states that in 1000 a Viking fleet on leaving England went to Normandy, and that in the next year the coasts of England opposite to Normandy were ravaged. This to some extent helps to confirm William of Jumièges at this point.

[55] Will. Jum., Bk. v, chap. 1 (ed. Marx, p. 73).

[56] Compare the lurid account given by Rodulf Glaber (ed. Prou, p. 43) with that supplied by the *Gesta Episc. Cameracensium* (*Mon. Germ. Hist.* SS, vii, p. 464).

[57] 'Translatio S. Maglorii', ed. Merlet (*Bibl. Éc. Chartès*, lvi, pp. 247–8).

[58] Will. Jum., Bk. v, chap. 11 (ed. Marx, pp. 85, 86).

[59] *Ibid.*, Bk. v, chap. 12 (ed. Marx, p. 87). See also C. Pfister, *Robert le Pieux* (1885), pp. 214, 215.

[60] See Lot, *Fidèles ou Vassaux?* (1904), pp. 177–237, which in general is here followed in this matter as opposed to Flach, *Origines de l'ancienne France*, (1917), iv, pp. 111–72.

[61] Bouquet, *Rec. Hist. Franc.*, ix, p. 536.

[62] *Annales* (ed. Lauer, pp. 39, 55, 75).

[63] *Ibid.*, p. 84.

[64] Richer (ed. Waitz [1877], p. 53).

[65] Dudo (ed. Lair, p. 209).

[66] During the two years which followed the murder of William Longsword, Louis d'Outre-Mer was in Rouen no less than five times, and on one occasion for a considerable period (cf. Lauer, *Louis d'Outre-Mer*, p. 131).

[67] Dudo (ed. Lair, pp. 167, 168). Rollo's baptismal name was Robert.

[68] 'Princeps Francorum, Brittonum atque Nortmannorum' (*Annales Floriacenses* s.a. 956).

[69] Flodoard, *Annales* (ed. Lauer, pp. 86, 87).

[70] *Ibid.*, p. 148.

[71] L. Halpen, *Rec. des ætes de Lothaire et de Louis V* (1908), p. 53, no. xxiv.

[72] Bouquet, *Rec. Hist. Franc.*, ix, p. 731.

[73] Cf. Lot, *Derniers Carolingiens*, p. 215.

[74] Will. Jum., Bk. v, chap. 15 (ed. Marx, pp. 93, 94); Bouquet, *Rec. Hist. Franc.*, x, p. 270 (a chronicle of Auxerre). King Robert's charter of 30 May 1006 is dated at Fécamp (*Gall. Christ.*, xi, Instr., cols 8–9).

[75] See the *Vita Roberti regis* (Bouquet, *Rec. Hist. Franc.* x. 106); cf. *Chron. of Auxerre* (*ibid.*, x, 270).

[76] The letter of Odo to King Robert (Bouquet, *op. cit.*, x, 501) discusses the part played by Duke Richard in this famous affair. Duke Richard is there styled as *fidelis*.

[77] *Gesta Episc. Cameracensium* (*Mon. Germ. Hist.* SS, vii, p. 462), confirmed by Vernier, *Chartes de Fumièges* i, 25, no. x.

[78] Will. Jum., Bk. vi, chap. 7 (ed. Marx, p. 105), confirmed by Lot, *Saint-Wandrille*, pp. 52–4, no. 13.

[79] See above.

[80] Duke Richard I's charter for St Denis (Bouquet, *Rec. Hist. Franc.*, ix, p. 731)

alleges that a gift at Berneval to St Denis was originally made by *avus meus Robertus nomine*. The reference is to Rollo by his baptismal name.

[81] See above.

[82] See especially the *Lament* printed with facsimiles and discussed in J. Lair, *Étude sur la vie et la mort de Guillaume Longue Épée* (1893).

[83] Will. Jum., Bk. ii, chap. 7 (ed. Marx, p. 38) and cf. the authorities quoted by H. Prentout (*Étude*, pp. 30 *sqq.*).

[84] Will. Jum., Bk. iii, chap. 8 (ed. Marx, p. 39), confirmed by Vernier, *Chartes de Jumièges*, i, pp. 16–19, no. vii.

[85] *Translatio B. Agili Resbaciensis*, cited by Aubrey of the Three Fountains (*Mon. Germ. Hist.* SS, xxiii, p. 762).

[86] See Adémar of Chabannes, ed. J. Chavanon, pp. 139–40, and cf. p. 198.

[87] Flodoard, *Annales* (ed. Lauer, p. 63).

[88] *Gallia Christiana*, vol. xi *passim*; for Coutances, see *Gall. Christ.*, xi, Instr. 217.

[89] L. Halphen, *Rec. des actes de Lothaire et de Louis V*, p. 53, no. xxiv.

[90] T. Bonnin, *Cartulaire de Louviers* (1870), i, p. 1, no. i.

[91] F. Pommeraye, *Hist. St Ouen*, p. 404; Vernier, *Chartes de Jumièges*, i, no. xii, at p. 35.

[92] Lot, *Saint-Wandrille*, pp. xxxi–xxxvi, and authorities there cited.

[93] *Gall. Christ.*, xi, cols 513–14.

[94] A preliminary reference may here perhaps be usefully made to the 'Inventio et Miracula Sancti Wulfranni' which was apparently composed in the time of Duke William II, and which has recently been edited by Dom J. Laporte (*Soc. Hist. Norm. Mélanges*, 1938). This contains (pp. 28 *sqq.*) an account of Mainard and his influence.

[95] Cf. A. Robinson, *Times of St Dunstan* (1923), pp. 132 *sqq.*

[96] Cf. D. Knowles, *Monastic Order in England* (1940), pp. 83–99.

[97] 'Liber de Revelatione' (Migne, *Pat. Lat.*, vol. 151, cols 718, 719). Cf. H. Prentout, *Étude*, pp. 405, 406.

[98] Printed J. F. Lemarignier, *Privilèges d'exemption* (1937), pp. 291–3.

[99] C. H. Haskins, *Norman Institutions* (1918), pp. 252–3; Lemarignier, *op. cit.*, pp. 50–6. Their opinion that the clause is an interpolation is doubtless correct, but the matter does not appear to me to have been finally settled. That the charter was in fact issued by Richard I and not by his son, as has been sometimes suggested, is shown by the subscription of *Radulfi fratris comitis*. This seems to be the half-brother of Richard the Fearless.

[100] 'Chron. Fiscamn.' (Migne, *Pat. Lat.*, vol. 147, col. 480); 'Chron. S. Benign.' (*ibid.*, vol. 141, col. 864).

[101] C. H. Haskins, *op. cit.*, pp. 253–5, with illustration; *Gall. Christ.*, xi, Instr., cols 8, 9. Facsimile of original in Lemarignier, *op. cit.*

[102] The development of the exemption is discussed in Lemarignier, *op. cit.*, pp. 32–64.

[103] *Monasticon Anglicanum*, vi, 1073.

[104] Lemarignier, *op. cit.*, pp. 241–5.

[105] On this see the remarkable article by Watkin Williams in *Downside Review*, lii (1934), pp. 520–45.

[106] 'Chron. S. Benign.' (Migne, *Pat. Lat.*, vol. 141, col. 885).

[107] See Watkin Williams, *op. cit.*, pp. 537 *sqq.*

[108] *Gall. Christ.*, xi, cols 26–30; 333–4; 571; 766.

[109] G. H. White, *R. Hist. Soc. Trans.*, 4th ser., xxii, p. 81.

[110] Cf. *Gall. Christ.*, xi, col. 870.

[111] Lemarignier (*op. cit.*), in stressing the absence of Papal action in respect of Fécamp in 1006, appears to me to take too little cognizance of conditions at Rome at this time. After the death of Sylvester II in May 1003 there succeeded to the Papacy first John

XVII, who reigned only seven months, and then John XVIII, who survived until 1009. Both these popes seem to have been almost powerless and under the strict control of the counts of Tusculum; and their reigns are wrapped in great obscurity (R. L. Poole, *Studies in Chronology and History*, pp. 147, 155; cf. F. Gregorovius, *The City of Rome in the Middle Ages*, Eng. trans., vol. iv, pt. i, p. 7). Jaffé, *Reg. Pontif. Rom.*, gives no instrument under John XVII, and under John XVIII sixteen instruments of which six are for France. The absence in 1006 of a bull directed to a northern province is not surprising.

[112] R. L. Poole, *op. cit.*, p. 201.

[113] Pflugk-Hartung, *Acta pontificum inedita* (1881), i, p. 10. Some doubts have, however, been expressed respecting the authenticity of this act.

[114] Esp. C. H. Haskins, *op. cit.*, chap. i.

[115] D. Knowles, *Monastic Order*, pp. 87–99.

[116] Will. Jum., ed. Marx, pp. 320–9, and cf. G. H. White in *Genealogist*, N.S. xxxvii, p. 59.

[117] *Ord. Vit.* interp. Will. Jum., Bk. vii, chap. 3 (ed. Marx, p. 157).

[118] Will. Jum., Bk. v, chap. 10 (ed. Marx, p. 84). For the date see Pfister, *Robert le Pieux*, p. 215. It is alleged that Tosny was given him by Hugh, Archbishop of Rouen until 989 (*Gall. Christ.*, xi, col. 25, quoting *Acta Archiep. Rothom.* from Mabillon, *Analecta*, ii, p. 437). There seems here to be a serious chronological difficulty, but Ralf was probably the original grantee of Tosny. Tosny, it may be noted, is just across the Seine from Les Andelys, which was an archiepiscopal demesne of old standing.

[119] Vernier, *op. cit.*, i, p. 41, no. xii. For the family see Douglas, *Domesday Monachorum* (1944), pp. 65, 66.

[120] *Ord. Vit.*, ed. Le Prévost, iii, pp. 41, 42, 257.

[121] L. Delisle, *Hist. du Château et Sires de Saint-Sauveur-le-Vicomte* (1867), Preuves, pp. 4–6; Round, *Cal. Doc. France*, no. 703.

[122] Between 1017 and 1025 charters for Fécamp were witnessed by a certain *vicecomes* named Thurstan (Haskins, *op. cit.*, p. 256; Bonnin, *Cartul. de Louviers*, i, p. 3, no. 2), who also, between 1023 and 1032, attested charters for Le Mont Saint-Michel (*Cartul. des Îles Normandes*, pp. 5–8, no. 3; pp. 182–4, no. 114). This Thurstan was clearly a man of importance, and, although the proof is somewhat complicated, it seems possible to identify him with Thurstan Goz, ancestor of Hugh, Earl of Chester. Thus William of Jumièges states that a Thurstan whom he describes as *praeses* of the Hiémois rebelled against Duke William during the minority of that duke (Bk. vii, chap. 3, ed. Marx, p. 118); and Orderic interpolating this passage (*ibid.*, p. 160) observes that this Thurstan was surnamed 'Goz', and had a son named Richard. Similarly in his own history Orderic twice asserts that Richard, *vicomte* of the Avranchin, was son of Thurstan (ed. Le Prévost, ii, pp. 60, 105), and this same Richard is shown in charters to have been the son of Thurstan Goz (*Cart. Antiq. Baioc.*, Livre Noir [1902], i, pp. 3–4; Bertrand de Broussillon, *Maison de Laval* [1895], i, p. 39, no. 27).

[123] Before 1022 a certain Anschitil witnessed Gunnor's charter for Le Mont Saint-Michel, and between 1028 and 1034 another charter for the same house was attested by 'Anschetillus Baiocensis vicecomes' (Round, *Cal. Doc. France*, nos 703–4). He survived until after 1031, for between that year and 1035 he attested two ducal grants for St Wandrille (Lot, *Saint-Wandrille*, pp. 53, 56, nos 13, 14). After his death his office continued in his family, for among the rebels at Val-ès-Dunes in 1047 was Ranulf, *vicomte* of the Bessin, and it is reasonable to suppose that this was the son of Anschitil, since about 1042 Duke William had restored to *Rannulfo filio Anschitilli* land in Guernsey which his father had given to Le Mont Saint-Michel (Will. Poit., ed. Giles, *Scriptores*, p. 80; Delisle, *op. cit.*, Preuves, p. 19, no. 17). He married Alice, daughter of Duke Richard III (*Robert Torigny*, ed. Delisle, i, p. 34) and was succeeded as *vicomte* of

the Bessin by another Ranulf (II) who was presumably his son, and who occurs in or before 1066 (Bertrand de Broussillon, *Maison de Laval*, i, pp. 39–42; Davis, *Regesta*, no. 4). This Ranulf II married Maud, daughter of Richard, *vicomte* of the Avranchin (*Ord. Vit.*, iv, p. 422), and it was his son, Ranulf III, who became *vicomte* of the Bessin at some date after 24 April 1089 (see *Cart. Antiq. Baioc.*, ed. Bourrienne, pp. 7–8), and who in due course became Earl of Chester (see *Complete Peerage*, iii, p. 166).

124 Richard II's charter for Judith is printed in Martène and Durand, *Thesaurus novus Anecdotorum* (1717), i, col. 122.

125 For Ferrières see Will. Jum., Bk. vii, chap. 1 (ed. Marx, pp. 116, 155); *Ord. Vit.*, i, p. 180. Chambrais, whose name was later changed to Broglie, adjoins Ferrières, and was, at a subsequent date, the *caput* of the barony.

126 See Richard II's charter for Bernay, the best printed text of which is in *Mém. Soc. Norm. Antiq.* (1828), iv, pp. 377–83. There seems no reason to distrust the information given in this charter, but the long list of witnesses may be inflated.

127 Robert of Torigny, 'De Immutatione ordinis monachorum' (*Monasticon Anglicanum*, vi, p. 1063).

128 The record of a plea in the time of Duke Richard II printed as an appendix to L. Valin, *Le Duc de Normandie et sa cour*, at p. 257, reveals the situation of the estate which was alienated at this early date. The central manor is 'Douvrenc' which is Douvrend (Seine-Inf., arr. Dieppe, cant. Envermeu), and which appears in other Rouen documents as belonging to the cathedral (cf. Martène and Durand, *op. cit.*, i, col. 146, and Bouquet, *op. cit.*, 4to continuation, Pouille . . . de Rouen, p. 40). The dependent estates include 'Montciit', 'Montane', 'Extrie Montes', 'Dowrendel', 'Puteolis', 'Hugonis mesnil' and 'Baslei'. These are Monthuit, Montigny, Étrimont, Douvrendel, Pulcheux, Humesnil, Bailly-en-Rivière. It should be noted also that the plea concerning this estate was held in a wood called 'Blanca', and in 1815 there was still in the vicinity of Douvrend a wood called 'Le Clos Blanc' (J. B. D. Cochet, *Rép. archéol.* . . . *de la Seine-Inférieure* [1871], p. 27).

129 F. Chalandon (*La Domination normande en Italie*, at p. 52) mentions Ralf de Tosny as arriving at Salerno, whilst at p. 49 he places the seige of Salerno late in 1015 and early in 1016. This date should be preferred to that given (1012) in the 'Chron. Mon. Cassinensis' (*Mon. Germ. Hist. SS*, vii, p. 652), since in 1013 or 1014 Ralf was apparently conducting the defence of Tillières (Will. Jum., Bk. v, chap. 10, ed. Marx, p. 84).

130 *Cartul. des Îles Normandes*, p. 5, no. 3.

131 Thus the family held Troarn, where before 1050 Roger I of Montgomery founded a church of secular canons (*Ord. Vit.* ii. pp. 21–2: the date is shown by a charter of Roger given on the day of the dedication of the church which contains the confirmation of Hugh, bishop of Lisieux (R. N. Sauvage, *Saint Martin de Troarn*, p. 347, Preuves, no. i); although Sauvage relates it to the foundation of the later abbey the occurrence of Bishop Hugh who died in October 1049 shows it to refer to the earlier foundation. But a charter of Duke Richard II (Bonnin, *Cartulaire de Louviers*, no. ii, at p. 4) had previously confirmed to Fécamp: 'Troadum et quicquid ad ipsum pertinet'. Similarly 'Almasniacus', which was likewise confirmed to Fécamp by Richard II, is clearly Almenèches, where Roger II of Montgomery established on his estates an abbey of Benedictine nuns. Finally before his death Duke Richard II confirmed to the abbey of Jumièges land, toll, and a fair at Vimoutiers (Vernier, *Chartes de Jumièges*, i, no. xii, at p. 35), but Roger I of Montgomery seems to have acquired these shortly after the Duke's death, since between 1028 and 1035 he restored to the monks the market at that place (Vernier, *op. cit.*, i, p. 43, no. xiii: the editor refers this charter wrongly to Roger II, whom he strangely describes as 'Comte de Montgomery').

132 The document printed as No. 1 in the *Cartulaire de Louviers* compiled by Bonnin indicates that Richard I gave to St Taurin *de dominico suo* land *apud Molas*. This is very

possibly Meules (Calvados, arr. Lisieux, cant. Orbec), which in due course became the *caput* of the Norman barony of Baldwin son of Count Gilbert. One of Baldwin's tenants in England in 1086 was Roger 'de Moles' (D.B. i, fol. 106).

133 Robert of Torigny interpolating Will. Jum. (Bk. viii, chap. 37, ed. Marx, p. 324). The pedigree suggested by Robert cannot be correct, but a connection between the two families may be assumed.

134 In 1086 Roger 'de Abernon' held Molesham (Surrey) and Freston (Suffolk) from Richard fitz-Gilbert (D.B. i, fol. 35; ii, fol. 395b). A charter of Theobald, Archbishop of Canterbury (*Monasticon Anglicanum*, vi. 1659), enumerates among the gifts of the men of the lords of Clare certain benefactions 'ex dono Radulfi de la Cressimera'. Both Abenon and La Cressonnière are within three miles of Orbec.

135 In 1106 Gerold de Normanville witnessed a charter of Henry, count of Eu, giving the manor of Hooe, Sussex, to the Priory of St Martin de Bose (Round, *Cal. Doc. France*, no. 399). Normanville is some fifteen miles south of Neufchâtel-en-Bray. Neufchâtel is the ancient Drincourt, and a charter in the cartulary of Holy Trinity, Rouen (ed. Deville, p. 423, no. ii), the date of which may be roughly placed *c.* 1040–50, shows William the younger, brother of Robert, Count of Eu, as having a contingent interest in Drincourt.

136 D.B. i, fols 257, 257b. *Ord. Vit.*, ii, p. 427, gives particulars which place the family of Pantulf at Noron within the Hiémois, where Roger I of Montgomery was *vicomte*.

137 Vernier, *Chartes de Jumièges*, i, p. 43, no. xiii.

138 *Ord. Vit.*, iii, pp. 426, 427; *Gall. Christ.*, xi, Instr., col. 132. A branch of the family is found in Yorkshire on those lands which at the time of Domesday had been held by Berengar de Tosny of Belvoir (Farrer, *Early Yorkshire Charters* [1914], i, p. 466 sqq.). For further evidence of the early connection between Clères and Tosny in England see Round, *Cal. Doc. France*, no. 626. Before the Conquest Roger I of Clères made a grant to Saint-Ouen of land at Blainville in the vicinity of Clères with the assent of his lord, Ralf de Tosny (Le Prévost, *Mémoires . . . sur Eure*, iii, p. 467).

139 *Ord. Vit.*, i, p. 180; ii, pp. 40, 41.

140 *Ord. Vit.*, iii, pp. 426, 427. The editor wrongly identifies 'Rogerius de Clara', here mentioned, with Roger de Clare, son of Richard fitz-Gilbert. The families of Clères (Seine-Inf., arr. Rouen, cant. Clères) and of Clare (Suffolk) are of course quite distinct.

141 See Duke Richard II's charter for St Quentin (*Nouveau traité de Diplomatique*, iv, p. 225).

142 Arfast's charter for Saint-Père of Chartres (*Cartulaire*, ed. Guérard [1840] i, p. 108) names these *milites* as 'Rollo et Angoht et Unbeina'. The names are apparently Scandinavian (see E. Björkman, *Nordische Personennamen in England* (1910), pp. 4, 14, 113, 169, 170).

143 Le Prévost, *Mémoires . . . sur Eure*, iii, p. 467; Haskins, *op. cit.*, p. 19.

144 See Haskins, *op. cit.*, chap. i, and F. M. Stenton, *Anglo-Saxon England*, pp. 549–51.

145 Ed. Giles, *Scriptores . . . Willelmi Conquestoris* (1845), pp. 121, 122.

VIII

Rollo of Normandy

Rollo, ancestor of the dukes of Normandy, is a figure familiar both in history and in legend. He fired the imagination of his medieval posterity, and afterwards for more than three centuries he has supplied the material of a copious and controversial literature.[1] During the latter half of the nineteenth century, disputes respecting him were stimulated by Scandinavian politics, and today the student is confronted with rival and contradictory accounts of his career sponsored by scholars as distinguished as Steenstrup,[2] W. Vogel,[3] Alexander Bugge[4] and Henri Prentout.[5] In England, these controversies have in the main produced an uneasy silence,[6] and it therefore deserves note that the most important contribution to Rollo's biography was in fact made by an Englishman. The problem of Rollo is bound up with that of Dudo of St Quentin who between 1015 and 1026[7] compiled his 'panegyric' of the Norman dynasty.[8] In 1865 J. Lair made his learned attempt[9] to rehabilitate Dudo as an historical source, and his conclusions were generally accepted by Steenstrup[10] and in part by Vogel.[11] But they had already been successfully impugned in 1880 by Sir Henry Howorth, who showed conclusively how little reliance could be placed upon any statement made by Dudo about Rollo.[12] Since the appearance of this article it has been clear that Rollo's biography must be constructed independently of the dean of St Quentin. But Howorth added to his destructive criticism a new account of Rollo's life which, though it apparently enjoys wide currency in this country, is none the less more easy to criticize. Certainly, English scholars do not appear to be either decided or unanimous about Rollo,[13] and it may therefore be seemly to attempt in an English periodical a fresh review of the evidence which relates to this remote progenitor of English kings.[14]

The origins of Rollo have been hotly disputed. According to Dudo he was the son of a nobleman in 'Dacia', and he had a brother named 'Gurim'. Both he and 'Gurim' fought with the king of 'Dacia' and in the struggle 'Gurim' was killed. Then Rollo went to 'Scanza' (? the Scandinavian peninsula) with six ships. From there (as it is added) he subsequently set sail for England where he entered into relations with 'Alstelmus', 'the most Christian King'. Afterwards, leaving England he conducted long campaigns in Frisia, and only on their completion did he enter Gaul where, after depositing the relics of St Himeltrude on the altar of St Vedast, he at length took possession of Rouen.[15] This story is manifestly improbable in all its details,[16] but since it seems likely that by 'Dacia' Dudo meant Denmark, a long line of Danish historians have contended that Rollo was a Dane.[17] There seems, however, no reason to trust Dudo on this matter more than elsewhere. The dean of St Quentin had some cause to assign a Danish origin to Rollo since when he wrote there was an alliance between Duke Richard II and the Danish king, Sweyn Forkbeard.[18] Nor can his statement here be confirmed. Saxo Grammaticus who, in the twelfth century, might have been expected to speak of Rollo's connection with Denmark if he believed in it, is wholly silent on this point,[19] and even William of Jumièges, who transcribed so much of Dudo's narrative, is somewhat cautious in his treatment of this matter.[20] The theory that Rollo came from Denmark rests in the last resort upon Dudo's uncorroborated testimony.[21] As such it is deeply suspect.

It is therefore significant that during the middle ages there was a powerful tradition that Rollo came from Norway and that he was Rolf the son of Rögnvald, earl of Möre. This opinion is, for instance, asserted in a series of emphatic statements in the Heimskringla. Thus the *Life of Harold Fairhair* remarks:

Rögnvald had for his wife Hild the daughter of Rolf Nevja and their sons were Rolf and Thorir. . . . Rolf was a great Viking: he was so big that no steed could bear him, and he therefore walked wherever he went, so that he was called Rolf 'the Ganger'.[22]

For his lawlessness he was in due course exiled from Norway, and therefore he

afterwards crossed the sea to the Hebrides, in the British Isles, and from there went south-westward to France, where he harried and possessed himself of a great earldom. He settled many Norsemen there, and it was afterwards called Normandy. From Rolf are descended the earls of Normandy. Rolf the Ganger's son was William, the father of Richard, the father of another Richard, the father of Robert Longsword, the father of William the Bastard, king of the English, from whom are descended all the later kings of the English.[23]

Similarly, the Life of St Olaf, speaking of Richard II of Normandy, adds:

Richard, earl of Ruða [Rouen] was son of Richard, son of William Longspear, and he was the son of earl Rolf 'the Ganger' who had won

Normandy. He in turn was the son of Rögnvald the Great, earl of Möre.[24]

The *Kings' Lives* represent opinions current in the thirteenth century, and their evidence on this question must therefore be approached with all the scepticism demanded by an imaginative source of a late date. But when compiling them it seems very possible that Snorri Sturlason edited material derived from the earlier work of Ari the Learned,[25] and certainly that careful and scholarly writer, who was born in 1067 and died in 1148,[26] was in this matter decided in his opinion. Among the sons of Rögnvald he says:

> Another was Ganger-Rolf, who conquered Normandy. From him came the earls of Rouen and the kings of the English.[27]

Such testimony merits, at least, respectful consideration.

The undoubted difficulties which lie in the way of its acceptance do not, moreover, appear to be insuperable.[28] Thus it has been suggested as very strange that Norman writers of a later date do not allude to Rollo's nickname of 'Ganger', or to the story of how he came by it.[29] But the probable absence[30] in Dudo of any reference to the name is sufficient to account for its omission in later Norman writers who took almost everything concerning Rollo from Dudo's book. Both the nickname and the story attached to it have the appearance of a legend which obtained currency after the death of a hero. If this be so, and Rollo was not so described in his lifetime, he would not have brought the nickname with him to Neustria, and, since the fable was obviously of either Norwegian or Icelandic origin, there is no reason why Dudo should ever have heard of it. In any case, he would have had good reason to suppress it in view of his own story of Rollo's career.

More seriously to be considered is the fact that Richer of Rheims in a difficult passage refers to Rollo as to 'filio Catilli'.[31] This statement, which is nowhere confirmed, may, however, easily be given greater weight than it deserves. It must be placed in its proper setting in Richer's book. Richer, for the period before 970, is an untrustworthy writer whenever he adds to the statements of Flodoard whose work he used.[32] He admittedly relied upon legends, and this 'Catillus', who figures largely in the earlier chapters of his book,[33] is clearly a legendary figure[34] who has been held to conceal the personality of Hasting[35] or perhaps of Hundaeus.[36] Even if 'Catillus' can here be taken as representing the Scandinavian name *Ketil*,[37] Richer's isolated statement does not inspire confidence. Until it receives some confirmation from a more trustworthy source it may be set aside without undue misgiving.

Thirdly, it has been suggested[38] that the name which Ari reproduces in the form 'Hrólfr' would probably be Latinized as 'Radulfus', not 'Rollo'. But there is little weight in this objection. Hrólfr itself appears to be derived from some such name as 'Hróð-wulk', and a hypocoristic form of this, presumably 'Hrolle', probably lies behind the Latin 'Rollo'. In any case there appears to be positive evidence that the name Rolf was in fact sometimes Latinized as Rollo.[39] Thus Le Prévost prints[40] part of a charter of Richard II, Rollo's great grandson, in favour of St Ouen of Rouen. In this confirmation Richard alludes to previous possessions of that abbey 'quae omnia noster atavus Rolphus praenominato loco partim restituit et dedit'. If this charter be genuine, its testimony on this matter would be conclusive. But even if it be a fabrication – and the charters of St Ouen are not above suspicion – it would be odd if a forger should use such an exceptional form unless he got it from earlier documents. 'Rollo' can, with little difficulty, be accepted as a Latin form of 'Rolf'.

The argument in favour of the Norwegian tradition of Rollo's origins does not, however, depend on the answers which may be made to objections thereto, but on more weighty considerations. For, when all due qualifications have been made, the evidence of the Sagas on this question cannot in truth be lightly set aside. They embodied the traditions of a seafaring folk who frequented the northern ports and were certainly well acquainted with Rouen. Here they recorded the exploits of a man who was involved in the making of Normandy, one of the most notable achievements of the race. In matters of genealogy, moreover, the Sagas are always worthy of a particular attention, and it is impossible to suggest that this story was invented for the glorification of a particular family. Even if unconfirmed, the tradition here recorded would deserve respect. When it is found to be independently confirmed it promotes conviction.

Perhaps the greatest obstacle to the elucidation of early Norman history lies in the fact that it is generally impossible to relate the Scandinavian to the Frankish evidence. But in this crucial matter it actually seems possible to do so. Ari the Learned not only speaks of Rollo as Rolf the son of Rögnvald,[41] he also, in another passage, states that Rolf's daughter, Kathleen, married Beolan, a king in Scotland.

> Another son of Othere was Helge. He married in Scotland and won there as his booty Nithbeorg, daughter of King Beolan and of Kathleen, daughter of Ganger-Rolf.[42]

The mother of a woman named Kathleen would almost certainly be an Irish-Scot since the name is Keltic, and an Irish-Scot at this period would be a Christian. The story told by Ari therefore suggests that Rolf while campaigning in Scotland took to wife a Christian woman. Turn now to the Frankish *Lament for the Death of William Longsword* which is nearly contemporary with the events which it describes.[43] Speaking of William

Longsword, who was the son of Rollo, this poem states that William was born outside France and of a Christian mother at a time when his father was still pagan.[44] The suggestion of the Landnámabók is thus confirmed by an epic poem composed in Gaul in the tenth century. The fact would seem to be a powerful, if not a conclusive, argument in favour of the identity of Rollo with Ganger-Rolf.

The Norwegian origin of Rollo seems to have remained a belief in the ducal family at a later date. In the time of St Olaf, the dukes of Normandy apparently claimed kinship with the leading men of Norway, and set great store by it so that men from Norway were allowed to live in Normandy in freedom and peace:[45] and William of Malmesbury writing about 1115, and therefore before the *Kings' Lives* assumed their present form, tells much the same story as they do.[46] Formal proof is impossible in view of the paucity of the evidence, but despite all difficulties the chain of related testimony appears to leave little doubt as to the origins of Rollo. It would seem that he was Ganger-Rolf, and apparently the son of Rögnvald, earl of Möre. While in Scotland he married a Christian woman and by her he had a daughter named Kathleen who became the wife of Beolan. William, Rollo's son, being either the brother or the half-brother of Kathleen, was also born overseas, but was afterwards to succeed his father in Normandy.

Such conclusions respecting Rollo himself should not be taken as implying that all, or even most, of the Viking settlers in Normandy in the time of Rollo were of Norwegian descent. After his recognition, Rollo apparently gave land not only to his own personal followers but also to other men from overseas.[47] Moreover, the general course of Scandinavian expansion westward in the ninth and tenth centuries would suggest that apart from those invaders who penetrated to the Seine basin by way of the valley of the Loire, the bulk of the settlers in Normandy would in all probability be Danes. Certainly, the Great Army which towards the end of the ninth century divided up Northumbria and East Anglia established in those districts a population which was predominantly Danish,[48] and equally certainly this same Great Army conducted its operations indiscriminately on both sides of the Channel.[49] The question must not be regarded as completely closed, since there are some indications of the presence of Norwegian settlers in the Seine valley,[50] and, after the Norman Conquest, it was officially stated in England that the ancestors of 'nearly all the Norman barons' came from Norway.[51] Such statements should not, however, be given undue weight, and it is probably safe to conclude that in the early tenth century the bulk of the new settlers in Normandy were of Danish stock, but that men from Norway (in a proportion not known) were intermingled among them, particularly among the aristocracy that surrounded Rollo, the Norwegian chief.

The date of Rollo's first appearance in the Seine valley is very hard to establish. In one of the few paragraphs of his book that contains a date, Dudo asserts that Rollo took possession of Rouen in 876,[52] and this statement has been repeated by many writers, both medieval and modern.[53] In truth, it is completely false,[54] and must be set aside together with the whole of Dudo's story respecting the adventures of Rollo in Gaul during the last quarter of the ninth century.[55] Rollo, who was certainly alive at least as late as 925,[56] cannot have arrived in Gaul until long after 876. A later tradition recorded by a monk of Limoges while interpolating the eleventh-century chronicle of Adémar of Chabannes[57] places his arrival in the years 896–900, but even this is probably too early. It is unlikely that he left Norway earlier than 900,[58] and before coming to the Seine valley he had a considerable career as a Viking. He certainly visited Scotland,[59] and the *Historia Norvegiae* written about 1200, but embodying earlier material, asserts that while in Scotland he raided Northumbria.[60] It is also stated that he went to Ireland,[61] and this statement is perhaps supported by the remark of the *Heimskringla* that he crossed the sea from Norway to the Hebrides and from there subsequently went 'south-west' to France.[62] Nothing could be more plausible than this hypothesis. Ireland was a constant lure for raiders in Scotland at this period and it was also the starting-point for many raids upon Gaul.[63] Moreover, during the first decade of the tenth century the Norse power in Ireland was beginning to wane, and many Viking chiefs, such as Bard and Erik who sacked Tours in 903,[64] made their way from Ireland to France about this time. Rollo may well have followed in their wake. This suggestion which is supported by the common tendency of so much converging evidence is also in harmony with what is known of the ages of Rollo's children, some of whom (it will be remembered) were born before their father arrived in Gaul. It seems, for instance, improbable that William Longsword was born before about 905,[65] and on all grounds it is unlikely that Rollo reached Gaul much if at all before that year.

Several scholars in company with Sir Henry Howorth[66] have indeed asserted that Rollo's first appearance in the Seine valley did not take place until much later even than this, because there seemed to be an absence in the Frankish chronicles of any unequivocal reference to him as present in Gaul before 921, in which year Richer of Rheims[67] speaks of him as being a leader of the pirates in Neustria, with a possible implication that he was not yet in possession of the lower Seine.[68] But this isolated passage in Richer is neither unambiguous nor deserving of great credence, and the implication of the chroniclers' apparent silence might very easily be exaggerated. Neither the Annals of St Vedast nor those of St Bertin were being continued in this period, and the only notable contemporary chronicler of this time is Regino of Prom whose work stops in 906,[69] and who in any case was not directly concerned with the affairs of northern

Gaul. In effect, as will appear below, the conclusion that Rollo was not in Gaul before 921 is inadmissible.

A diploma of Charles the Simple[70] assigns to the abbey of St Germain des Près the monastery of La Croix-St Ouen situated on the Eure together with its possessions:

praeter partem ipsius Abbatiae uam annuimus Nortmannis Sequanensibus, videlicet Rolloni suisque comitibus pro tutela regni.

This diploma, moreover, contains the following dating clause:

Datum II Idus Mart. Indictione VI anno XXVI regnante Karolo Rege glorioso, redintegrante XXI, largiore vero hereditate indepta VI.[71] Actum Compendio palatio in Dei nomine feliciter. Amen.

In short, this text, dated 14 March 918, speaks of a previous concession to Rollo and to the Normans of the Seine, and if it be authentic in its present form it is conclusive evidence that Rollo and his followers were settled in Normandy before that year. The printed text of this charter is derived from an original in Paris[72] which has apparently never been reproduced in facsimile, and is now unavailable, so that it must be approached with all proper caution. But since it has been accepted as genuine by Mabillon,[73] Giry[74] and Ferdinand Lot,[75] it would be difficult to cite stronger testimony in favour of its authenticity, and there appears to be nothing either in its form or matter to justify doubt.[76] Unless, therefore, further research should pronounce it to be spurious it supplies irrefragable testimony as to the latest date which could be assigned to Rollo's advent into Gaul.

The evidence from the chroniclers, moreover, when examined, is found to tend in the same direction. Before 970, as has been seen, Richer is an unreliable guide whenever he glosses Flodoard, and in this matter the testimony of Flodoard is against him. Flodoard wrote some time after 952, and then compiled annals for the period 919 to 966.[77] He also composed a history of the church of Rheims.[78] In the course of these works he makes four statements relating to the origins of Normandy. Firstly, he states that at some period in the reign of Charles the Simple a definite agreement was made between that prince and the Vikings of the Seine valley.[79] Secondly, he records that as a consequence of that agreement these same settlers received baptism.[80] Thirdly, he remarks that the conversion (and therefore also the agreement) followed after a great battle at Chartres where the Vikings were defeated.[81] And fourthly (in another place), he alludes to Rollo as being in 925 *princeps* of the Northmen in the neighbourhood of Rouen.[82] These four statements, which may be accepted at their face value, deserve close attention.

It will be seen that Flodoard makes no specific allusion to the presence

of Rollo in France before mentioning him in connection with events in
925. Nevertheless, he relates the agreement between Charles the Simple
and the Vikings directly to the battle of Chartres. The date of that battle
becomes therefore of cardinal importance to the elucidation of this
chronology. Dudo here as elsewhere is untrustworthy, since he confuses
that battle with earlier campaigns waged by the Normans of the Loire.
Other later writers give varying dates, but in general the balance of later
tradition was in favour of 911, and this is confirmed by the reliable Annals
of Ste Colombe of Sens which state that the battle took place on 20 July
911.[83] This date must be accepted.[84] Now, according to Flodoard, the
agreement followed this defeat of the Vikings, and there is ample evidence
to suggest the motives which inspired Charles to conclude it. Such
agreements were an essential part of his policy.[85] Moreover, in 911 he had
good reasons for desiring a stabilization of the north, for he had long
planned an invasion of Lorraine,[86] and in the very next year he was to put
that plan into execution, strengthened by the death of Louis the Child,
who died on 24 September 911.[87] If, then, the battle of Chartres took
place on 20 July 911 the negotiations which followed it must have been
concluded before 1 January 912, at which date Charles the Simple was at
Metz[88] engaged in his new venture in Lorraine. It would appear, therefore,
that despite the criticism which has been levelled against it, the traditional
date given for this famous agreement is correct. The treaty between
Charles the Simple and the Vikings of the Seine was made in the autumn
of 911.

This being so, there only remains the question whether Rollo himself
was involved in these events. Charles's diploma, supported by the whole
weight of subsequent tradition, asserts that this was the case, and without
violently offending probability it would be very hard to gainsay it. Moreover, there were undoubtedly Viking raids into central France about the
year 910. These particularly affected the neighbourhood of Bourges and of
St Benoît-sur-Loire,[89] and it is thus significant that the eleventh-century
author of the *Miracula S. Benedicti* actually speaks of depredations which
were committed by a 'King Renaud' who (it is added) later died at Rouen.[90]
If Rollo was in truth involved in this campaign, his most natural route
northward would have brought him before the walls of Chartres. On all
grounds it seems certain that Rollo not only took part in the settlement
with Charles in 911, but that he was present at the battle which made
that settlement possible.

According to Dudo, whose statement here lacks any independent
confirmation, these negotiations culminated in a personal interview
between Charles and Rollo at St Clair-sur-Epte.[91] This is very possible
since such formal meetings (like that between Alfred and Guthrum) were
not uncommon, and St Clair is not a place that would seem likely to be

selected if the story were an invention. On the other hand, it must be noted that in 965[92] a famous interview did without doubt take place on the Epte between Richard I of Normandy and Lothair.[93] Dudo, who frequented the court of Richard I at a later date, would have been well acquainted with this event, and it would be in no wise contrary to his constant practice if he should have used this example to fabricate a similar episode in the life of Rollo.[94] Certainly, in view of the unwarranted precision which is usually given to 'the Treaty of Saint Clair-sur-Epte', it deserves emphasis that the only positive evidence connecting the agreement with a personal interview or with the village of Saint Clair-sur-Epte comes from a source which is very suspect. That the celebrated interview actually took place, and that the so-called treaty was ratified at the place from which it takes its conventional name are historical assumptions which, though very possibly true, are unproved.

The 'Treaty of Saint Clair-sur-Epte' has thus been rashly designated, and it is also very easy to be too precise as to the agreement which was undoubtedly made in the autumn of 911 between Charles and the Northmen of the Seine. No text of 'the treaty of St Clair-sur-Epte' exists, and it is doubtful whether its terms were ever reduced to writing since, in the tenth century,[95] and in particular in this region of northern Gaul,[96] the practice of making written records of legal transactions appears to have been lapsing into desuetude.[97] Dudo, who is so loquacious about the alleged meeting between Rollo and Charles, is both laconic and obviously inaccurate in describing its results.[98] All that remains certain is that a cession of territory was made, and that this was followed by the formal conversion of Rollo and many of his followers.

What were the lands which were then granted? In his *History of the Church of Rheims*, Flodoard expressly remarks that the territory then ceded to the Vikings consisted of Rouen, together with several districts on the sea coast which were dependent upon that city.[99] This statement is precise, for Flodoard knew very well the extent of the province of Rouen, and if he had meant to imply that the whole of that province was bestowed he would have said so.[100] His words indicate that only a part of this province was granted,[101] and this is confirmed by other evidence. It will be recalled that Charles's diploma of 918 indicates that in that year only part of the lands of the monastery of St Croix-St Ouen,[102] situated on the Eure, were in Scandinavian hands. The force of this testimony is in this connection, however, diminished by the fact that nothing is known as to the exact location of the ancient possessions of this abbey.[103] It remains certain none the less that before 924 the lands which had been ceded to the Vikings in this region did not extend beyond the Orne. In 923 the dynastic wars of Gaul gave an opportunity to Rollo and his followers to barter their support. They did so; and as a result in 924 a new grant of

E

land was made to them by King Rudolf. Flodoard is perfectly clear as to what this implied. It was in 924, he says, that the Bessin and Maine were added to the lands which the Seine Vikings already held.[104]

Nor was even this the final settlement.[105] It should be remembered that at this period the political filiation of the region comprised in the dioceses of Coutances and Avranches was not yet determined, and there were, indeed, strong indications that this wide area might finally be attached not to the Viking province to the east of it but to Brittany. As early as 867, Charles the Bald, in his efforts to withstand the Northmen, had granted to the Breton king Solomon the county of Coutances,[106] and five years later the Avranchin – *Pagus Abrincatinus* – had certainly passed under Breton control.[107] Since that time all this region had been subject to Viking raids, and between 919 and 924 the clergy of Dol, together with those of Avranches and Bayeux, fled from the pagans carrying with them the relics of their patron saints.[108] This devastation was, however, primarily the work of the Vikings of the Loire not those of the Seine,[109] and after 919 it is said that the whole of Brittany was overrun by invaders from the south.[110] The formal cession of the county of Nantes to the Vikings of the Loire in 921[111] might even have perpetuated these conditions and attached both Brittany and also the two westernmost dioceses of medieval Normandy permanently to a state thus constructed in north-western Gaul. But in 931 a general revolt of the Bretons took place.[112] Its suppression resulted in a new extension of the dominion of the Seine Vikings. This was, however, the achievement not of Rollo, but of his son and successor William Longsword, who in 933 having commended himself to Rudolf of Burgundy was granted 'the lands of the Bretons situated on the sea coast'.[113] The history of the previous decades leaves no doubt as to what this final grant implied. The district thus designated comprised the Côtentin and the Avranchin. Not until 933 – after the death of Rollo – was the western frontier of medieval Normandy at last marked out.

The acquisition of Normandy by the Vikings only took place gradually, and was only partially accomplished in the time of Rollo. In 911 Rollo received Upper Normandy between the Epte and the sea. After 924 he possessed the Bessin and Maine. But, as it appears, he never acquired the Côtentin or the Avranchin which were attached to Normandy by his son. Nevertheless, in several respects, this final development was prepared in the previous decades. The revision of the western frontiers of Normandy is not merely to be regarded as an expansion of the Seine Vikings; it implied at the same time the reassertion of the ancient unity of the arch-diocese of Rouen, itself based upon the old Roman province of *Lugdunensis secunda*, with its seven *civitates* of Rouen, Bayeux, Avranches, Evreux, Sées, Lisieux and Coutances.[114] The frontiers of Normandy established after so much difficulty in 933 may have at that time seemed unstable, but they were based upon ancient tradition, and they had the sanction of ecclesiastical usage. They were therefore to endure.

The future development of the province founded in the time of Rollo was thus conditioned by the conversion of Rollo and his followers to Christianity. According to Dudo, Rollo was baptized by Franco, archbishop of Rouen, in 912 after the departure of Charles, his sponsor being Robert of Paris.[115] The date is probably correct unless the baptism, like the agreement of which it formed an essential part, was performed in the latter months of 911. The name of the archbishop has, however, given rise to grave doubts.[116] The chronology of the archbishops of Rouen at this period is very uncertain, and it has been suggested that Dudo is here confusing the baptizer of Rollo with Franco, bishop of Liège, who baptized Gotfried the Viking in 881.[117] But there was, apparently, about this time an archbishop of Rouen named Franco who in the succession followed Witto and preceded Gunhard.[118] It is difficult, however, to be certain that Franco was dead before 939, and the date of his accession is unknown. Moreover, there is some evidence to suggest that Witto, his predecessor, was himself directly connected with the conversion of the Normans of the Seine.[119] Whilst therefore Dudo's evidence, albeit unconfirmed, can be made compatible with contemporary chronology, it cannot, even here, be regarded as decisive. What remains certain is that Rollo was converted either by Franco or Witto, archbishops of Rouen, early in 912, or possibly in the latter months of 911.

With Rollo many of his companions were baptized. He was apparently followed to the font by 'his companions and the soldiers of his army'[120] and gave instructions that these should be instructed by competent teachers in the Christian religion. But if, as William of Jumièges also suggests,[121] the conversion was general, it was clearly at first in practice only formal. Orderic Vitalis paints a gloomy picture of the Norman Church as controlled by the followers of Rollo,[122] and there can be no doubt that his picture represents the truth. The ecclesiastical life which had flourished in this province in the seventh century had been all but destroyed, and during the lifetime of Rollo there were few signs of a revival. The bishoprics were in a state of disintegration, and the *lacunae* in the surviving lists of their holders are highly significant. At Lisieux there is a gap from 832 to 990; at Avranches from 862 to 990; at Sées from 910 to 936,[123] and in the time of Rollo the bishopric of Coutances-St Lô appears to have lost all connection with a district that had lapsed into paganism, and, as it appears, five successive bishops of that see resided in Rouen.[124] With regard to the monasteries the situation was even worse. The houses were desolate, the congregations dispersed. Some maintained a precarious existence by migration. Thus the monks of Jumièges departed to Haspres in the diocese of Cambrai,[125] and those of Fontenelle went to Boulogne bearing with them the relics of St Wandrille.[126] During the reign of Rollo it is probable that not a single monastery remained in the Norman land. Little credence should thus be given to later stories of Rollo's benefactions to the Church. At the time of his conversion Rollo is said to have made gifts to churches in Rouen, to Bayeux, to Evreux, and to Mont St Michel,[127] but since many of these places were situated in territory which he did not then possess, such largesse would have been impossible even if it had been intended. Doubtless the archbishop of Rouen was able to exact some promises from the newly converted Viking, but it is unlikely that Rollo was ever ready to part in large measure with the spoils of conquest. According to one version of the *Lament for William Longsword*, Rollo appears to have reverted to paganism before his death,[128] and Adémar of Chabannes later recorded the tradition that just before he died he ordered the sacrifice of a hundred Christian captives to propitiate the Viking gods he had once abandoned.[129] What value should be given to such statements is doubtful,[130] but certainly pagan practices were widespread in this region during the decades subsequent to the conversion, and they were long sporadically to survive.

Nevertheless, the conversion of Rollo with his followers was the most important feature of the arrangements of 911–12. It fixed the destinies of Normandy and determined the influence which this province was later to exercise upon Europe. The future fortunes of the dynasty which was then established were to be linked with those of the Latin and ecclesiastical centre of Rouen. Even in the period immediately following the agreement the significance of this became apparent. It was reflected in the gradual advance westward of the Norman frontiers until at the Couesnon they corresponded with the ancient boundary of the ecclesiastical province of Rouen. For similar reasons the eastern limit of the Norman territory, fixed apparently from the start at the Bresle, was, by contrast, never to change. But this frontier none the less needed to be defended at the close of Rollo's reign. In 925, according to Flodoard,[131] the 'Normans of Rouen' 'broke the treaty' of 924, and ravaged the territory of Beauvais and Amiens penetrating as far as Noyon. At the same time, disturbances broke out in Normandy itself. As a result, the men of Paris, under the leadership of Hugh the Great, raided as far as the neighbourhood of Rouen, and from the east a yet more formidable threat developed. Arnulf of Flanders, with the support of Herbert of Vermandois, having collected troops both from the north-eastern sea-board of Gaul and from the neighbourhood of Rheims, advanced towards the Bresle. Rollo replied by constructing a fortress at Eu, and sending a thousand men there for a garrison. In the resulting siege these Vikings troops were heavily defeated and most of them killed.

These events are the last which in the Annals are specifically associated with Rollo. The date of his death is, however, unknown. Richer of Rheims states that he was killed at the siege of Eu.[132] The passage which records this event may, however, have been derived from a careless reading of Flodoard,[133] and in the manuscript it was later struck out.[134] But it is not clear that it did not represent Richer's own opinion,[135] and it has perhaps been too summarily set aside. Certainly, no specific act of Rollo is recorded in any reputable source as having taken place subsequent to 925, and, equally certainly, in 927, it was William Longsword and not Rollo who commended himself to Charles the Simple.[136] Nevertheless, the Annals of Flodoard do contain one further reference to Rollo. In his account of what occurred in 928, after describing the manner in which certain magnates were summoned to the presence of Rudolf of Burgundy, Flodoard adds: 'Filius tamen Heriberti, Odo, quem Rollo habebat obsidem, non redditur illi donec se committit Karolo pater cum aliis quibusdam Franciae comitibus et episcopis.'[137] This has generally been taken to mean that Rollo was alive in 928. But Flodoard's language at this point is not wholly unambiguous, and in view of what occurred in 927 it is probably unwise to regard it as conclusive.[138] Nor does Dudo help to solve the problem. His account of the latter years of Rollo's life is untrustworthy and totally unconfirmed, and his statement that Rollo lived for a 'lustre'[139] after handing over his government to William Longsword is intrinsically improbable and wholly uncorroborated. In short, Rollo was undoubtedly dead when William Longsword was conducting his Breton campaigns in 933, but, while the difficult passage of Flodoard perhaps makes it probable that he was living in 928, there remains the distinct possibility that he was dead when William commended himself to Charles in 927, even if he was not killed at the siege of Eu in 925.

Thus ended a career which, judged by its later consequences, must be ranked among the most momentous in medieval history. In view of the character and the paucity of the evidence, it would be signally foolish to advance through the fog of controversy to any categorical statement on the details of Rollo's life. Most certainly the purpose of this article is not to attempt any such dogmatism. Much remains doubtful, more unproved. The most that can be hoped is that this new review of the evidence has justified its author in offering the following very tentative suggestions for the further consideration of English scholars. Rollo was born in Norway, being, as it seems, a son of Rögnvald, earl of Möre. Exiled from his native land, he set out on a Viking's career which brought him to Scotland, and probably to Ireland. In the course of these wanderings he took to wife a Christian woman, by whom he had a daughter named Kathleen, and his son, William Longsword, was likewise born outside Gaul. It is most improbable that later he married either 'Popa' or Gisela. He was certainly not on the continent of Europe as early as 876, but he was undoubtedly there before 918, and there are convincing reasons for believing that he arrived in Gaul between 905 and 911. He was most probably present at the battle of Chartres on 20 July 911, and it can hardly be doubted that he took part in the negotiations between Charles the Simple and the Seine Vikings which certainly occurred in the autumn of that year. That he concluded these negotiations by means of a personal interview with Charles at Saint Clair-sur-'Epte is very possible, but not proved. The territory which he was granted in 911 was but a small part of medieval Normandy, for it seems to have extended merely from the Bresle to the Dives, or perhaps to the Orne. Only in 924 had the western frontier of Normandy advanced to the Vire; and only in 933 (after the death of Rollo) was it established at the Couesnon. By this gradual process was the dominion of the Vikings of the Seine made to conform to the ancient ecclesiastical province of Rouen whose fortunes became henceforward closely intermingled with those of the dynasty which Rollo founded. But neither Rollo nor his companions promoted a resuscitation of the Norman Church; pagan practices and sympathies continued among them; and towards the end of Rollo's reign fresh raids were conducted by them into France. In the warfare which followed Rollo organized the defence of Eu – the last recorded act of his life. He was dead by 933, but, though he may well have been alive in 928, it is very possible that he died before 927, and even, perhaps, as early as 925.

NOTES

[1] See G. Storm, *Kritiske Bidrag til Vikingetidens Historie* (1878), p. 130.

[2] *Normannerne*, i, pp. 128–63. This account was elaborated and expanded in his *Normandiets Historie under de syv første hertuger* (1925).

[3] *Die Normannen und das Frankische Reich* (1906).

[4] *Norges Historie* (1910), vol. i, pt. ii, pp. 171–3, and more particularly in his 'Gange Rolv og erobringen av Normandie', in *Historisk Tidsskrift* (1912), pp. 160 *sqq.*

[5] *Étude Critique sur Dudon* (1916). I am much indebted to this extensive discussion of much of the previous literature respecting Dudo and his subject-matter, though I cannot always accept the author's conclusions.

[6] Cf. Freeman, *Norman Conquest,* i (ed. 1870), p. 164, who remarks: 'I do not feel myself at all called upon to narrate in detail the exploits which are attributed to Rolf in the time before his final settlement.'

[7] J. Lair, 'Dudonis Sancti Quintini de Moribus et Actis Primorum Normanniae Ducum' (*Mem. Soc. Antiq. de Normandie*, 3rd ser., vol. 3, 1865, pp. 17–19).

[8] *Ord. Vit.* (Le Prévost), ii, p. 2: 'Bellicos siquidem actus trium ducum Dudo Vermandensis Decanus eloquenter enarravit; affluens que multiplicibus verbis et metris panegyricum super illis edidit et Richardo Gunnoridae gratiam eius captans transmisit.'

[9] J. Lair, *op. cit.*

[10] Steenstrup, *Normannerne*, i, p. 132; *Normandiets Historie*, pp. 37–86.

[11] W. Vogel, *op. cit.*, pp. 22–3.

[12] 'A Criticism of the Life of Rollo as told by Dudo of St Quentin' (*Archaeologia* [1880], xlv, pp. 235–50). I have not been able to accept all the conclusions of this article,

but I wish to pay grateful tribute to its critical acumen. All subsequent studies on Rollo are in some sense dependent upon it. An idea of its services to scholarship can be attained by contemplating the words of Palgrave written in 1851 (*Collected Works*, ii, p. 500): 'You may abandon the history of Normandy if you choose, but if you accept the task, you must accept Dudo or let the work alone.' Since 1880 those who have tacitly adopted Palgrave's attitude have lacked his ingenuous excuse. And I cannot refrain from the opinion that Steenstrup's learned review of early Norman history (*Normandiets Historie*, 1925) is vitiated by his persistent refusal to accept Howorth's conclusions upon Dudo as an historical source.

[13] Compare, for example, *Cambridge Medieval History*, iii, pp. 322, 365; F. M. Stenton, *William the Conqueror*, pp. 24–6; Kendrick, *History of the Vikings*, pp. 220, 221.

[14] I wish to thank Mr L. C. Loyd and Professors F. M. Stenton and Bruce Dickins for advice in connection with this article. It would be a poor return for their kindness were I thereby to imply that they are necessarily in agreement with all the opinions here expressed.

[15] Dudo (ed. Lair), pp. 138–53.

[16] Howorth, *op. cit.*, pp. 236–8. The action attributed to the Viking leader at the monastery of St Vedast is incredible. No confirmation is to be found of Rollo's appearance in Frisia, and Steenstrup's belief in it (*Normandiets Historie*, p. 28) seems unjustified. Nor will the story of Rollo's relations with 'Alstelmus' in England withstand criticism. For long it was considered that 'Alstelmus' represented Athelstan (Howorth, *op. cit.*, p. 239), but this is chronologically impossible, and a more plausible suggestion (W. H. Stevenson, *Asser*, p. 254, n. 1) is that the name stood for Guthrum, the Danish king of East Anglia who assumed the name Athelstan after his baptism. This also seems incredible since, according to Dudo, Rollo arrived in Gaul in 876, and Guthrum was not converted until 880. Possibly the late medieval tradition, expressed by Bromton (Twysden, *Scriptores*, col. 810), was right in equating the 'Alstelmus' of Dudo with King Alfred himself, thus implying that, here as elsewhere, the dean of St Quentin ascribed to Rollo the deeds of some other warrior – in this case either Guthred or Guthrum. The point is, however, hardly important, since there seems nothing to suggest that this episode in the life of Rollo ever took place.

[17] Especially Steenstrup, *Normannerne*, i, pp. 128 *sqq*. He was immediately criticized on this point by E. Beauvois, *Revue Historique*, iv, p. 424, but he reiterated his views in *Normandiets Historie*, pp. 37–40.

[18] William of Jumièges (ed. Marx), pp. 79–81.

[19] Cf. A. Bugge, *Norges Historie*, vol. i, pt. ii, p. 172.

[20] Ed. Marx, p. 2.

[21] So also does the view that Rollo came from Sweden as expressed by W. Roos, *The Swedish Part in the Viking Expeditions, ante*, vii, p. 241.

[22] *Heimskringla*, ed. F. Jónsson (1911), p. 56.

[23] *Ibid.*

[24] *Heimskringla*, ed. F. Jónsson (1911), p. 144. The Laxdœla Saga (*Orig. Island*, i, p. 246) gives Rolf a different father, but this opinion seems unique among the Sagas.

[25] Cf. Vigfusson and York Powell, *Corpus Poeticum Boreale* (1883), i, pp. lxxxii–lxxxviii; Vigfusson, *Sturlunga Saga* (1878), i, p. lxxvii.

[26] Cf. *ibid.*, i, pp. xxvii–xxviii.

[27] *Orig. Island*, i, p. 187; Annarr vas Gongo-Hrólfr, es vann Normandi. Frá hónum ero Rúðo-iarlar kommer ok Engla konongar.

[28] Steenstrup, *Normandiets Historie*, pp. 279–83.

[29] *Ibid.*

[30] Prentout (*op. cit.*, 129) suggests the passage in Dudo (ed. Lair, p. 174) indicates that Dudo knew of the legend, but this is doubtful.

[31] Ed. G. H. Pertz, *Mon. Germ. Hist., Script.*, (1839), iii, p. 578.

[32] Cf. F. Lot, *Les Derniers Carolingiens*, p. xvii.

[33] Ed. Pertz, *op. cit.*, pp. 570, 572.

[34] P. Lauer, *Louis d'Outremer* (1900), p. 268.

[35] *Ibid.* Waitz in his edition of Richer (1877), p. 5, suggests 'Wulf'.

[36] Lauer, *ubi supra*.

[37] *Ibid.*

[38] Cf. Kendrick, *History of the Vikings* (1930), pp. 220, 221.

[39] Toustain fitz Rou, whose English lands were to pass into the possession of the family of Ballon (Round, *Peerage and Family History*, pp. 181 *sqq.*), appears in Domesday Book as *Turstinus filius Rolv* (*D.B.*, i, fs 37, 75, 85, 100, 179). He was perhaps the *Turstinus filius Rol* whose gifts to the abbey of St Georges de Boscherville were later confirmed by Henry I (Round, *Calendar of Documents preserved in France*, no. 196). If, moreover, as Freeman asserts (*Norm. Conq.*, ii, p. 709; iii, p. 464; iv, p. 39; v, p. 796), and as Round thinks very probable (*Peerage and Family History*, p. 188), *Turstinus filius Rolf* is to be equated with William's standard-bearer at Hastings, then the interchange of forms would be clearer still, for this man is described by Orderic (ed. Le Prévost, ii. p. 147) as *Turstinus filius Rollonis*, and by Wace (*Roman de Rou*, ed. Andresen, v. p. 7657) as *Tousteins filz Rou le Blanc*.

[40] *Memoires et Notes . . . sur l'Eure* (1862-9), ii, p. 163; cf. Lot, *St Wandrille* (1913), p. lxi.

[41] *Orig. Island*, i, p. 187.

[42] *Ibid.*, i, p. 66: (Helge)herjaðe á Skottland, ok feck þar at herfange Niðbiorgo, dóttor Beolans konoungs ok Caðlinar, dóttor Gongo-Hrólfs.

[43] Ed. J. Lair, *Guillaume Longue-Epée* (1893), pp. 61–70, and by Lauer, *op. cit.*, pp. 319–23; cf. *ibid.*, pp. 276–83.

[44]
> Hic in orbe transmarino natus patre
> in errore paganorum permanente
> mater quoque consignata alma fide
> sacra fuit lotus unda

Lair to support his own theory amends 'orbe' to 'urbe', and is followed in so doing by Steenstrup (Lair, *op. cit.*, pp. 73–7; Steenstrup, *Normandiets Historie*, p. 83). There seems, however, no sufficient reason for this change.

[45] *Heimskringla*, ed. F. Jónsson (1911), p. 119.

[46] Ed. Stubbs, i, p. 138.

[47] Cf. Dudo (ed. Lair), p. 171.

[48] F. M. Stenton, 'Danes in England' (*Proceedings of the British Academy*, xiii, pp. 204, 205, 228, 229).

[49] Cf. esp. A.S. Chron. 'A', *sub. anno* 880 (equals 879) and *Asser* (ed. Stevenson), p. 48, with *Ann. Vedast.*, *sub anno* 879. There is abundant continental testimony that the attack on Gaul by the Vikings began immediately after their defeat by Alfred. (cf. *Mirac. S. Bertin.* – Bouquet, ix, p. 118). Fulk, archbishop of Rheims, writing in 886, says that it was then eight years since the scourge had ravaged the kingdom (Bouquet, viii, p. 156).

[50] The Frankish chroniclers here speak with an uncertain voice, since they allude to the invaders indiscriminately as *Nordmanni*, *Dani*, or, more generally, as *piratae* or *pagani*. But a more accurate acquaintance with such racial epithets might have been expected from the Normans themselves, and it is therefore curious that in the tenth century a Norman notable is sometimes described as *Danus* while the nickname *Noricus* does not seem to have been used as a distinguishing mark. The instances of 'Bernard the Dane' and of Ansfrid 'the Dane', ancestor of the earls of Chester, immediately come to mind (cf. William of Jumièges, ed. Marx, pp. 44, 53, 54, 55; Ord. Vit.,

ibid., p. 160; Ord. Vit., ed. Le Prévost, ii, pp. 60, 105). This might perhaps be taken to suggest that a man of Danish stock was then exceptional in Normandy, at any rate among the upper class.

[51] *Leges Edwardi Confessoris* (Liebermann, *Gesetze der Angelsachsen*, i, p. 661).

[52] Dudo (ed. Lair), p. 151.

[53] It appears, for instance, as a Latin interpolation to A.S. Chron. 'E', *sub anno* 876, and as a Saxon interpolation to the Latin annal of 'F' for the same year. It was added to the manuscript of Asser's Life of Alfred (ed. Stevenson, p. 38), and it was copied by Florence of Worcester (ed. B. Thorpe, 1848, i, p. 94), by the Annalist of St Neots (Stevenson, *op. cit.*, p. 134) and by others (cf. Ord. Vit., ed. Le Prévost, ii, p. 360).

[54] Cf. Howorth, *op. cit.*, pp. 240–4.

[55] According to Dudo's story, it was Rollo who led the Viking attack on Paris in 885–7, and who during these years also sacked Evreux and Bayeux. After the sack of the latter town (it is added) he married Popa the daughter of Berenger, count of Rennes, and by her (according to the same account) he had a son, William Longsword. All this may be set aside. The leader of the Viking host outside Paris is known to have been Siegfried, not Rollo (Abbo, v, pp. 32 *sqq.*). And if Rollo was not at the siege of Paris he certainly did not take part in the contemporary Viking expeditions against Evreux and Bayeux. Nor was William born in France but overseas before Rollo came there. The whole story of Popa therefore, in its turn, becomes incredible, and the name, itself suspicious, was possibly invented by Dudo from the analogy of Sprota, a Breton woman who did in fact bear children to William Longsword. Dudo's account of Rollo's early adventures in Gaul was in fact constructed largely from the Annals of St Vedast, and in the main by assigning to Rollo the deeds of others. It was fabricated to explain the appearance of Rollo in Gaul at least a quarter of a century too soon.

[56] See below.

[57] Ed. J. Chavanon (1897), p. 139.

[58] It would seem that Harold Fairhair was only established in power about that time; Vigfusson and York Powell, *Corpus Poeticum Boreale* (1883), ii, pp. 487–500.

[59] See above.

[60] *Monumenta Historica Norvegiae*, ed. J. Storm, p. 90.

[61] *Ibid.*

[62] *Heimskringla*, ed. Jónsson, p. 56.

[63] A. Bugge, *Norges Historie*, vol. i, pt. ii, p. 173.

[64] A. Eckel, *Charles le Simple* (1899), pp. 67, 68, quoting manuscript authority.

[65] Cf. Lair, *Guillaume Longue-Epée*, p. 6.

[66] Howorth, *op. cit.*; cf. Vigfusson and York Powell, *Corpus Poeticum Boreale*, ii, p. 493.

[67] Ed. Pertz, *op. cit.*, p. 578.

[68] Howorth, *op. cit.*, p. 247.

[69] R. L. Poole, *Chronicles and Annals* (1926), p. 38: 'I doubt whether a single word of history, beyond the briefest entries in Easter Tables, was written in France or Germany between 906 and 940.'

[70] Printed in Dom Bouquet, *Receuil des Historiens . . . de France*, ix (Nouvelle edition, 1874), 536.

[71] Corrigendum vii.

[72] Cf. F. Lot, *Fidèles ou Vassaux* (1904), p. 179, who speaks of the 'original' and cites it as Archives Nationales K. 16, no. 9.

[73] Mabillon, *Ann. Bened.*, iii, p. 697. He does not seem specially to have cited this diploma also in his *De Re Diplomatica*, but the king's style and the system of dating agree with what he there requires from the instruments of Charles the Simple. See also the *Nouveau Traité* for Gozlinus, the notary, who appears in this charter.

[74] A. Giry, *Manuel de Diplomatique* (1894), p. 324, n. 2.

[75] Lot, *ubi supra*.

[76] In face of such authoritative testimony in favour of the charter further comment would appear superfluous. But the 'protocols' and 'eschatocols' appear to be in order, and the reference to Rollo seems in itself to favour authenticity. The mention of Rollo and his companions is introduced as an exception limiting the territorial extent of the grant. If the diploma were spurious it must have been fabricated at a later date, and the forger's object would surely have been to produce written evidence to support the abbey's title either to lands already in its possession or to which it was making a claim. Since it would be practically impossible at a later date to ascertain what exactly the king had granted to Rollo before 14 March 918, a fabricated instrument would, in order to achieve its purpose, have needed to define the lands in some much more definite manner than has here been done.

[77] R. L. Poole, *op. cit.*, p. 38.

[78] Printed in *Monumenta Germ. Hist., Script.*, xiii, 409 *sqq*. Long extracts are given in Bouquet, viii, pp. 154-75.

[79] *Annales* (ed. Lauer), p. 16; *Hist. Rem. Eccl.* (*Mon. Germ. Hist., Script.*, xiii, p. 577; Bouquet, viii, p. 163).

[80] *Annales*, p. 16.

[81] *Hist. Rem. Eccl.* (*Mon. Germ. Hist., Script.*, xiii, p. 577; Bouquet, viii, p. 163).

[82] *Annales*, p. 31.

[83] Bouquet, ix, p. 40.

[84] Cf. Prentout, *op. cit.*, pp. 445-7.

[85] He had attempted similar negotiations with the invaders of the Seine in 897 (*Ann. Vedast.*, *sub anno* 897; Flodoard, *Hist. Rem. Eccl.* – *Mon. Germ. Hist., Script.*, xiii, p. 565). In 921 he was to conclude a like treaty with the settlers in the Loire valley (Flodoard, *Annales*, p. 6).

[86] A. Eckel, *Charles le Simple* (1899), p. 74.

[87] E. J. Dümmler, *Geschichte des Ostfränkischen Reiches* (1862-88), ii, p. 452.

[88] See the charter for St Maximin of Trèves (Bouquet, ix, pp. 514, 515).

[89] Cf. Bouquet, viii, p. 230. See also Prentout, *op. cit.*, p. 188.

[90] Migne, *Pat. Lat.*, cxxxix, cols 806, 807.

[91] Dudo (ed. Lair), p. 168.

[92] Prentout, *op. cit.*, pp. 447-51. Contrast Lot, *Les Derniers Carolingiens* (1891), pp. 354, 355.

[93] See the diploma of 7 February 966 printed in Bouquet, ix, p. 729.

[94] Perhaps it is worth noting that in his description of the events of 912 Dudo makes Rollo confer gifts on the monastery of Mont St Michel. It is impossible that he should then have done so (see above, p. 132). But the meeting of 965 between Richard and Lothair was in fact followed immediately by the re-establishment of this monastery (Bouquet, ix, p. 729). Mainard the abbot, then established at Mont St Michel, apparently survived until 991 (cf. P. Gout, *Le Mont St Michel* [1910], i, p. 109), and Dudo may even have met him.

[95] H. Bresslau, *Handbuch der Urkundenlehre* (1912), xi, pp. 489 *sqq*.

[96] Cf. the evidence cited by L. Valin, *Le Duc de Normandie et sa Cour* (1910), p. 145.

[97] Cf. Lot, *St Wandrille*, p. lxi.

[98] Dudo (ed. Lair), p. 169. He says that Rollo was given Gisela the daughter of Charles in marriage, and that he was granted the whole of Brittany for the sustenance of his followers. Both these statements are in the highest degree improbable. Among the six daughters of Charles the Simple one was named Gisela, being the fourth daughter by his first wife Frederune (*Genealogia Arnulfi Comitis* – *Mon. Germ. Hist., Script.*, ix, p. 303). It is generally accepted that Charles only married Frederune in 907

(Mabillon, *De Re Diplomatica*, p. 558), and since Dudo implies that Gisela was legitimate and that she was adult when she became Rollo's wife, the whole story would thereby be made impossible. In fairness it needs to be added that the evidence for the date of Frederune's marriage is not as completely conclusive (see Steenstrup, *Normandiets Historie*, p. 61) as Prentout (*op. cit.*, p. 206) suggests, but even so it seems impossible to accept at this point the story of Dudo, who perhaps here fed his imagination on the account given by Regino of Prüm (ed. Kurze, p. 120), of a marriage between Godfried the Viking and Gisela daughter of Lothair II. As for Dudo's statement respecting Brittany it is mainly interesting because in the eighteenth century it provoked a famous controversy between R. de Vertot and G. A. Lobineau. Not until many years after 911 did Brittany come under the attention of the Vikings of the Seine. At this time Brittany was hardly withstanding the attacks of the Vikings of the Loire (see above, p. 130). Dudo's statement is probably to be explained by the fact that he wrote when Norman pretensions to overlordship over Brittany were being successfully made by his patron Richard II.

[99] *Hist. Rem. Eccl.* (*Mon. Germ. Hist., Script.*, xiii, p. 577; Bouquet, viii, p. 163).

[100] Ach. Deville, *Dissertation sur l'étendue du territoire concedé à Rollon* (*Mem. Soc. Antiq. Norm. années 1831, 1832, 1833*, Partie i, pp. 47 *sqq.*). Dudo on this matter seems to give two contradictory opinions. In one place (ed. Lair, p. 169) he says the land was marked out between the Epte and the sea. This suggests Upper Normandy. In another place (*ibid.*, p. 170) he suggests a far more extensive grant.

[101] It is unnecessary here to consider afresh the terms on which these lands were held by Rollo, since the matter has been exhaustively discussed, particularly by French scholars. In opposition to the opinions of Flach (*Origines de l'ancienne France*, iv, pp. 109-73) and of Steenstrup (*Normandiets Historie*, pp. 54, 55) I share the view of Lot (*Fidèles ou Vassaux*, pp. 177-237) and of Prentout (*op. cit.*, pp. 207-50) that from the first the Norman dynasty held their land by some sort of dependent tenure. The implications of this may well, however, have been barely understood by Rollo (cf. M. Bloch, *La Societe Féodale* (1939), i, p. 272), and certainly Rollo acted in fact as an independent prince. In Frankish theory a vassal, in practice he was constantly unfaithful to his lord.

[102] Eure, arr. Louviers, cant. Gaillon.

[103] Cf. T. Stapleton, *Rotuli Scaccarii Normanniae* (1840), i, p. xlix. Contrast Eckel, *Charles le Simple*, p. 76, and Prentout, *op. cit.*, p. 201.

[104] Flodoard, *Annales* (ed. Lauer), p. 24: 'Nordmanni cum Francis pacem ineunt sacramentis per Hugonem et Heribertum comites, Seulfum, quoque archiepiscopum absente rege Rodulfo: eius tamen consensu terra illis aucta Cinomannis et Baiocae pacto pacis eis concessae.'

[105] Cf. Howorth, *op. cit.*, p. 246.

[106] Ann. Bert., *sub anno* 867.

[107] Mabillon, *Acta SS. Ord. Bened.*, Saec. iv, pars ii, p. 246. For this district in the ninth century, see A. Le Prévost, 'Anciennes Divisions Territoriales de la Normandie' (*Mem. Soc. Antiq. Norm.*, 2nd ser., i, p. 46).

[108] Cf. R. Merlet in 'Les Origines du Monastère de S. Magloire à Paris' (*Bibl. École de Chartes*, vol. 56, pp. 243-8).

[109] See Ach. Deville, *op. cit.*, p. 51.

[110] *Chronicon Namnetense,* ed. R. Merlet (1896), p. 81.

[111] Flodoard, *Annales* (ed. Lauer), p. 6.

[112] *Ibid.*, p. 50.

[113] *Ibid.*, p. 55: 'Willelmus princeps Nordmannorum eidem regi se comittit; cui etiam rex dat terram Brittonum in ora maritima sitam.'

[114] Cf. T. Stapleton, *Magni Rotuli Scaccarii Normanniae*, i, p. xxxvii.

[115] Dudo (ed. Lair), p. 170.

116 F. I. T. Licquet, *Histoire de Normandie* (1835), i, pp. 85–8; Prentout, *op. cit.*, pp. 252, 253.

117 Cf. G. A. Lobineau, *Histoire de Bretagne* (1707), ii, col. 77.

118 Cf. Prentout, *op. cit.*, p. 252.

119 At some time during his pontificate, Hervey, archbishop of Rheims from 900 to 922, sent to Witto, archbishop of Rouen, instructions on how to deal with recent converts in his archdiocese who had lapsed into paganism (Flodoard, *Hist. Rem. Eccl. – Mon. Germ. Hist., Script.*, xiii, p. 577; Bouquet viii, p. 163). At about the same time Hervey also addressed a letter to a Pope John on the same subject, and the reply has been preserved (J. F. Pommeraye, *S. Rothomagensis ecclesiae concilia* [1677], p. 47). It is impossible to assign an exact date to these transactions (cf. Howorth, *op. cit.*, p. 235), but it seems probable (cf. Prentout, *op. cit.*, p. 255) that the pope concerned was John X (914–28), and certainly these missives describe a semi-pagan society such as would have resulted from a formal conversion taking place in 912. It should, however, be remembered that ever since 897 when Charles entered into his first alliance with the Seine Vikings to the great disgust of Fulk, archbishop of Rheims (Flodoard, *Hist. Rem. Eccl. – Mon. Germ. Hist., Script.*, xiii, p. 565), there had been a movement in progress for the conversion of these pagans. And in that year 'Hundaeus' apparently actually underwent the ceremony of baptism (*Ann. Vedast. sub anno* 897).

120 Dudo (ed. Lair), p. 170.

121 Ed. Marx, pp. 29, 30.

122 Ord. Vit. (ed. Le Prévost), ii, p. 397. The neophytes baptized at the same time as Rollo, having acquired their parishes by force of arms, were, he says, always ready to defend their possessions by the same means. Small wonder (he adds) that they frequented the beds of concubines and loved their brats better than their books.

123 *Gallia Christiana*, xi, cols 474, 629, 765.

124 *Ibid.*, xi, col. 868.

125 Cf. William of Jumièges (ed. Marx), pp. 38, 39.

126 Cf. Lot, *St Wandrille*, pp. xxxi, xxxvi.

127 Dudo (ed. Lair), p. 171.

128 Ed. Lair, *Guillaume Longue-Epée*, p. 61:

> Moriente infidele suo patre
> surrexerunt contra eum belliquosae.

This is the reading of the Clermont-Ferrand MS. Lair (*op. cit.*, 66), Lauer (*Louis d'Outremer*, p. 320), and Steenstrup (*Normandiets Historie*, pp. 79–82) prefer, however, the reading of the Florence text which gives 'infideles'.

129 Ed. J. Chavanon, pp. 139–40, cf. p. 198.

130 Steenstrup, *Normandiets Historie*, pp. 79–82.

131 *Annales* (ed. Lauer), p. 32.

132 Ed. G. H. Pertz, *op. cit.*, p. 583, n. *e*.

133 Cf. Prentout, *op. cit.*, p. 277.

134 Pertz in his edition of Richer, *loc. cit.*

135 He refers in another place (ed. Pertz, p. 584) to Rollo's being killed – de cujus interfectione iam relatum est.

136 Flodoard, *Annales* (ed. Lauer), p. 39.

137 *Ibid.*, p. 41.

138 I think, for example, that Prentout (*op. cit.*, pp. 277, 278) is too dogmatic at this point.

139 Dudo (ed. Lair), p. 174.

IX

Edward the Confessor, Duke William of Normandy and the English Succession

I

Prominent among the ultimate causes of the Norman Conquest – that 'great turning point in the history of the English nation'[1] – must be placed the relations which were established between Edward the Confessor and Duke William of Normandy; and certainly no topic of English medieval history has been more fervently discussed.[2] The triangular connection between Edward, Harold and William, portrayed so early in the stitchwork of the 'Bayeux Tapestry' had already before the end of the middle ages become thickly overlaid with contrasting legends, and in the seventeenth century the same theme was made the sport of venomous and prolonged controversy among lawyers and politicians.[3] Moreover, the polemical ardours thus evoked for long pervaded the work of historical scholars, and even today it sometimes seems strangely difficult to dissociate the study of these vital events – and of the texts which record them – from considerations which are at best extraneous, and at worst anachronistic. Perhaps, therefore, although the subject is time-worn, some excuse may be found for a new attempt to elucidate in part a few of the features of Anglo-Norman relations in the time of Edward the Confessor by means of a fresh and strictly historical examination of the evidence.

It is 'beyond serious doubt'[4] that at some period of his reign the Confessor recognized Duke William as his heir, and it would not be easy to suggest any more probable time for this important act than during the English crisis of 1051–2. For this reason, no episode in the Confessor's reign has been made more familiar – and few have been regarded as of greater moment – than the dramatic visit which Duke William is said to have paid to England with a large retinue in 1051. It is described with emphatic clarity in manuscript 'D' of the Anglo-Saxon Chronicle:

> Then forthwith Count (eorl) William came from overseas with a great force of Frenchmen, and the King received him with as many companions as suited him, and let him go again.[5]

This has naturally attracted the attention of all modern historians of this period. Thus Freeman, who discusses the matter at length,[6] made this the dividing point in his treatment of the Norman reign of Duke William,[7] and spoke of the visit as 'marking one of the most important stages in our history'.[8] Similarly (to select only a few of the more prominent names) Lingard,[9] Thierry,[10] Palgrave,[11] Lappenberg,[12] J. R. Green,[13] Sir Charles Oman[14] and Sir Frank Stenton[15] have all accepted the visit as an established fact, and seen in it an event of crucial consequence to the developing question of the English succession which was not to be settled until after 1066.

To question a story of such proleptic significance, and one which has been received with such authoritative unanimity into the canon of English historical doctrine, would indeed be rash. None the less it can only be regarded as particularly unfortunate that the account of the duke's visit as given in manuscript 'D' of the Anglo-Saxon Chronicle appears to receive no independent confirmation in any contemporary or nearly contemporary source. 'Florence of Worcester'[16] seems the only chronicler of this age who makes any allusion to this noteworthy event, and he does so in a manner which leaves little doubt that he is merely transcribing, or paraphrasing, the information supplied by 'D'. Not until very much later does the story begin to be repeated, as when Wace, writing about 1170. included it among many others in his metrical eulogy of the Norman dukes.[17] In short, belief in the visit – and in its consequences – must stand, or fall, by the credence given to thirty-three clear and emphatic words in one – and in only one – of the surviving manuscripts of the Anglo-Saxon Chronicle relating to the year 1051.

The silence of the other writers of the time about this spectacular event is the more remarkable in that so many of them were deeply interested in the history of which it is alleged to have formed an important part. Particularly is this the case with the Norman chroniclers of the eleventh century who were especially concerned to emphasize the cordial relations between the Confessor and Duke William, and boastfully prone to enlarge upon any of the duke's exploits which might indicate the respect in which he was held by foreign princes, or help to justify his later acquisition of England. Yet, both William of Jumièges and William of Poitiers, although they give circumstantial accounts of the manner in which the Confessor established the duke as his successor, are completely silent about any visit of the Conqueror to England during Edward's reign. The former writer gives a wholly different account as to how the succession was established,[18] whilst the latter says that a purpose of the journey later taken by Earl Harold to Normandy was that the duke who had previously received the allegiance of certain English magnates *in his absence* might now in person accept it from one of the most powerful men of England.[19] It is, indeed, implicit in the narratives both of William of Jumièges and William of Poitiers that Duke William never set foot in England before he landed here in 1066. The fact deserves attention. Nothing could better have fitted the Norman chroniclers' version of Anglo-Norman relations than a visit by Duke William to England in 1051. It is, therefore, little short of astonishing that they failed to record it.

Nor is the corresponding silence of the English chroniclers of the next generation much easier to explain, for these also were deeply concerned with everything that assisted the establishment of the Norman monarchy in England. Thus Eadmer,[20] followed here by Simeon of Durham,[21] discusses the relations between the Confessor and the duke, but makes no allusion to any conversation ever having taken place in England between them. William of Malmesbury,[22] in his turn, narrates the history of 1051 at considerable length, but is equally silent about an episode which to an historian of his logical temper might have appeared as the fitting conclusion to the events of that year. Again, the *Vita Æduuardi Confessoris* whose interest was in the monarch, his wife and Earl Godwine, and which considers in some detail the implications of the revolution of 1051–2,[23] never mentions the presence of the Norman duke in the Confessor's company at any time during the reign of the sainted king. If Duke William did in fact come to England, with a large following in 1051, and if he at that time (as is usually supposed) received in person a promise of the succession, then the most representative English writers of the generation immediately following the Norman Conquest either did not know the fact or did not think it worthy of mention.

Finally, the testimony of the Anglo-Saxon Chronicle itself needs to be considered. As is well known, there are four manuscript versions of the Anglo-Saxon Chronicle which deal with the events of 1051. These are 'C', 'D', 'E' and 'F'. Of these 'D' – and 'D' alone – makes any allusion to Duke William's visit. 'F' being a bilingual Canterbury text needs here no separate comment, since it may be considered in connection with 'E' to which it is closely related, and whose original in the main it epitomizes.[24] 'C', on the other hand, is the distinct version compiled at Abingdon, and it might reasonably have been expected to record so signal an event. Its account of 1051[25] is, however, short, and its silence on this matter, though surprising, might perhaps be explained – in part at least – by the brevity of the annal. With 'E', however, the case is very different. For 'E' not only gives the longest of all accounts of 1051, but (as will be recalled) it was at this time being compiled at Canterbury,[26] and throughout this period it is distinguished by its many unique and detailed references to the affairs of south-eastern England.[27] 'E', for instance, alone among the manuscripts gives a precise and detailed account of the raid by Lothen and Yrling in 1048[28] – a raid on Kent and Essex which is barely mentioned in 'C'[29] (without the names of the leaders), and wholly omitted in 'D'. Again, in respect of the events of 1051 itself, 'E', as might be expected, gives by far the greatest prominence, among the versions, to the disturbances round Dover which are wholly neglected both by 'C' and the *Vita Æduuardi*, and passed over much more briefly by 'D'.[31] Thus 'E' knows, and speaks of, the progress of the Dover riot, comments on the fact that Eustace and his men put on their armour before they reached the town, and states the number of casualties on both sides.[32] 'E' is, in short, the chronicler whose normal practice it is to record in exceptional detail anything that specially affected the south-east. But, if Duke William in fact came over with a large band of magnates in 1051, he must surely have landed somewhere in Godwine's earldom east of Southampton Water, and it is a matter for wonder that his progress through the south-east with a great company could have passed utterly without notice by the annalist who was always particularly concerned to narrate events which took place in that region.

By contrast, the chronicler whose work has survived in the existing manuscript 'D', certainly displays no special knowledge of contemporary events in south-eastern England. He had his own sources of information respecting Scandinavian affairs,[33] but so far as England was concerned, his particular interests lay elsewhere than in the south-east. This is not the place to consider whether (as has been traditionally supposed) the bulk of his work was compiled within the Worcester diocese,[34] or whether (as would now seem more probable) it derived in the main from some northern centre such as York.[35] Nor, fortunately, is it necessary in this instance to enter at all into that general controversy. For the annal in 'D' relating to 1051 is precisely that which, without any hesitation, can be ascribed unequivocally to a northern source, since in describing the king's summons of troops to London earlier in the year, 'D' specifically remarks:

> The folk throughout all this northern region, in Siward's earldom and in Leofric's, were organized to go there.[36]

In so far as the events of 1051 are concerned, 'D' is emphatically 'the northern chronicler', and, as Sir Frank Stenton rightly observes of his work at this point, 'the northern chronicler seems to have known little about events in Kent'.[37] So much the more remarkable is it, therefore, that 'D' should supply the sole notice of an event which must have been of special notoriety in the south-east. It can hardly be suggested that in the conditions of 1051, Duke William could have sailed up the east coast, landed somewhere in Yorkshire, and thus passed through the 'northern region' *en route* to visit the Confessor in the south of England.

There seems, therefore, no escape from considering the possibility that this very surprising and unique notice in 'D' may have been the result of an interpolation made subsequently to the original compilation of the chronicle. 'D', it will be recalled, is a manuscript written in many hands;[38] it is unskilfully compiled;[39] it is 'from first to last very inaccurately and carelessly written';[40] and it is 'full of mistakes and omissions'.[41] Again, 'D' only assumed its present form at a comparatively late date, and almost certainly after 1100.[42] Consequently, even when, as in the present instance, there is no trace of any interpolation into the existing manuscript of 'D', it is always possible, in the case of this text, that entries 'may have been inserted at the latest stage of composition'.[43] Moreover, the folio on which the notice of Duke William's alleged visit occurs is written in the fifth of the hands which Sir George Warner detected in this manuscript,[44] and it would be very rash to place this hand much, if at all, before 1100. An interpolation embodied at this point in 'D' would thus at least be possible, and a comparison of the three extant accounts in the Chronicle of events at the close of 1051 does not remove the suspicion that perhaps it may have been made. After describing the fall of the house of Godwine 'D', 'E', and 'F' at this point all notice *in the same order* (i) the fall of Godwine's family, (ii) the dismissal of Edith (the king's wife and Godwine's daughter), and (iii) the establishment of William, the king's priest, as bishop of London in place of Sparrowhawk. It is only 'D' which arbitrarily inserts between (ii) and (iii) the short entry about the coming of that other William – the duke of Normandy.

To account for this interpolation (if such it be)[45] would undoubtedly not be easy. A plausible suggestion might be hazarded that the entry was perhaps due to an inaccurate transcription of a passage in the lost original of 'D' which itself may have been carelessly set out, or which in some other way gave to the later copyist an opportunity to dramatize the events of the Confessor's reign in the light of subsequent events. Such speculations are, however, profitless in the absence of proof. Nor are they required since one thing at least seems certain. A theory that this entry had been transported bodily from another annal in the original of 'D' could not be sustained since all the objections which can be urged against the notice in this place would apply with greater force if it were assigned elsewhere. If Duke William's visit ever occurred, it must be placed chronologically where 'D' puts it. For William of Normandy could hardly have visited England on such an errand in any year after the triumphant return of Earl Godwine in the summer of 1052, and the circumstances of Norman history make it equally improbable that the young duke could have come to this country at any time before 1050. Moreover, the whole relevance of the story, as it is generally accepted, implies that the visit took place after, and very shortly after, the banishment of the earl of Wessex, that is to say 'in the winter of 1051 or the spring of 1052'[46] – or (to speak more precisely) after the 'autumnal equinox' when Earl Godwine was exiled,[47] and before

24 June 1052[48] when the earl launched from Flanders the expedition which
was to lead to his return. It is, therefore, pertinent to inquire what was
the likelihood of Duke William's making this sparsely recorded visit at
such a time.

Now, there seems nothing in the contemporary sequence of Norman
events which would make it theoretically impossible for Duke William to
have left his Duchy between these dates, but if the course of Norman
history from 1047 to 1053 be reconsidered, it must appear wholly surprising that he should have done so. For during all this period Duke William
was engaged in a most hazardous and uninterrupted struggle for survival.
In 1047 he had only escaped complete destruction through the intervention
of the French king, and after Val-ès-Dunes his position remained extremely perilous. Guy of Burgundy continued to hold out at Brionne for
a considerable time, and only after a long struggle was the duke able to
re-establish himself even in the valley of the Risle.[49] During these years,
too, he was engaged in warfare in Maine, and his reinstatement at Rouen
can hardly be placed much if at all before the beginning of 1050.[50] Nor
was this the end of his difficulties, for it was precisely during 1050 and
1051 that Geoffrey Martel, in Duke William's despite, established himself
as the most powerful force in north-western Gaul, and early in 1051 – the
crucial year in this inquiry – three events occurred which brought the
Angevin menace to the very borders of Normandy. On 26 March 1051
there died Count Hugh of Maine.[51] As a result, Geoffrey Martel entered
Le Mans in person and took possession of the city.[52] Finally, Bishop
Gervais of Le Mans in exchange for his liberty surrendered to Geoffrey
the castle of Château-de-Loir,[53] which had hitherto been a primary
obstacle of his northward progress. Thus, by the autumn of 1051, at the
time of the exile of Earl Godwine from England, the count of Anjou
found himself at last fully established in Maine, and he was beginning
actively to threaten the Norman frontiers.

Moreover, the peril of Duke William was at this time further enhanced
both by the political conditions prevailing within his Duchy, and also by
the changing policy of the king of France. At home, the duke had to face
the notorious disaffection[54] of his uncles the count of Arques and the
archbishop of Rouen, and their open rebellion was in due course to be
made even more menacing by the fact that it was to be conducted with
the active support of the French king. Thus during these same two years
– 1051-2 – the duke of Normandy was being robbed of that protection
by his suzerain which in 1047 had alone enabled him to survive. It is
fortunate, therefore, that this vital change can also in its turn be dated with
some precision. In 1050 King Henry and Count Geoffrey were still at war,[55]
but 'in the winter of 1051 and the spring of 1052' the *rapprochement*
between them against the duke of Normandy must have been clearly

foreshadowed. Nor was its consummation to be delayed. For a dated charter of King Henry issued at Orleans, and witnessed by Geoffrey Martel and his wife who were then in the royal entourage, shows that the reconciliation between the count of Anjou and the king of France had taken place before 15 August 1052.[56]

If, therefore, the celebrated visit of Duke William to England in fact occurred, it would have to be placed between the seizure of Le Mans by Geoffrey Martel (after 25 March 1051) and the conclusion of the offensive alliance against Normandy of the count of Anjou with the king of France (before 15 August 1052) – a time of immediate and increasing peril for the duke, when he was faced by the loss of his overlord's support, and by the imminent threat of a great rebellion headed by the two most powerful of his magnates. A decision by the duke to leave Normandy at this juncture with a large company of his followers would occasion astonishment, for it is obvious that such an enterprise could then only have been undertaken at extreme hazard. The presence of Duke William in England at any time during the winter of 1051–2 might even appear so intrinsically improbable that before it could be accepted for truth, it would have to be supported by stronger evidence than can be cited in its favour. Further testimony would seem to be required before the famous visit of Duke William of Normandy to England during the winter of 1051–2 can with any confidence be regarded as an established fact.

II

The bearing of this conclusion upon the whole interpretation of Anglo-Norman relations during the period immediately preceding the Norman Conquest will be obvious. And if on this matter 'D' can no longer be regarded as an infallible text, the evidence of the other authorities which have hitherto been disparaged by comparison with 'D' may deserve a fresh evaluation even if this should lead to results which must be regarded as tentative. In particular, the Norman chroniclers merit careful consideration. The precise connection between the narratives of William of Jumièges and William of Poitiers has never been fully elucidated, but there is clearly some relation between them and the most attractive hypothesis is that William of Poitiers knew and used the work of William of Jumièges, and elaborated it on occasion out of his own knowledge or according to his own ideas.[57] However this may be, the combined testimony of these two writers is not here to be disregarded. Both William of Poitiers and William of Jumièges may fairly be described as contemporary witnesses of these events, and their accounts were apparently set down within ten years of the battle of Hastings. They deserve to be heard.

William of Poitiers speaks in some detail of Edward's promise of the

English throne to Duke William in three separate passages in his narrative.
In an allocution which he places in the mouth of the duke before Hastings,[58] he says that the Confessor had made William his heir; that this
had been confirmed by an oath taken in the Confessor's presence by many
English magnates among whom are mentioned Archbishop Stigand, and
the earls Godwine, Leofric and Siward; that as a further guarantee of this
grant a son and a grandson of Earl Godwine were delivered to the duke
as hostages; and that in due course Earl Harold himself was sent to
Normandy to ratify these arrangements in person. Secondly, and in
another place,[59] William of Poitiers remarks that Harold, whose brother
and nephew had previously been given to the duke as hostages, was sent in
person to Duke William in order to confirm the earlier promise of the
succession, and that Harold took an oath to that effect, the precise terms
of which are then described. Finally, this same writer observes in a third
passage that at the time of his accession the Confessor relied much on
Norman support (though Duke William himself had never come to
England), and that in gratitude Edward had formally declared the duke
his heir. Wherefore with the assent of his magnates he sent Robert,
archbishop of Canterbury, who was the agent of this grant (*huius delegationis
mediatorem*) and who brought with him the son and grandson of the most
powerful Earl Godwine as hostages.[60]

Now, William of Poitiers was a boastful writer with a deplorable taste
for rhetoric, and his words have therefore to be treated with great caution,
the more especially in respect of the speech which he attributes to William
before Hastings. His association of Archbishop Stigand and the great earls
with a formal oath taken in favour of the duke may therefore be without
much misgiving dismissed as embroidery. But with these qualifications
the story as told by William of Poitiers does not seem unreasonable, and
it comes from a writer who with all his faults is properly accepted as an
authority for many of the chief events of the Norman Conquest.[61] It
should be noted therefore that four principal points emerge from the
stories that he tells:

1. That a promise of the succession was given by the Confessor to the
   duke – perhaps with the assent of certain magnates in England.
2. That a son and grandson of Earl Godwine were sent to William as
   hostages.
3. That Robert of Jumièges, archbishop of Canterbury, was sent to
   make formal announcement to the duke of this bequest.
4. That later Earl Harold was similarly sent by the Confessor to confirm
   these arrangements.

As to the first of these points, there can be no reasonable doubt that the
promise was in fact given, for this is vouched by a sufficient number of

authorities, and it has been accepted by almost all modern historians of the Confessor's reign.[62] The second point is more disputable and less important, but this also receives some curious confirmation in that Eadmer,[63] albeit telling a somewhat different story, likewise mentions the sending of these hostages, and *independently* adds their names – Wulfnoth and Hakon – which are nowhere mentioned by William of Poitiers. It is, however, in respect of his third and fourth points that William of Poitiers is here most interesting, and in particular for his statement that in connection with the original request of the English kingdom to Duke William, the Confessor sent Robert of Jumièges, archbishop of Canterbury to Normandy as *huius delegationis mediatorem*.

It is, indeed, at this point that the evidence of William of Jumièges himself[64] falls to be considered; for in conjunction with the other testimony it enables a coherent account to be established. Archbishop Eadsige, it appears, died on 29 October 1050, and Robert of Jumièges was appointed to Canterbury at mid-Lent in 1051.[65] But in the course of the same Lent Robert went to Rome for his pallium,[66] and he came back to England from Rome 'one day before the eve of the Feast of St Peter' – that is to say on 27 June 1051.[67] Now, it is surely highly probable that the new archbishop, who was a Norman, and who had formerly been abbot of Jumièges, should have passed through Normandy in the course of his journey to Rome, and it is entirely in keeping with all the conditions of the time that, on the orders of the Confessor, he should have combined this journey with the 'King's errand'.[68]

The story here told by William of Jumièges thus seems to do less violence to chronology and probability than do any of the other accounts of these momentous events. If it were to be accepted, it would be necessary to conclude that a declaration of the succession in favour of Duke William was made by the king early in 1051, and that before the end of Lent, Robert of Jumièges, the new archbishop of Canterbury, was sent to make formal delivery of the grant to the duke of Normandy, whilst on his way to Rome. The act must in this case have taken place some time between mid-Lent and 21 June 1051. On this interpretation (as will be seen) the transaction would have to be regarded as a cause, rather than as a consequence,[69] of the struggle in England which broke into open hostility between the king and Earl Godwine in September of the same year.[70]

Nor does this itself seem improbable. The incident at Dover to which such prominence is given in manuscript 'E' of the Anglo-Saxon Chronicle (as to a lesser extent in manuscript 'D') might appear in itself an insufficient cause for the great political crisis which ensued. It will be recalled, moreover, that the Anglo-Saxon Chronicle as a whole gives a very confused account of the events of 1051 in that its various versions are irreconcilable with each other.[71] It may, however, be noted that two of the

Anglo Saxon annals relating to 1051 begin with a reference to the appointment of Robert of Jumièges,[72] and that neither 'C' nor the *Vita Æduuardi
Regis* even mention the affray at Dover. Indeed the *Vita*, whose claims
to be regarded as a nearly contemporary source seem now to be strengthened,[73] specifically relates the beginning of the troubles of 1051 to a
conflict between Earl Godwine and the new archbishop.[74]

The *Vita* is, in truth, a most perplexing and difficult text,[75] but in so far
as it 'seized the big motives', and suggests a 'bigger background',[76] to the
events of 1051, it undoubtedly offers additional support to the evidence of
William of Jumièges. It yet further increases the inherent probability that
the clear and factual statement of that Norman chronicler represents the
truth.

The events of 1051 were followed in Normandy by the great upheaval
which only ended with the duke's victory at Mortemer in February
1054.[77] In England they were followed by the reaction consequent on
Godwine's return, and, as it would seem, by the adumbration of a design
directed towards the eventual succession of the Atheling Edward. With
these happenings this essay is not concerned. But the Atheling's return to
England in 1057, and his sudden death before he ever reached the king,[78]
clearly marked the culmination and collapse of this policy and brought the
more strictly Anglo-Norman question once again to the front. For this
reason, it is interesting that William of Jumièges brings into a logical
sequence the original bequest to Duke William of the English succession
and the journey taken by Harold Godwineson to Normandy some time
after the Atheling's death. It is impossible, therefore, wholly to avoid the
suspicion that the re-examination of the evidence here attempted might
also react upon the vexed question of the famous oath taken by Earl
Harold to Duke William – perhaps the most picturesque episode in the
history of Anglo-Norman relations before the Conquest.

As is well known, the Anglo-Saxon annals are wholly silent about this
famous affair, and the testimony of the Norman writers thus here assumes
an even greater comparative importance. Before considering that testimony, it may, however, be useful to examine a version of Earl Harold's
Norman visit which has always been popular, and which has enjoyed a
wide general acceptance since it received the erudite approval of Freeman
himself. According to this interpretation, Harold's presence in Normandy
on this occasion was 'purely accidental'.[79] The earl, it would seem, was
out 'fishing'[80] off the Sussex coast in the neighbourhood of Bosham.
While thus 'merely yachting',[81] being engaged on a 'pleasure trip',[82] he
was blown out to sea by an unexpected wind, and carried diagonally
across the Channel – a distance of some sixty miles – to be wrecked on the
coast of Ponthieu. There he was imprisoned by the count until he was
rescued by Duke William. As a result of his misfortunes he was forced to

offer to William certain guarantees under oath, and in turn received certain favours from the duke. He then returned to England. It is a good tale. But it might have been supposed that very strong evidence would be needed before such a strange story could be accepted. Such testimony, however, is hard to find. The earliest evidence which can be cited in its favour appears to be that of William of Malmesbury[83] whose *Gesta Regum* was probably not completed much before 1125, and whose account of these events, which itself seems without any contemporary confirmation, contains in addition its own elements of confusion.[84] Moreover, being itself unsatisfactory, it is specifically contradicted by the Bayeux Tapestry which in this matter is of far greater value as evidence. Even an eleventh-century earl would hardly go fishing in a war galley complete with shields,[85] and it is not easy to believe that the artist of the Bayeux Tapestry could have resisted the temptation to portray a shipwreck if he believed one to have occurred.[86] The piscatorial activities of Harold Godwineson may perhaps now be consigned to oblivion.

Scarcely more credible are two other and later accounts of Harold's misfortunes. Henry of Huntingdon in a short notice states that Harold set out on this occasion for Flanders,[87] and this is interesting in that it would be very possible for a man on such a journey to be deflected from his course to the coast of Ponthieu. But Count Guy is not even mentioned in the story which is wholly unconfirmed, and it seems reasonable to suppose that Henry of Huntingdon, writing more than half a century after the event, was here confusing Harold's journey with another and distinct expedition of the earl to Flanders which did in fact take place.[88] Finally, Snorre Sturlason writing in Iceland or Norway in the thirteenth century has also been cited in this connection.[89] According to the story finally recorded in the *Heimskringla*, Harold, at this juncture, was starting for 'Bretland'.[90] If, as is suggested by Dr A. H. Smith, Wales is here meant, the earl's decision to proceed from a Sussex port becomes incredible, and in any case the account conflicts with all the other evidence. The saga does not mention Ponthieu, and brings Harold directly to the 'west of Normandy'.

Now it hardly needs emphasis that no one of these accounts, if taken singly, could inspire confidence.[91] Moreover, they are all (i) late in date, (ii) unconfirmed, and (iii) mutually contradictory. They have, however, one point in common. They all make Harold's presence in Normandy involuntary, and it was probably for this reason that they appealed so strongly to later English writers who sought to portray the earl of Wessex as the leader of the 'patriotic' party[92] – a man who, true to nineteenth-century notions of nationalism, must on no account be allowed to have connived at negotiations designed to bring a 'foreigner' to the English throne. It may even be the lingering influence of this anachronistic tradition which has made some more modern scholars so reluctant specifically to discard theories built upon such slender foundations. In any case, it is difficult otherwise to account for the respect shown to this late and confused testimony, when there is known to exist in the narratives of William of Jumièges and William of Poitiers, and in the Bayeux Tapestry, evidence of a nearly contemporary character which supplies a simpler, a more coherent, and (as will here be suggested) a much more credible description of this important episode in English history.

The statement of William of Jumièges is here once again short and clear. Earl Harold, he says, was sent over to Normandy at the command of Edward the Confessor to confirm in person the grant of the English succession which had previously been made through the agency of Robert of Jumièges, archbishop of Canterbury. Carried out of his course by the wind, the earl landed in Ponthieu and was thrown into prison by the count. Rescued by Duke William, he was brought with honour to Rouen. He stayed with the duke for some time, and during his sojourn in Normandy he 'performed fealty concerning the kingdom with many oaths'.[93] Finally, having received great gifts, he was sent back to the Confessor. This short account is nearly contemporary, and it is substantially confirmed by the Bayeux Tapestry. According to the Tapestry, there was nothing accidental about Harold's voyage. The earl has a formal interview with the Confessor before setting out.[94] He goes to a port most suitable for a voyage to Normandy.[95] His ships and his escort show signs of considerable preparation,[96] and the wind before which he sails is sufficient to account for his being blown out of his course.[97] The landing at Ponthieu, the imprisonment by Guy, and the rescue by Duke William all follow in due course;[98] and other details such as the Breton war and the knighting of Harold are added.[99] At length the earl takes an oath to William,[100] and what is equally significant he goes to Edward and makes his report immediately after his return to England.[101] Finally there is William of Poitiers who, after his fashion, embroiders the tale with rhetorical flourishes, but none the less speaks substantially in the same sense, and who concludes by adding the precise terms of the oath which Harold swore to the duke.[102] The earl is to act as William's *vicarius* at the Confessor's court; he is to do all he can after the Confessor's death to ensure the duke's succession; and in the meantime he is to maintain garrisons in certain strongholds – particularly at Dover.

If viewed objectively, this composite account supplied by these three early witnesses may surely command confidence. Doubtless these were Normans but they were not necessarily for that reason liars, nor is it possible for them to be uniformly so regarded;[103] and the Bayeux Tapestry 'being woven for public exhibition at a time when a number of the minor actors in the story were still alive' is 'unlikely to portray any incidents which are entirely fictitious'.[104] Moreover the story as here collectively told contains singularly few discrepancies.[105] Difficulty has been felt at Harold's undertaking this mission at such a time, but even if the detention of his relatives at Rouen as hostages[106] be not credited, it would not be hard to account otherwise for Harold's consent. In 1064 – the most probable date for the oath[107] – Harold was at the height of his power, but he was not omnipotent.[108] He was the chief subject of a king whose administrative energy was considerable,[109] and whose prestige was immense.[110] Even a strong earl might have hesitated to disobey him. Nor, in view of Harold's lack of royal blood, and in view also of his rivals both at home and in Scandinavia, could he regard his own succession to the English throne with any certainty. On all grounds he may have thought it prudent to obey the orders of his king, and perhaps at the same time to safeguard his own position in the event of the success of his most formidable rival.[111] These are speculations. Nor are they necessary. For whatever may have been the motives of Earl Harold there can be little doubt as to what were his acts at this juncture, and there can remain little doubt as to general credibility of the earliest testimony which records them.[112]

In considering the subject of this article, Freeman observed that it involves 'one of the most perplexing problems of all history',[113] and no finality is claimed for the solution here attempted. But perhaps some of these questions would be less perplexing if they were treated more dispassionately. If it be admitted that the Anglo-Saxon Chronicle, being, for all its merits, a fallible human production, cannot in all its contradictory versions be always treated as a sacrosanct text,[114] if the same standards of criticism be applied to the English and the Norman sources, and if the politics of the eleventh century be firmly dissociated from the preoccupations of the nineteenth, then there may emerge a story at once shorter and more coherent than the commentaries which have sometimes been constructed to explain it away. It is essentially the story as told by William of Jumièges. Edward the Confessor made a promise of the English throne to Duke William of Normandy, and in 1051 he sent Robert of Jumièges, the newly appointed archbishop of Canterbury, to ratify the grant in the presence of the duke who, himself, never came to England in that year. Later – and probably in 1064 – Earl Harold was sent by the Confessor to confirm that grant in person, and when on this mission he took his famous oath to the duke. To that story the other early authorities, William of Poitiers, the *Vita Æduuardi*, the Bayeux Tapestry and the Anglo-Saxon annals themselves, all add independent details which may be regarded as more or less credible: the relations between Robert and Edward,[115] and the former's journey to Rome in 1051;[116] the matter of the hostages;[117] the imprisonment of Harold by Guy, his rescue by William[118] and the terms of his oath.[119] But the story, in its main outlines, appears clear and coherent. Doubtless it challenges many preconceptions, and certainly its acceptance would entail a reconsideration both of the character and policy of Edward the Confessor, and of the revolution of 1051–2 which was the crisis of his reign. None the less, it is here advanced, albeit very tentatively, as the version of these momentous events which, in the present state of our knowledge, seems supported by the best evidence, and as the account which can best be made to accord with the known facts of Norman and English history at this time.

NOTES

[1] E. A. Freeman, *Norman Conquest*, (1870), i, p. 1.

[2] I wish to thank my friends Professor V. H. Galbraith and Mr James Sherborne for their kindness in reading and criticizing this paper. I wish, also, in this connection to thank my pupils in the Norman Conquest seminar at Bristol University who have so often, and so helpfully, subjected me, and the subject, to the stimulus of their arguments.

[3] For examples of this see D. C. Douglas, *The Norman Conquest and British Historians* (1946).

[4] F. M. Stenton, *Anglo-Saxon England* (1943), p. 553.

[5] Anglo-Saxon Chronicle, 'D' s.a. 1052 (equals 1051). See J. Earle and C. Plummer, *Two Saxon Chronicles Parallel* (1892), i, p. 176.

[6] *Norman Conquest*, iii (ed. 1869) Appendix 'R'. All students of these questions must feel indebted to the collection of evidence made by Freeman at this place, even if they cannot accept the conclusions he drew from that testimony.

[7] Cf. *Norman Conquest*, ch. viii with ch. xii.

[8] *Ibid.* (1870), ii, p. 309.

[9] *History of England* (ed. 1825), i, p. 410.

[10] *Conquest of England* (1847), i, p. 134.

[11] *Collected Works*, (1921), iii, pp. 160–2: an elaborate description.

[12] *History of England under the Anglo-Saxon Kings*, trans. B. Thorpe (1845), ii, p. 251 – relying in part on the pseudo-Ingulf.

[13] *Conquest of England* (1883), p. 531.

[14] *England before the Norman Conquest* (ed. 1910), p. 620.

[15] *Anglo-Saxon England* (ed. 1943), pp. 557–8.

[16] *Eng. Hist. Soc.* (ed. 1848), i, p. 207. This is repeated verbatim in the prologue to the *Gesta Regum* attributed to Simeon of Durham. (Ed. Rolls Series, ii, p. 168.)

[17] *Roman de Rou*, ed. H. Andresen, (1879), ii, p. 247, ll. 5425–32. The whole story seems here to be placed much later than 1051.

[18] *Will. Jum.*, vol. vii, ch. 13, ed. J. Marx, p. 132.

[19] J. A. Giles, *Scriptores Rerum Gestarum Willelmi Conquestoris* (1845), p. 130, ed. Foreville, p. 176.

[20] *Historia Novorum*, ed. M. Rule (Rolls Series, 1884), pp. 5–6.

[21] *Historia Regum*, ed. T. Arnold (Rolls Series, 1885), ii, p. 183. This is taken from Eadmer.

[22] *Gesta Regum Anglorum*, ed. W. Stubbs (Rolls Series, 1887), pp. 241–3.

[23] See *Lives of Edward the Confessor*, ed. H. R. Luard (Rolls Series, 1858), pp. 399–403.

[24] J. Earle and C. Plummer, *Two Saxon Chronicles Parallel*, ii, p. xxxviii. The text of 'F' for this annal can best be studied in the six-text version in the Rolls Series, ed. B. Thorpe (1861), i, pp. 313–15.

[25] Earle and Plummer, *op. cit.*, i, p. 172.

[26] F. M. Stenton, *Anglo-Saxon England* (1943), p. 681.

[27] For instance see Earle and Plummer, *op. cit.*, ii, pp. xlviii–xlix.

[28] 'E' s.a. 1046 (equals 1048). Text in Earle and Plummer, *op. cit.*, 1, p. 166.

[29] Earle and Plummer, *op. cit.*, *loc. cit.*

[30] 'D' s.a. 1049 (equals 1048). Text in Earle and Plummer *op. cit.*, i, p. 167.

[31] Cf. 'E' s.a. 1048 (equals 1051) with 'C' s.a. 1051 and with 'D' s.a. 1052 (equals 1051). The relevant texts will be found in Earle and Plummer *op. cit.*, i, pp. 170, 171–3, 174–5, and these may be set alongside the accounts given in the *Vita Æduuardi* (*Lives of Edward the Confessor*), ed. Luard, pp. 399–403.

[32] Earle and Plummer, *op. cit.*, i, pp. 171–3.

[33] Cf. for the period the unique notices of the request for aid by Sweyn Estrithson ('D' s.a. 1048, 1049 – equals 1047, 1048).

[34] Cf. Earle and Plummer, *op. cit.*, ii, p. lxxvi.

[35] F. M. Stenton, *Anglo-Saxon England* (1943), pp. 680–1.

[36] Earle and Plummer, *op. cit.*, i, p. 175 : 7.

[37] *Anglo-Saxon England* (1943), p. 555.

[38] Earle and Plummer, *op. cit.*, ii, p. xxxiii.

[39] *Op. cit.*, ii, p. lxxxi.

[40] *Op. cit.*, *loc. cit.*

[41] *Ibid.*

[42] *Op. cit.*, ii, p. lxxix.

[43] *Op. cit.*, ii, p. cxxi.

[44] *Op. cit.*, i, p. xxxiii.

[45] If, in fact this were a later interpolation, the words 'Willelm eorl' might invite the attention of glossators. Compare, for instance, the entry in 'D' for 1071 (equals 1070) with its reference to 'Francena kyning 7 Wyllelm eorl' – the reference in this case being to William fitz Osbern who assuredly was not an earl in 1051, but who might have been so styled by a later interpolator. It would in truth be less improbable for William fitz Osbern to have come to England in 1051 than for the duke of Normandy to have done so, the more especially as his brother Osbern (later to be bishop of Exeter) did settle in England during the reign of Edward the Confessor. (See William of Malmesbury, *Gesta Pontificum*, ed. N. E. S. A. Hamilton, Rolls Series, 1870, pp. 201, 202.) Suggestions such as this are, however, in the absence of proof, more tempting than profitable.

[46] F. M. Stenton, *Anglo-Saxon England* (1943), p. 557.

[47] *Anglo-Saxon Chronicle*, 'E' s.a. 1048 (equals 1051); Earle and Plummer, *op. cit.*, i, p. 174.

[48] *Ibid.*, 'E' s.a. 1052: Earle and Plummer, *op. cit.*, i, p. 177.

[49] *William of Jumièges*, bk. vii, ch. 7, ed. Marx, p. 123; *William of Poitiers* (Giles, *Scriptores*, p. 81; ed. Foreville, p. 18); Ord. Vit., ed. Le Prévost, iii, p. 342; iv, p. 335.

[50] On these wars and their chronology, see generally L. Halphen, *Comté d'Anjou au XIe siècle* (1906), pp. 70–5 and R. Latouche, *Histoire du comté du Maine pendant la Xe et XIe siècles* (1910), pp. 27, 28, 84.

[51] *Nécrologie – obituare de la cathedrale au Mans*, ed. Busson and Ledru (1906), p. 72. Cf. Halphen, *Comté d'Anjou au XIe siècle* (1906), p. 75, n. 1.

[52] *Actus Pont. Cenomm.*, ed. Busson et Ledru (1901), p. 366 – *Rec. Hist. Franc.*, xi, p. 138.

[53] *Actus Pontif. Cenomann.*, *loc. cit.*

[54] That the hostility of the count of Arques to the young duke was notorious long before it broke into open rebellion is brought out clearly by William of Poitiers (Giles,

Scriptores, p. 92; ed. Foreville, p. 52), and by Ordericus Vitalis (ed. Le Prévost, iii, p. 232). See also the evidence cited in Douglas, 'Earliest Norman Counts' (*ante*. lxi, p. 146).

55 Cf. Halphen, *op. cit.*, pp. 74 and 129.

56 *Rec. Hist. Franc.*, xi, p. 590. Cf. F. Soehnée, *Catalogue des Actes d'Henri I* (1907), no. 91.

57 I am myself convinced by the remarks in this sense given by J. Marx in his edition of *William of Jumièges*, and elaborated by him in *Mélanges d'histoire du Moyen Age offerts à M. Ferdinand Lot* (1925), pp. 543–9. These should, however, be contrasted with the opinion expressed by L. Halphen (*Comté d'Anjou*, pp. xii, xiii). Cf. also Foreville, *op. cit.*, pp. xxv–xxxviii.

58 Giles, *Scriptores*, pp. 129–30. Ed. Foreville, pp. 174–6.

59 *Ibid.*, pp. 107–8. Ed. Foreville, pp. 100–4.

60 Giles, *Scriptores*, pp. 95 *sqq.*; ed. Foreville, pp. 28 *sqq.*

61 *E.g.* the terms of Harold's oath, and the course of the battle of Hastings.

62 Cf. F. M. Stenton, *op. cit.*, p. 553.

63 Eadmer, *Historia Novorum*, ed. M. Rule (Rolls Series, 1884), pp. 5–6.

64 *Will. Jum.*, bk. vii, ch. 13; ed. Marx, pp. 132–3.

65 'C' s.a. 1050 referring to the Lent of 1051 by using the Lady Day reckoning for the beginning of the year.

66 'E' s.a. 1048 (equals 1051): Earle and Plummer, *op. cit.*, i, p. 171: 7 þæs sylfan Lentenes he for to Rome æfter his pallium.

67 'E' s.a. 1048 (equals 1051): Earle and Plummer, *op. cit.*, i, p. 172.

68 Compare the account of Aldred's mission given in 'D' for 1054 (Earle and Plummer, *op. cit.*, i, p. 185): þæs ilcan geres for Aldred b' to Colne ofer sæ þæs Kynges ærende. The purpose of this visit was very possibly the recall of Edward the Atheling.

69 It was a neglect of this possible explanation which led Freeman, over-hastily, to reject the story of William of Jumièges (and of Ordericus) out of hand. 'They doubtless had in their minds,' writes Freeman, 'the time when Robert really did cross from England into Normandy. But that perilous passage was not made in the king's errand, or on any errand at all; it was the hurried flight of a public enemy, hastening to save himself from the vengeance of the English people' (*Norman Conquest* [ed. 1869], iii, p. 371). But, as has been seen, there is no need to place the visit of Robert of Jumièges to Duke William at the occasion so picturesquely described by Freeman. It could have taken place at the time when the archbishop went with full power to Rome to seek the *pallium*.

70 Both 'D' and 'E' mention in this connection the 'second Feast of St Mary', i.e. the Nativity of the B.V.M., 8 September.

71 B. Wilkinson, 'Freeman and the Crisis of 1051' in *Bulletin of the John Rylands Library*, vol. 22, no. 2, Oct. 1938.

72 See *Anglo-Saxon Chronicle*, ed. B. Thorpe (Rolls Series), i, p. 312.

73 Marc Bloch (*Analecta Bollandiana*, xli, pp. 3 *sqq.*) suggested that the *Vita* should be referred to a date subsequent to 1103, and his opinion deserves respect. But his arguments in this case would seem to have been inadequate. Two very remarkable articles have at all events been written to contest it. R. W. Southern, 'The First Life of Edward the Confessor' (*Eng. Hist. Rev.* [1943], lviii, pp. 385–400) and E. K. Henningham, 'The Genuineness of the Vita Aeduuardi Regis' (*Speculum*, xxi [1946], pp. 419–56). Both contend for a date shortly after the death of Edward the Confessor.

74 *Lives of Edward the Confessor*, ed. H. R. Luard (Rolls Series, p. 399).

75 For a full consideration of this fascinating and extraordinary production see the articles by R. W. Southern and E. K. Henningham cited above.

[76] R. W. Southern, *op. cit.*, pp. 393, 394. The short entry of 'C' should perhaps be excepted from this comparison for this is in keeping with the fuller account of the *Vita*. See Earle and Plummer, *op. cit.*, i, p. 172.

[77] It is possible that the revolt of William, count of Arques, long expected, broke out before the end of 1052; and throughout 1053 there was fighting not only in Upper Normandy but also in Maine. The king of France was in Upper Normandy on 25 October 1053. See the obit of Ingelran of Ponthieu who was killed in the action of St Aubin (C. Brunel, *Rec. Actes des Comtes de Ponthieu*, 1930, p. iv). The great double invasion of Normandy took place early in 1054, and the decisive battle of Mortemer was fought before Lent (Ord. Vit., ed. Le Prévost, iii, p. 237) which in that year began on 16 February (cf. also *Will. Poit.*, Giles, *Scriptores*, p. 95; ed. Foreville, 'pp. 54–8, for these events). It is obvious that Duke William could have found few opportunities to concern himself at all with English affairs during this period.

[78] *Anglo-Saxon Chronicle*, 'D' and 'E' s.a. 1057.

[79] E. A. Freeman, *Norman Conquest*, (1869), iii, p. 221.

[80] *Ibid.*, p. 678.

[81] *Ibid.*, p. 678.

[82] *Ibid.*, p. 221.

[83] *Gesta Regum*, ed. W. Stubbs (Rolls Series, 1887), i, pp. 278, 279.

[84] At the beginning of his story, William of Malmesbury mentions the idea that Harold had been sent by the Confessor to Normandy in connection with the duke's succession. He then discards this notion in favour of his own theory about fishing. But after the earl has been imprisoned, William of Malmesbury returns in some sense to the earlier view, and says that the earl while in fetters sent messages to Duke William supplicating the duke to effect his release on the ground that he had in truth been sent over to ratify the promise of the succession.

[85] Plates V and VI (quoting the conventional numeration as given for example in F. R. Fowke, *The Bayeux Tapestry*, 1875). These are not fishing boats, nor is there anything that could be described as a tempest. It is perhaps also a little difficult to understand why men should keep their sails up, and sail thus behind a brisk wind, if in fact they were being carried in a direction immediately opposite to their wishes. One of these vessels is furnished with thwarts for oars, and the other has a series of holes in it which may well be rowlocks.

[86] Plates VI and VII. There is no suggestion of a shipwreck. A man throws out an anchor, and the earl, landing without mishap, is arrested with his retinue by mounted men. The whole question of this shipwreck might repay study. The story which was later developed into a legend clearly has its origin in a passage in William of Poitiers. But even this is not wholly unambiguous. It might be interpreted in the sense that Harold, having reached Ponthieu inadvertently, was thereupon treated (according to the barbarous custom of the country which the writer rhetorically describes) as a shipwrecked mariner. This, at all events, is the account given in William of Jumièges and the Bayeux Tapestry.

[87] *Historia Anglorum*, ed. 1879, Rolls Series, p. 1965.

[88] See P. Grierson, 'A Visit of Earl Harold to Flanders in 1056', *ante* (1936), li, pp. 90–6.

[89] Cf. E. A. Freeman, *op. cit.* (1869), iii, p. 678.

[90] The story is given in the 'Saga of Harold Hardraada' in the *Heimskringla*. The account can be conveniently examined in translation in *Heimskringla*, ed. E. Monsen and A. H. Smith (1932), p. 555.

[91] I do not need to notice here further developments of these legends which are still later in date, and which are embodied in writers such as Matthew Paris. Those curious in these matters will find examples given in Freeman, *Norman Conquest*, vol. iii, note 'R',

but later medieval narratives such as these can hardly be considered as adding to the essential evidence on this question.

[92] E. A. Freeman, *op. cit.* (1870), ii, p. 292, where, speaking of Duke William's alleged visit in 1051, he remarks: 'We may be sure that every patriotic Englishman looked with an evil eye on any French-speaking prince who made his way to the English court.'

[93] *Will. Jum.*, bk. vii, ch. 13.

[94] Plate I (using the conventional rotation).

[95] Plate III.

[96] Plates IV and V.

[97] Plate VI.

[98] Plates VII–XVI.

[99] Plates XX–XXIII; XXV.

[100] Plate XXVII.

[101] Plate XXIX–XXX. Much has been written on the question whether Harold is here depicted as being in disgrace at this interview.

[102] Giles, *Scriptores*, p. 108; ed. Foreville, p. 104. As Sir Frank Stenton observes (*William the Conqueror*, 1928, p. 156), 'this is the one contemporary account of Harold's oath which we possess'.

[103] William of Poitiers and the Bayeux Tapestry are frequently and properly accepted as good evidence for other events in these years. See Stenton, *Anglo-Saxon England*, p. 687.

[104] Stenton, *op. cit.*, p. 569.

[105] The most important is perhaps that relating to the place where the oath was taken. *The Bayeux Tapestry* (Plate XXVI) says 'Bagias', which, though the form is curious, probably signifies Bayeux. William of Poitiers says 'Bonnevillam' which is most probably the castle of Bonneville-sur-Touques (Calvados, arr. and cant. Pont l'Evêque). Orderic at a later date seems to have been doubtful about all this for he places the oath at Rouen (ed. Le Prévost, ii, p. 117).

[106] *Will. Poit.* (Giles, *Scriptores*, pp. 107, 108; ed. Foreville, pp. 100–4). Cf. Eadmer, ed. M. Rule (Rolls Series, 1884), p. 6.

[107] Cf. Freeman, *Norman Conquest* (1869), iii, p. 694.

[108] It will be recalled that the Northumbrian revolt was very soon to break out.

[109] The very numerous surviving writs of the king (cf. F. E. Harmer, *Anglo-Saxon Writs*, 1952) are good evidence of this.

[110] Perhaps the best example of this is to be found in his success in imposing the unpopular Tostig on the Northumbrians for eleven years. But the phrases in the *Vita* are also significant in this respect. To some at least this man was king 'ex Dei gratia et hereditario jure': he had been chosen king by God before he was born and consecrated 'non tam ab hominibus quam divinitus'. On this matter see R. W. Southern, *op. cit.*, p. 389.

[111] *William of Poitiers* (Giles, *Scriptores*, p. 109; ed. Foreville, p. 104) gives some additional support for this view when he says that after the oath, the duke at Harold's request confirmed the earl in all his possessions.

[112] It is no part of the purpose of this article to consider the probability that on his death-bed Edward the Confessor finally designated Harold as his heir. That is a distinct question which would demand a separate treatment.

[113] *Norman Conquest*, (1869), iii, p. 696.

[114] Even if it be the ghost, Æ, or the 'democrat of Peterborough' (cf. Freeman, *op. cit.*, iii, p. 581).

[115] *Vita Æduuardi* (ed. Luard, *op. cit.*, pp. 399–403).

[116] *Anglo-Saxon Chronicle* 'E' s.a. 1048 (equals 1051).

[117] *Will. Poit.* (Giles, *Scriptores*, p. 107; ed. Foreville, p. 100).

[118] *The Bayeux Tapestry*, Plates VII–XVII.

[119] *Will Poit.* (Giles, *Scriptores*, p. 108; ed. Foreville, p. 104).

X

The Norman Conquest
and English Feudalism[1]

It is now more than forty years since John Horace Round inaugurated a
new epoch in English feudal scholarship by discovering the origins of
English knight-service not in Anglo-Saxon custom but in the bargains by
which the Conqueror fixed the number of knights due for his service from
each of his greater followers.[2] The doctrine was at the time a startling
heresy;[3] it has since been developed into the severest orthodoxy; and we
are now authoritatively taught[4] that after the Norman Conquest and as its
result a new social structure was rapidly and widely established in England
by means of a military reorganization that ignored Old English precedent
at every point. Even those who are most concerned to display the vitality
of English society during 'the last phase of Anglo-Saxon history' are
rigid in their refusal to extend Old English influence into this department
of social growth, and there are today, among the successors of Round,
some who would deduce from his theory of knight-service implications
wider than those suggested by its original author. 'It is hardly possible,'
writes Dr Darlington, 'to speak of any trend towards feudalism in England
before 1066,'[5] and Jolliffe categorically asserts the 'absence' of feudalism
in Anglo-Saxon England.[6] In the greatest work which during the present
century has been devoted to this subject, Professor Stenton is much more
cautious. The break between the two societies, he remarks, was 'far from
absolute'.[7] But his readiness to appreciate the evidence in its totality, and
his unique equipment for doing so, make his conclusions only the more
significant. 'Feudalism' is a word of vague connotation; it demands
definition; but 'it is turning a useful term into a mere abstraction to apply
the adjective "feudal" to a society which had never adopted the private
fortress, nor developed the art of fighting on horseback, which had no
real conception of the specialization of service, and allowed innumerable
landowners of position to go with their land to whatever lords they
would'.[8] In this sense, English feudalism is to be regarded as 'essentially
a creation of the eleventh century'.[9]

F

No student of English history in the Middle Ages can afford to neglect these conclusions. Feudal law adhered to the structure of English medieval life *velut ossa carnibus*,[10] and the origins of English feudalism are thus in a sense those also of the English constitution. To assert that formal feudalism was in England not the product of centuries of growth but a conscious creation made by alien conquerors within a restricted period is not merely to comment upon a point of legal antiquarianism. It is to offer an interpretation of a large part of English medieval development. It is perhaps seemly therefore to illustrate this interpretation afresh if only because its very importance may have led in some quarters to unexpected exaggeration. Anglo-Norman studies are today dominated by a lively consciousness of the cataclysm which marked the genesis of English feudalism, and the unanimity here achieved by scholars in opposition to the views of their predecessors is so remarkable that it may now be apposite to take note of some of the obstacles which they have surmounted.

It must, for example, always remain difficult to regard English feudalism as in any exact sense a Norman creation in as much as the social organization of England after the Norman Conquest was even in its military aspects so notably different from that coexisting in contemporary Normandy. 'Resemblance between two societies can only be superficial,' remarks Professor Stenton, 'when one expects a man to fight in his lord's quarrel and the other makes the beginning of private war a cause of forfeiture.'[11] From the time of the Conquest the monarchy exercised over English feudal arrangements a coordinating control for which it would be hard to find a parallel elsewhere.[12] William's action in assessing the quotas of knights due from his magnates was in itself a revolutionary act inaugurated by the royal initiative, and at a later date feudal society in England was to show itself exceptionally susceptible to monarchical control. English feudalism always possessed its own distinguishing features, and not the least of these was the dominating position assumed therein by the king.

There is, moreover, some reason to believe that the royal influence so characteristic of Anglo-Norman feudalism was during its formative period even more pervasive than is sometimes supposed. Normally, the king undoubtedly left in the hands of his tenants-in-chief the task of making such sub-infeudations as they deemed necessary to comply with the demands of the royal service.[13] But it seems clear that, on occasion, and particularly when dealing with ecclesiastics, William did not shrink from sometimes intervening directly in the construction of the mesne fiefs of selected sub-tenants.[14] A very early charter of Bury St Edmunds, for example, reveals a particular knight being enfeoffed on the Abbey lands by the special command of the king,[15] and Domesday displays at Potterne in Wiltshire a 'miles' similarly established by the royal order on the estates of the bishop of Salisbury.[16] Such action was sometimes designed to enable prelates to endow their own followers and relatives with the lands of the church.[17] Thus the Abingdon chronicler makes this a special complaint against Abbot Ætuelhelm,[18] and Frodo, the brother of Abbot Baldwin, held land of Bury St Edmunds by military service *regis ipsius iussu*.[19] But more often the royal intervention in such sub-infeudations was exercised in opposition to the ecclesiastical tenants-in-chief themselves. When, for instance, the king sent from Normandy a writ to the abbot of Peterborough bidding him enfeoff Eudo the son of Hubert de Ryes at Easton, the abbot protested.[20] But he was forced to yield, and Eudo duly appears in Domesday as possessed of the estate.[21] Similarly at Aldwinkle St Peter in Northamptonshire, Ferron in 1086 held a Peterborough fief by the king's command in opposition to the wishes of the same abbot,[22] and in Cambridgeshire it was likewise the will of the king that at Harleston intruded Picot, the dreaded sheriff, on to the Ely estates.[23]

Evidence of this character deserves perhaps more consideration then it has yet received. The intervention of the king in the construction of subordinate fiefs was something quite distinct from his allocation of quotas to his tenants-in-chief. The latter was a practice common to feudal Europe; the former was exceptional. By the end of the eleventh century the monarchy in Gaul, for instance, had long ceased to exercise any control over the enfeoffments made by its immediate tenants.[24] That in England William could, and occasionally did, do so is a fact of considerable importance. It illustrates from a new angle a divergence between the feudal practice of England and that of the continent even in the first phase of English feudalism. William's followers brought with them into England not a clear-cut scheme of social reorganization but the recollection of diverse social customs emanating from the many lands from which they came. The Conqueror could refer to his East Anglian subjects as 'English, French and Danish';[25] Breton names long persisted in the Richmond fee in Lincolnshire;[26] and even in the twelfth century a lord could address his Cambridgeshire tenants as 'French, English and Flemish'.[27] The assimilation of these elements in the new society was ultimately complete. But it was not immediate,[28] and it was not from Normandy nor Brittany nor Flanders that the special characteristics of English feudalism derived.

It might therefore have been tempting to suppose that Anglo-Norman feudalism owed something to the earlier traditions of the country in which it was developed, the more especially as Anglo-Saxon England was no stranger to many of the institutions which in western Europe later contributed to the feudal organization of society.[29] The benefice appears early on English ecclesiastical lands, and the immunity in various forms was well known to Anglo-Saxon law. No student of Domesday can assert that this country knew not commendation, or that on the eve of the Conquest dependency between man and lord was not widespread. The relationship of homage was familiar to Anglo-Saxon England as to the whole Germanic world. These developments were, doubtless, too vague in their implications, and too sporadic in their incidence, to bear detailed comparison with the ordered arrangements of Anglo-Norman feudalism. But it is, none the less, true that the Norman invaders found themselves confronted in England with a body of customs regulating dependency and that, for whatever reason, the feudal society which they developed in this country bore from the first a special character.

The social reorganization of England after the Norman Conquest involved the establishment of a class of warriors whose position depended upon their possession of a particular form of military equipment and upon their ability to use it: the central figure of Anglo-Norman society was the mounted knight. The replacement of the *thegn* by the *knight*[30] was indeed perhaps the most remarkable innovation of the Conquest. For the thegn was a typical product of the Old English past. His social position derived from his high wergild; his service followed from his rank; and when he fought, he fought on foot.[31] By the beginning of the twelfth century his place in England had been taken by men[32] who underwent apprenticeship in mounted warfare as a condition of their status, who performed military service by contract in return for the estates they held, and who were distinguished from their fellows not by reason of their noble birth but because of their proficiency in arms. Here was a transition which undoubtedly involved drastic and widespread alteration in the social structure of England. Darlington does not shrink from describing it as 'one of the most sudden and far-reaching revolutions that this island has witnessed'.[33]

The character of even this fundamental change must, however, sometimes have been blurred in the practice of the late eleventh century. Certainly it was not always fully appreciated by those who drew up the legal documents of the period. Geoffrey de Ros for instance took his name from Rots canton, Tilly sur Seuilles; he was a member of a family which had enjoyed the special favour of Odo;[34] and in company with that bishop he had come to England. He was among the most important of the new military tenants in Kent; and he became also one of the knights of Canterbury.[35] But a comparison between the *Domesday Monachorum* of Canterbury and the Exchequer Domesday shows that the royal clerks who drew up the latter record could actually describe this man as a thegn.[36] It would of course be in the highest degree misleading to over-emphasize the implications of an isolated example of Domesday terminology, but such errors of description at least suggest that the compilers of Domesday

were not always so alive as are some modern scholars to the legal distinctions between the thegn and the knight. Sometimes it was difficult for
them to be so. Another of the military tenants of Canterbury was for
example Ægelwin the son of Brihtmar,[37] and his previous history can in
part be traced. In the time of King Edward he had been a tenant of the
bishop of London at Stepney, and there he remained after the Norman
Conquest.[38] He was an important man in contemporary London, and as
such he witnessed in the house of Eadmer, 'the one handed', the famous
agreement[39] which is the chief evidence for connecting Bishop Gundulf
of Rochester with the building of the Tower of London. In his name and
from his origins, Ægelwin, son of Brihtmar, was as representative of the
older social order as was Geoffrey de Ros of that which supplanted it:
yet while the latter could be wrongly described in an official document as
a thegn, so could the former appear alongside of men such as Hugh
de Montfort and William de Braiose as a knight of a Norman archbishop.

During the first age of Anglo-Norman feudalism, the knights of
England constituted no homogeneous class. If the warrior enfeoffed
with land was unknown in Anglo-Saxon England, he was also in a
minority even among the knights who settled in England immediately
after the Conquest. The presence of large numbers of unenfeoffed knights
in Anglo-Norman England appears ever more clearly in the documents.[40]
These men were represented for instance in the mercenary troops who, as
William of Poitiers remarked, played so large a part in the battle of
Hastings,[41] and they were of the company of those 'armed and mounted'
men who rioted in London during the coronation of the Conqueror.[42]
William dismissed many of them from his personal service about 1068,[43]
but more settled in England, taking a prominent place in the new society
as the armed household retainers of the great magnates of the land.
Henry of Huntingdon describes how as a boy he admired the military
entourage of Bishop Robert of Lincoln;[44] Wulfstan of Worcester had
milites in his household;[45] besides his great enfeoffed tenants Abbot
Baldwin probably maintained knights at Bury St Edmunds;[46] and at
Westminster a number of knights resided in the immediate neighbourhood
of the abbey and perhaps were fed at the abbot's table.[47] When between
1094 and 1104 Arnulf of Hesdin ratified in his English house at Norton
his father's gifts to the Priory of St George at Hesdin, he assembled as
witnesses to the transaction 'many knights of his *familia*'.[48] The presence
of these men was often a menace to the peace of the land. The armed
French retainers of Abbot Thurstan committed sacrilege in 1083 by
shedding the blood of the monks in the church of Glastonbury,[49] and just
as the knights quartered at Ely were a perpetual source of disturbance,[50]
so also did the misbehaviour of the household knights of Bishop Walcher

of Durham help to precipitate the northern rebellion of 1080.[51] These household knights, who can thus be traced widespread through contemporary accounts of Anglo-Norman England, were certainly trained in a technique of warfare unpractised by their predecessors in this country. But their social position was not very different from that of the retainers of an Anglo-Saxon noble or in particular from that of the housecarls who filled a notable place in late Old English society.

Even in respect of those knights who were actually enfeoffed with land, the transition between the two social organizations must sometimes have been less sudden in contemporary practice than it has occasionally become in modern theory. The knight's fee was the institution which distinguished most sharply the new feudal order from the older military system it supplanted, and the widespread establishment of such fees was in a sense the measure of the feudal consequences of the Conquest. It would be in the highest degree unwise to minimise in any way the magnitude of the tenurial changes which these enfeoffments involved but it would be equally rash to assume that during the last quarter of the eleventh century the tenure of the Anglo-Norman knight had everywhere in England assumed a uniform character. No feature of the later knight's fee was for example more universally recognized than its hereditary quality,[52] but even this appears sometimes to have been lacking during the first phase of Anglo-Norman feudalism, and it deserves considerable emphasis that of the two earliest records of English enfeoffments,[53] one leaves the question of succession studiously vague,[54] whilst the other definitely creates a life tenancy of the estate with which it deals.[55] These may perhaps be regarded as exceptional documents,[56] but in face of their testimony it becomes impossible to postulate a hereditary tenure for the enfeoffed knight as existing uniformly through England before the twelfth century. And in as much as this uniformity was resisted or delayed so far were older notions of beneficial tenure allowed after the Norman Conquest to affect even the most characteristic of the new military tenures of the Anglo-Norman state.[57]

The nature of the feudal transition consequent upon the Conquest could, in fact, be aptly illustrated by the extent to which this vital question created confusion and controversy. Evidence derived from lay fiefs is here, perhaps, inevitably lacking, but the life leases which were certainly granted upon church lands during this period suggests that the prelates of England were not unnaturally alarmed at an institution which appeared to involve the permanent alienation of ecclesiastical lands and to contribute to 'the servitude of the church'.[58] The point was vexing contemporary Europe. In France towards the end of the eleventh century ecclesiastical magnates were wont on occasion to transfer fiefs away from the heirs of their former possessors, and the strict heredity of French fiefs was only slowly established.[59] In the Empire, less than thirty years before the Norman Conquest, Conrad the Salic found it necessary to issue his famous decree to safeguard the succession of his lesser military tenants,[60] and his admiring biographer indicated the joy which this caused, though, significantly, here too it was the great ecclesiastics who most resisted the legislation.[61] After the Norman Conquest, the ecclesiastics of England must in a similar fashion have been anxious to oppose the establishment of hereditary military tenures upon the lands of the Church, and they could take some support from Old English precedent. Late in the tenth century Oswald of Worcester had effected a notable reorganization of his estates by defining the holdings of his greater tenants in such a manner as might prevent the establishment of military tenures in perpetuity on his lands.[62] A hundred years later his successors in the Church were, apparently, in very different circumstances, to attempt the same task, and this time to fail. For a time, however, the transformation remained, as it seems, incomplete. During the last quarter of the eleventh century, the conception of the benefice as a simple usufruct was not uniformly superseded by the newer notion of the hereditary fief. The Anglo-Norman knight was by no means always enfeoffed with land and, even when he was so endowed, it was not always in hereditary right.

In many ways, therefore, the sharpness of the transitions involved in the military reorganization of England by the Normans might in practice be modified. Nor did the arrangements involved in the institution of knight service constitute the only means whereby the Norman settlement was effected. Even in the upper ranks of society the events of 1066 must sometimes have caused little tenurial change upon many large estates. On the lands of Bury St Edmunds it is, for example, occasionally possible to trace a continuity of tenure throughout the period of the Conquest,[63] and a most important series of correlated texts shows unmistakably that Saxon thegns seated upon the estates of St Benet of Holme could be succeeded by Norman magnates holding their lands upon the same terms as did their predecessors.[64] These practices were probably exceptional,[65] and they must certainly be regarded as secondary to the general feudal policy of the Conqueror. But their very existence challenges attention, and it is difficult to escape the conclusion that the endowment of the followers of King William occasionally did not take the form of grants of land to be held *in capite* by knight service, but of tenures which the recipients enjoyed under conditions similar to those of the Saxon notables who held them before the Norman Conquest. When this occurred, the tenurial transformations implicit in the Conquest must have been gradual rather than abrupt.

The Norman Conquest set up in England a new aristocracy who held the bulk of their possessions by a tenure with which Saxon England was

scarcely acquainted, and who were themselves distinguished by proficiency in a technique of warfare unfamiliar to the men whom they had
beaten in battle. But their establishment concerned, in the first instance,
only a small class in the community, and for long the vast bulk of the
people of England were but indirectly affected by the change. Domesday
Book shows unmistakably that the agrarian structure of England was in
all essentials the same in 1086 as it had been in the days of King Edward,
and well into the twelfth century the peasant life of Kent,[66] East Anglia[67]
and the Danelaw[68] continued to be conditioned by the same individual
customs which had long distinguished the several provinces of the Old
English state. Even if the honour rather than the province be taken as the
unit for examination, the same conclusions will be reached. In the great
honour of Bury St Edmunds the primary results of the Norman Conquest
were almost entirely confined to the intrusion of a small but very important
class of men holding their lands by a special form of military tenure.
Below them in the social scale it was an Anglian and a Scandinavian
population which remained, and the influence of the Norman settlement
upon the peasantry was very slight.[69]

The first phase of English feudal history can only be interpreted in the
light of these facts. The new aristocracy for long constituted only a small
minority amid an alien population, and the feudal superstructure which
the Normans created remained for a generation a precarious erection. The
central theme of Anglo-Norman history is not an opposition between
King and Baronage. It is the effort made by both the king and his greater
tenants, together with the knights who owed them allegiance, to maintain
their very existence in the land which they had conquered. To do this they
had at times to make a temporary and not unwilling compromise with
existing customs; they had to suppress dissension in their own ranks.
Their success was ultimately assured, but the issue was long in doubt,
and the feudal order which they at last secured and made uniform was not
the facile product of a sudden creation but the achievement of long years
of hazardous enterprise.

The course of that prolonged effort could best be traced in the extensive
litigation which was so notable a feature of the reign of William the
Conqueror. The full history of that litigation has still to be written.[70]
But it looms large in the documents of the age and its political significance
was certainly very great. The notable pleas of the time such as those of
Kentford and 'Ildeberga',[71] the great trials in Worcestershire and Kent,
were only outstanding examples of the consistent attempt which was made
during the reign to harmonize the divergent ideas which were dictating
the development of the new social structure of England. In this work
there was no desire to neglect tradition. Just as between 1072 and 1079,
John, archbishop of Rouen, vindicated the rights of the Priory of Bellesme

by reference to the sworn remembrance of men of great age,[72] so also was Æthelric, the aged South-Saxon bishop, brought by the king's command in a waggon to Pennenden Heath in 1072 in order 'to declare the ancient customs of the laws'.[73] This far-reaching litigation was characteristic of the first age of English feudalism. It reflected the slow and difficult imposition of the new feudal order on a society which in many ways was not yet ready for it.

After twenty years of Norman rule, the new feudal order was still not secure, and it had become imperative that these endless controversies involved in its maintenance should at last be settled by an authoritative statement of ownership and possession. There can be little doubt that the Domesday Inquest itself was related to this problem or that its procedure was evolved somewhat easily out of the feudal litigation which preceded it.[74] At Ely, at Canterbury, at Worcester and probably at Evesham and at Abingdon a continuous series of legal investigations led up to the events of 1086,[75] and in the final great inquiry the same methods of proof were employed by men who for the most part had had a large experience of similar work in the earlier trials.[76] Not only because of the *clamores* it records is Domesday Book to be regarded as the result of a great judicial eyre, and the questions at issue were those which vitally concerned the stabilization of the new feudal institutions.[77] The date at which the inquiry was instituted is in this connection also significant. For it was in December 1085 that the project for the Domesday Inquest was discussed at the Gloucester curia, and in the following August, while the inquiry was actually being conducted throughout England, there met the Salisbury gemot whereat 'all the landholding men of any account throughout England whosesoever men they were' came to the king and 'they all bowed to him and became his men and swore oaths of fealty to him that they would be faithful to him against all other men'. There is no need to exaggerate the constitutional importance of the Oath of Salisbury, but it was certainly an exceptional feudal measure.[78] It stands in direct relation to that other exceptional feudal measure – the Domesday Inquest – which it was hoped might terminate the disputes persisting within the feudal kingdom and so enable its social structure to be preserved.

For two decades after the Conquest, the Normans in England had to defend a precarious feudal order not only at home, but also against the constant menace of a lethal attack from overseas. In this task, too, their success was for long doubtful, and no conception of Anglo-Norman social development can be adequate which does not take full account both of the perpetual contemporary threat of Scandinavian invasion and of the persisting Scandinavian population in England which so notably increased its danger. This was the period when Sweyn Estrithson and his sons were making Denmark once more a formidable power in the north, and the Danish court swarmed with English exiles who pointed to a past tradition of Scandinavian conquest, and to the rewards which might once again follow from a successful invasion. The initial structure of English feudalism was erected under the abiding shadow of this impending catastrophe. It was, probably, the fear of such an attack which brought William hurriedly back from Normandy in 1068,[79] and the rising of the North in 1069 was rendered especially dangerous through the cooperation of the Danish fleet.[80] In 1070 it was only through the ancient expedient of bribery that William could persuade the Danish ships to depart,[81] and five years later the Danish fleet again appeared off the east coast to help the rebellion of Earl Ralph of Norfolk.[82] Twice during these years did York actually fall into Scandinavian hands, and the invaders could always count upon finding support in England.[83] When in 1069 the Danes proceeded to York they were (according to Orderic) welcomed by the countryside through which they passed,[84] and after the host had dispersed into Lindsey it was there feasted by its resident compatriots.[85] In a similar fashion the Old English Chronicle graphically describes the cordial reception of Osbeorn's troops by the men of the Fens.[86] Not without reason did William of Malmesbury later refer to Scandinavia as the chief obstacle to William's enjoyment of his kingdom.[87]

There can be no question that the feudal organization of England by the Normans was throughout closely connected with this perpetual menace, or that its special features are thus partly to be explained. The feudal reconstruction of the Abingdon tenures was, for example, certainly influenced by the demand for the rapid services of stipendiary knights to meet the invaders,[88] and the slow process of sub-infeudation in those districts of England most subject to Scandinavian attack was probably due to the desire of lords to keep knights in their households ready for instant defence.[89] But here also the threat to the new order did not reach its climax until the end of the reign when Saint Cnut of Denmark, Olaf of Norway and Count Robert of Flanders planned an attack upon England comparable to the great invasions of the previous century.[90] William was under no illusions as to the magnitude of the danger. In 1085, according to the Old English Chronicle, he 'passed over into England with such a force of horsemen and footmen from France and Brittany as had never sought this land before'.[91] He did not have to meet the dreaded attack, for the Scandinavian host was prevented from sailing. But the rebellion which took place in the Danish fleet in 1085 and which lead to the murder of Saint Cnut was one of the decisive events of English feudal history. It permitted the feudal organization of Norman England to be stabilized in such a manner that it might survive.

The crisis in the early history of English feudalism probably came not at the beginning of the reign of William the Conqueror but at its close.

It was not until then that the new social structure was saved from the dangers of internal disruption and external attack. In 1085–6 under the menace of a threatened invasion, the Domesday Inquest was planned and carried out in such a manner that the feudal controversies arising out of the Conquest might in the future be limited. In 1086 the Salisbury gemot met. In 1086, again, the Scandinavian danger reached its climax. These events, which were all interconnected, mark the end of the first period in the history of English feudalism. It was a period when the new regime in England was neither stable nor uniform, a period of development during which compromises needed to be made and older ideas inevitably exercised their influence upon the new administration. Not until after the death of the Conqueror were the immense initial difficulties of the Norman settlement overcome, and then the process of feudal organization could be more rapid and more confident. During the reign of Rufus, there was, as Stubbs observed, a 'hardening' and 'sharpening' of feudalism in England.[92] By the time of Henry I the new order could at last be deemed secure and England began everywhere to conform to the pattern proper to a feudal state. The formal feudalism of medieval England derived from the Norman Conquest, but the revolution which marked its beginnings was neither assured nor fulfilled until the twelfth century.

NOTES

[1] The article is based on an address delivered to the Eighth International Congress of Historical Sciences at Zürich, 31 August 1938.

[2] Round, *Feudal England*, pp. 225 *sqq.*, an essay based upon articles which had previously appeared in the *English Historical Review*.

[3] Round could have cited in his favour certain opinions expressed by seventeenth-century historians such as Spelman and Nicolson, but he was correct in his claim (*e.g. Commune of London*, p. 56) that his theory was in direct contradiction to 'the view of modern historians'.

[4] Stenton, *English Feudalism* (1932), pp. 121, 122 *et passim*. It is hardly necessary for me to add that the present paper is derived directly from this book. It is in particular a commentary upon its fourth chapter. Such additional evidence as I have here cited is in the main incidental to the argument, and when I have ventured to give a different emphasis to certain aspects of Anglo-Norman feudalism, I have always done so with extreme diffidence. Professor Stenton is therefore not necessarily to be considered as in agreement with all the individual opinions which are here expressed, but my general debt to his teaching on this subject will be apparent to anyone who reads these pages. It is a debt which has if possible been increased by his kindness in having read through this paper in proof and in having thus allowed me to profit once again by his advice.

[5] R. R. Darlington, 'Last Phase of Anglo-Saxon History', *History*, xxii, p. 2.

[6] *The Constitutional History of Medieval England* (1937). See the illuminating article in the index: 'Feudalism – absence of in pre-Norman England'.

[7] Stenton, *op. cit.*, p. 122.

[8] *Ibid.*, p. 215.

[9] *Ibid.*, p. 12.

[10] The telling phrase is that of Fabian Philipps (*Government of England* [1687], p. 213). This substantial folio is one of the most remarkable books ever devoted to the history of English feudalism.

[11] Stenton, *op. cit.*, p. 14.

[12] Cf. Valin, *Le Duc de Normandie et sa Cour* (1910), pp. 60 *sqq.*

[13] This is implicit in the whole argument of Round's famous essay. 'Every baron,' adds Professor Stenton, 'was free to make his own plans for the raising of his contingent' ('The Changing Feudalism of the Middle Ages' in *History*, xix, p. 298). The generalization was doubtless intended to apply only to lay magnates, but perhaps in view of the ecclesiastical evidence here cited it needs some qualification.

[14] Douglas, *Feudal Documents from the Abbey of Bury St Edmunds* (British Academy, 1932), pp. xcv-c.

[15] Douglas, 'A Charter of Enfeoffment under William the Conqueror', *Eng. Hist. Rev.*, xlii, pp. 245 *sqq.*

[16] D.B., i, fol. 66. Episcopus Sarisberiensis tenet Poterne – De eadem terra huius Manerii tenent II Angli VI hidas et unam virgatam terrae. Unus ex eis est miles iussu regis et nepos fuit Hermanni episcopi.

[17] In the earlier half of the eleventh century Robert, bishop of Coutances, had made himself notorious for such practices: non solum praebendas dictorum canonicorum servitio ecclesiae non reddidit, verum etiam haec et alia in feodum et hereditatem nepotibus et consanguineis et sororibus suis non large sed prodige distribuit. (*Gallia Christiana*, vol. XI, 'Instrumenta', col. 218.)

[18] Misit abbas Ethelelmus in Normaniam pro cognatis suis quibus multas possessiones ecclesiae dedit et feffavit. (*Chronicon Monasterii de Abingdon*, Rolls Series, ii, p. 283.)

[19] Douglas, *Feudal Documents*, p. 4.

[20] *Chronicon Petroburgense* (Camden Soc. 1849), p. 168; Cf. Round V.C.H. (Northants, i, p. 284).

[21] D.B., i, fol. 227 where the estate is described as pertaining to the fief of Eudo with the note that 'the land belongs to Peterborough Abbey'.

[22] D.B., i, fol. 222: Hac terra fuit T.R.E. de victu monachorum. Ferron tenet per iussum regis contra uoluntatem abbatis.

[23] D.B., i, fols 191, 200.

[24] Cf. Luchaire, *Institutions monarchiques*, ii, pp. 25 *sqq.*; Flach, *Les Origines de l'ancienne France*, ii, p. 560.

[25] Douglas, *Feudal Documents*, Charter No. 3.

[26] Stenton, *English Feudalism*, p. 24.

[27] *Op. cit.*, p. 28.

[28] Cf. Steenstrup, *Normandiets Historie under de syv forste hertuger* (1925), pp. 291 *sqq.*

[29] Cf. Fustel de Coulanges, *Les Origines du Systeme Feodal* (ed. Camille Jullian, 1922); Guilhiermoz, *Essai sur l'Origine de la Noblesse en France* (1902); Mitteis, *Lehnrecht und Staatsgewalt* (1933).

[30] On this see Stenton, *op. cit.*, chapter iv.

[31] Earl Ralph the Timid in his warfare against the Welsh courted disaster when he made his English thegns fight, Norman fashion, on horseback: 'Anglos contra morem in equis pugnare iussit.' (Florence of Worcester, sub. anno 1055). The English thegn might use horses to take him to the battle but in the actual engagement his practice was, as at Hastings, to fight on foot.

[32] But see modif. by Douglas 1951.

[33] Darlington, *op. cit.*, p. 3.

[34] *Gallia Christiana*, xi, p. 207; Orderic Vitalis, ed. Le Prévost, ii, pp. 129, 243; iii, p. 266; iv, pp. 269, 270; *Antiq. Cartul. Eccl. Baioc. – Livre Noir* (Soc. Hist. Norm.), i,

pp. 30–2. I am indebted for these references to the kindness of Lewis Loyd.

[35] *Domesday Monachorum*, fol. 14 (Cf. *V.C.H. Kent*, iii, p. 269).

[36] D.B., fol. 3 (Otford); D. Mon., fol. 3b (*V.C.H. Kent*, iii, p. 260). Cf. A. Ballard, *An Eleventh Century Inquisition of St Augustine's, Canterbury* (Brit. Acad. Records, vol. iv), p. xvii.

[37] *Domesday Monachorum*, fol. 7b (Cf. *V.C.H. Kent*, iii, p. 269).

[38] D.B., i, fol. 127b: Terra Episcopi Lundoniensis – Stibenhede – In eadem villa tenet Aluuinus filius Britmar i molendinum quod valet *xx* solidi. Quando recepit similiter. T.R.E. similiter. Ipsemet tenet de Willelmo episcopo.

[39] *Textus Roffensis*, ed. Hearne (1720), p. 212.

[40] Stenton, *English Feudalism*, pp. 139–42.

[41] William of Poitiers, *Gesta Willelmi Ducis* (ed. Giles, 1845), p. 146.

[42] *Op. cit.*, p. 142: Ceterum, qui circa monasterium in armis et equis præsidio dispositi fuerunt, ignotae nimio strepitu accepto, rem sinistram arbitrati prope civitati imprudentia flammam injecerunt.

[43] Stenton, *op. cit.*, p. 142. About 1077, according to Orderic Vitalis when William met the rebellion of Robert, he confiscated the lands of the rebels and used their rents for employing mercenaries against them (ed. Le Prévost, ii, p. 287).

[44] Henry of Huntingdon *Ep. ad Gualterum de Contemptu Mundi* (see Henrici Huntend. Hist. Angl. – Rolls Series – p. 299).

[45] *Vita Wulfstani*, ed. Darlington (Camden Soc., 1928), p. 55: 'habebat ipse in curia sua milites multos'.

[46] D.B., ii, fol. 372. See also Douglas, *Feudal Documents*, p. cvi.

[47] Armitage Robinson, *Gilbert Crispin* (1911), p. 41.

[48] Round, *Calendar of Documents preserved in France*, No. 1326.

[49] Old English Chronicle, sub. anno 1083. Cf. Stenton, *op. cit.*, pp. 132, 133; Douglas, *op. cit.*, pp. civ, cv.

[50] *Liber Eliensis* (ed. Stewart, 1848), p. 275; Cf. J. Bentham, *Antiquities of Ely* (1771), p. 106.

[51] Simeon of Durham *Historia Dunelmensis Ecclesiae* (*Opera Omnia* – Rolls Series – i, p. 116): 'ut autem qualiter nefanda episcopi sedes peracta sit ex ordine retexatur, statuto die quo et hi, scilicet milites antistitis qui fecerant injurias et qui fuerant in pacem redirent'.

[52] Stenton, *op. cit.*, p. 154; Valin, *Le Duc de Normandie et sa Cour*, p. 59.

[53] Stenton, *op. cit.*, *loc. cit.*

[54] Douglas, *Eng. Hist. Rev.*, xlii, pp. 245 *sqq.*; *Feudal Documents*, pp. 151, 152.

[55] V. H. Galbraith 'An Episcopal Land-Grant of 1085' (*Eng. Hist. Rev.*, xliv, pp. 353–72.

[56] On this matter I have permitted myself some disagreement with Professor Galbraith. See Galbraith, *op. cit.*, and Douglas, *Feudal Documents*, pp. xcv n.

[57] In Southern Italy, after the establishment of the feudal institutions of the Normans 'earlier Lombard tenurial usage co-existed with the newer Norman practice'. See Jamison, *Communications presentées au VIIIe Congrès International des Sciences Historiques*, i, p. 90.

[58] *Historia Anglorum sive Historia Minor*, ed. Madden (Rolls Series), i, p. 13.

[59] Luchaire, *Institutions Monarchiques*, ii, pp. 4 *sqq.*; Flach, *Les Origines de l'ancienne France*, ii, p. 560; W. M. Newman, *Le Domaine royal sous les premiers Capetiens* (1937), p. 24. See also Douglas, *op. cit.*, p. ciii n.

[60] *Mon. Germ. Hist.*, Leges, Sect. iv, Constitutiones, i, pp. 90–1. See also Lehmann, *Das Langobardische Lehnrecht* (1896), for a discussion of the effects of this edict on feudal society.

[61] *Die Werke Wipos*, ed. Bresslau: *Gesta Chuonradi II Imperatoris,* chap. vi, p. 28.

⁶² Maitland's view that the arrangements made by Oswald anticipated later feudal organization has now been generally rejected. See Stenton, *op. cit.*, pp. 122 *sqq.*; Douglas, *op. cit.*, pp. civ, cv.

⁶³ Douglas, *op. cit.*, esp. p. cxvi.

⁶⁴ The history of one such estate during the period of transition is told with a wealth of detail, that is perhaps unique, in the wills of the two thegns Edwin and Ketel, in Domesday Book, in a charter of Godric Dapifer, and finally in a charter of Abbot Anselm of St Benet, Holme, who between 1133 and 1140 confirmed Ralph the son of Godric in his possession. In this case there emerges with especial clarity the record of a continuity of tenure which the Norman Conquest apparently did little to impair. (Cf. Douglas *Feudal Documents*, pp. cxii–cxv, where these texts are criticized in detail.)

⁶⁵ Arrangements of this kind were not unknown in contemporary Normandy. Between 1091 and 1126 Abbot Gerard of Saint Wandrille granted to Witgar and his wife the usufruct of an estate in return for a payment and on condition that at their deaths the land should return to the monastery. (Lot, *Études critiques sur l'abbaye de Saint-Wandrille, Bibl. de l'École des Hautes-Études*, fasc. 204, 1913, p. 100, Doc. No. 44.) Cf. also the authorities cited by Génestal in *Rôle des Monastères comme Etablissements de crédit*.

⁶⁶ Jolliffe, *Prefeudal England: the Jutes* (1933).

⁶⁷ Douglas, *Social Structure of Medieval East Anglia* (1927), esp. pp. 205–19.

⁶⁸ Stenton, *Danelaw Charters* (Brit. Acad., 1920).

⁶⁹ Douglas, *Feudal Documents*, pp. cxvii–cxxxii.

⁷⁰ Some of the material for this history has been collected in Bigelow, *Placita Anglo-Normannica* (1879).

⁷¹ Cf. Brady, *Animadversions upon a Book called Jani Anglorum Facies Nova*, p. 191 in *Introduction to the Old English History* (1684); Round in *Domesday Commemoration Studies* (1886), ii, p. 542; *ibid.*, in *V.C.H. Worcestershire*, i, pp. 255 *sqq.*; Inq. Com. Cant., ed. Hamilton, pp. 192–5.

⁷² Round, *Calendar of Documents preserved in France*, no. 1190; For another example of the Norman use of this practice see Round's essay on *The Bayeux Inquest of 1133*, printed posthumously in *Family Origins* (1930), p. 205.

⁷³ *Anglia Sacra* (1691), i, p. 335.

⁷⁴ Douglas, *Odo, Lanfranc and the Domesday Survey* in *Essays presented to James Tait*.

⁷⁵ Cf. Douglas, 'The Domesday Survey', *History*, xxi, p. 256.

⁷⁶ Cf. Douglas in *Essays presented to James Tait*, pp. 55–7.

⁷⁷ *Ibid.*, *History, loc. cit.*

⁷⁸ The best account of the significance of the Salisbury assembly is in Stenton, *English Feudalism*, pp. 111–13, to which the reader is here referred.

⁷⁹ Orderic Vitalis, ed. Le Prévost.

⁸⁰ Freeman, *Norman Conquest*, iv (1871), pp. 247–71.

⁸¹ Florence of Worcester, sub. anno 1069.

⁸² Freeman, *Norman Conquest*, iv (1871), p. 585.

⁸³ The racial individuality of those districts of England which had been subject to Scandinavian settlement has been sufficiently established by Professor Stenton and others, and it needs no further emphasis here. New illustrations of the Scandinavian affinites of the East Riding at this period can be found in A. H. Smith's recently published *Place Names of the East Riding of Yorkshire* (1937), pp. xxii *sqq.* According to a remarkable story in the *Heimskringla* (508–9) it would appear that the speech of this district in the eleventh century was intelligible to a raiding Norwegian.

⁸⁴ Orderic Vitalis (ed. Le Prévost).

⁸⁵ *Ibid.*

86 Old English Chronicle, sub. anno 1070.

87 *Gesta Regum*, Bk. iii, Sect. 246.

88 *Chronicon Monasterii de Abingdon* (Rolls Series), ii, p. 11: Dein fama percrebuit Danos classem, qua Angliam oppugnarent, parasse. Quare militibus, quos Solidarios vocant, undecumque collectis, ubique locorum et in episcopiis et abbatiis tamdiu administrari victualia regis imperio jubetur, quoad rei veritas indice vero praedicetur. Cumque plurimum hac in expectatione anni tempus volveretur, nullaque Danorum impetitio solida certitudine affutura sciretur, solidarii remunerati regio donativo ad propria remeare sinuntur.

89 Stenton, *English Feudalism*, p. 138 n.

90 On the significance of this see the full discussion by Stenton (*op. cit.*, pp. 148-150).

91 Old English Chronicle, E, sub. anno 1085, D, sub. anno 1086. Professor Stenton calls attention to the importance of this entry (*op. cit.*, *loc. cit.*). The statement is surely highly remarkable as having been written within living memory of the invasion of 1066.

92 Stubbs, *Constitutional History* (1891), i, pp. 324-328. See also the highly suggestive article of R. W. Southern: 'Ranulf Flambard and early Anglo-Norman Administration', R. Hist. Soc. *Transactions*, 4th Series, xvi, pp. 95-128.

XI

The Norman Achievement

━━━━━━━◆◆◆◆◆◆◆◆━━━━━━━

I

So much has been written on the Norman Conquest of England that it
may well be doubted whether more can usefully be said about it. Nevertheless, it may be profitable to inquire whether some new light can be
thrown on the Norman intrusion into English history if it be considered
in connection with the general Norman expansion – so rapid and so vast –
which took place between 1050 and 1100. The Norman conquest of
England, the Norman conquests in southern Italy, the establishment of the
Norman kingdom in Sicily, have all been individually and exhaustively
discussed; and scarcely less attention has been paid to the Norman
relations with the Hildebrandine papacy, with the developing cleavage
between the Eastern and Western Churches, and with the origins of the
Crusades. But despite Haskins's more general survey which appeared some
fifty years ago, comparatively few attempts have been made to link
together these scattered exploits of a single people during the latter half of
the eleventh century, or to consider how far, if at all, between 1050 and
1100 they formed part of a single enterprise.

The fact deserves some emphasis. It is as legitimate as it is usual to
assess the historical importance of the Normans in connection with the
secular and ecclesiastical institutions which they influenced, and in
relation to the later development of the countries which they conquered.
It may, however, be true to say that the Norman impact upon England,
and upon Europe, can now be further elucidated if it be examined from
the point of view of the Normans themselves who, during the space of
little more than half a century, carried the influence of a single province of
France into so many lands.

No complete explanation has ever been given why this small racial
group was able, so rapidly and so widely, to extend its dominion by a
process of expansion which has even been compared with that of the
original inhabitants of Latium. How is it that within a few decades

Norman rule could have been stretched not only over England, Sicily and much of southern Italy, but also into Scotland and Wales, Greece, Syria and Palestine? Certainly the question is easier to ask than to answer, but a bare recital of a few selected dates might of itself prompt speculation whether the Norman Conquest of England should not be regarded as a part of a wider enterprise. Robert Guiscard started his fantastic career in Italy in the same year as William began his effective rule in Normandy after Val-ès-Dunes, and Duke William received from Edward the Confessor the promise of the English succession only two years before the Norman victory over Leo IX at Civitate initiated the new relations between the Normans and the papacy which were to prove so influential in England, in Constantinople and at Rome. Again, the capture of Bari by the Normans which marked the collapse of Byzantine administration in Italy, took place only five years after the battle of Hastings, and in the next year, while William was advancing into Scotland, the Normans took Palermo. That was in 1072, and in 1073 Archdeacon Hildebrand, who had sponsored the alliance between the papacy and the Normans, ascended the papal throne. These chronological connections could in fact be very widely illustrated. Robert Guiscard, for example, seized Durazzo, and began his invasion of the Eastern Empire only four years before William's hasty return from Normandy to England in 1085 to repel the threat of an invasion from Scandinavia, and to plan the Domesday Survey. And very soon, the sons of both Guiscard and the Conqueror, Bohemund and Robert, were to be associated in the First Crusade.

The close sequence of these widely scattered events is indeed remarkable. Of itself it might suggest that the Norman achievements of these decades were the result of a unified endeavour. It might also invite consideration how far the successful expansion of Norman influence is thus to be explained, and how far its character and manifold consequences derived from that fact.

II

Such an inquiry must inevitably start with some comparison between the Norman intrusion into England on the one hand, and into Italy and Sicily on the other, the more especially as the long-term results of that intrusion were in one respect very similar. The kingdom of England and the kingdom of Sicily were, in the middle of the twelfth century, to be the strongest and most mature governments in western Europe, and it would be hard to deny that in both cases this owed much to the earlier Norman conquest. On the other hand, both in England and in Sicily the later development depended largely upon earlier institutions which the Normans did but utilize and strengthen. Twelfth-century England enjoyed a full legacy from the Anglo-Saxon past, and no one can visit Palermo or Monreale, or above all Cephalu, without being aware of the debt of Norman Sicily to Saracenic and Byzantine inspiration. It might almost seem as if the Normans tended to be absorbed into the civilization of the countries they conquered but that in so doing they imparted an essential stimulus to earlier developments which apart from the Normans might never have reached fruition.

Leaving this aside, however, it might at first appear that the differences between the Norman intrusions into English and Italian history were more notable than any similarities between them. The Norman impact upon England began with a dynastic alliance; it reached its climax with an expedition carefully organized by a Norman duke; and it resulted in the conquest of an ancient kingdom whose unity it preserved and fortified. By contrast, the Norman impact upon Italy began with isolated acts of brigandage; and it operated upon a large number of contending states in a wide region where there were two religions, and two systems of ecclesiastical government; where three languages were spoken and where three systems of law were operative. Here at first a few isolated Norman lordships were established dependent upon the settlements at Aversa and Melfi, and only later by one of the most notable achievements of political consolidation known to history did the Norman government established first at Plesisma and then at Palermo impose an overriding political unity over all these lands which had previously been divided and distraught.

Widely different also were the circumstances which attended the coming of the Normans into England and into the Mediterranean lands. Whatever may be the relative value of the various legends relating to the first appearance of the Normans in Italy, there is no doubt that they arrived as savage marauders whose brigandage was indiscriminate and uncontrolled, and whose violence spared neither age nor sex. According to Leo IX, they were 'worse than the Saracens' in the atrocities they inflicted on their fellow Christians, and Anna Comnena at a later date gave a lurid picture of the savage cruelties of Robert Guiscard during his early career in Calabria. These were, of course, enemies of the Normans, but Amatus of Monte Cassino and Geoffrey Malaterra, in their turn, provide plenty of examples of Norman brutality, and John, abbot of Fécamp, declared to the pope in 1053 that so hated had the Normans become in Italy that it was unsafe for any Norman to travel in the peninsular even as a pilgrim.

It is important not to misconceive the shrill temper of much eleventh-century literature, but there seems little doubt that the terrible sack of Rome by the Normans in 1084 was in keeping with much of the earlier conduct of the Normans in Italy. The city, by Robert Guiscard's orders or at least with his connivance, was given over to indiscriminate pillage, and since on two occasions during the engagement much of Rome was deliberately fired, the destruction of the monuments of antiquity must have been very great. When Hildebert, archbishop of Tours, visited the city some sixteen years later, he was moved to declare: 'The idols and palaces have fallen, the people have sunk into servitude, and Rome scarcely remembers Rome.'

A contrast with England is here at once suggested. Before 1066, England suffered nothing from Norman violence, and when the Normans came here they were under firm leadership. The distress caused by William's early campaigns, and more particularly by his horrible harrying of the North, is assuredly not to be minimized, but after 1072 there was no indiscriminate destruction, and whilst the dispossession of the native nobility was indeed tragic, its replacement by a highly comparative aristocracy imported from overseas was effected without general anarchy, and with an overt respect for legal precedent. The Conqueror's rule over England was undoubtedly harsh, but the good order he maintained was noted with gratitude in the Anglo-Saxon Chronicle, and he was in fact always in control of the situation as were none of his contemporaries in Italy and Sicily. Here, however, a distinction must be made. In southern Italy neither Richard of Capua nor Robert Guiscard could in their early days assert authority as of right over the other Norman leaders, but in Sicily, Robert Guiscard and his brother Count Roger had no rivals of their own race, and could enfeoff their followers with land at will dictating the terms on which it was to be held. The results of this were, however, to lie in the future. In the closing years of the eleventh century, the contrast between the south and England remained very notable. William the Conqueror, avaricious himself, was able and determined to hold in check the rapacity of his followers.

None the less, when all this is said, certain characteristics between these two conquests made by men of the same race are immediately apparent. Everywhere during the central decades of the eleventh century the Normans were showing their own special qualities as skilled warriors who were also able on occasion, as at Civitate and Hastings, to submit themselves profitably to disciplined leadership. Their efficiency as troops was in fact immediately recognized in Italy by the constant demands made for their services – demands which they were prepared to meet with a complete lack of scruple. They fought for the Lombards against the Greeks, and for the Greeks against the Saracens, and there were Normans fighting on both sides during the crucial operations round Bari in 1071. These were of course men of minor importance, but in the early days the same temper was shown by the leaders themselves. Between 1030 and 1045 Rainald of Aversa was constantly changing his allies, and whilst the two eldest sons of Tancred of Hauteville fought for the Greeks against the Saracens in

Sicily about 1038, Roger, the youngest of their half-brothers, was in 1060 in close alliance with Ibn at Timnah, Emir of Syracuse.

Clearly the fighting qualities of the Normans were widely respected and there seems no reason to suppose that in character or in equipment the typical Norman warrior between 1050 and 1070 was essentially different in Sicily and in Sussex. No Bayeux Tapestry, alas, exists to illustrate the Mediterranean adventures of the Normans, but evidence on this matter is not wholly lacking. The importance of mounted troops in William's expedition to England in 1066 is well known, and as Anna Comnena and others were quick to point out, the Normans were likewise famous in the Mediterranean lands for their prowess on horseback. Many of the greatest Norman successes were in fact to be won by mounted men against infantry fighting in close order, and here a direct comparison can perhaps be made between the battle of Hastings in 1066 and the battle of Civitate near Benevento thirteen years earlier. William of Poitiers describes how the Norman victory in Sussex was achieved by the repeated charges of the Norman knights against Harold's massed infantry. And at Civitate very similar tactics seem to have produced the same result. According to both William of Apulia and one of the biographers of Leo IX, the Norman attack was here also made on horseback against foot soldiers. The chief resistance was offered by the Swabian troops who had been recruited by the pope, who, like Harold's troops at Hastings, fought with the utmost bravery. And their method of combat was the same. Even as Harold's infantry had been *densius conglobati*, so also were the Swabian and Italian at Civitate ranged in the closest formation – 'like a wall,' it is said – and at the last they formed themselves 'into squares' before they were finally overwhelmed. Both Civitate and Hastings were won by Norman horsemen over massed infantry.

Such comparisons are arresting, but it must be remembered that both in England and in Italy the successes of the Normans depended not only on their own prowess as horsemen, but also on their plentiful use of mercenaries. A notable article by Prestwich has recently demonstrated the importance of mercenaries in Anglo-Norman warfare between 1066 and 1086, and in like manner the Normans in Italy made wide use of mercenaries recruited from the lands they sought to conquer. Mercenaries from Apulia were in the army of Robert Guiscard when he marched against Bari in 1071. Similarly, Roger the Count after 1072 frequently had Saracen troops in his pay, and when in 1081 Robert Guiscard and his son Bohemund crossed the Adriatic to assault Durazzo they took with them many soldiers of Greek and Calabrian origin.

The widespread employment of mercenaries, who usually fought on foot, and who were to be used with such good effect by Bohemund in the First Crusade, may also have influenced the practice of the Normans of

using ships to assist their operations on land. At Bari the final success of
the siege in 1071 resulted from the defeat at sea by Calabrian sailors of a
relieving force sent from Byzantium; and at Palermo in 1072 a Moslem
fleet was successfully beaten off by ships in the pay of the Normans. In
contemplating these 'amphibious' operations one is immediately reminded
of the cooperation between the fleet and the land force of William the
Conqueror when late in 1072 he made his successful advance into Scotland.
Indeed, the implications of this comparison could be stretched yet further.
In both Italy and Sicily one of the chief problems for the Normans lay in
the difficult task of transporting horses by sea for the use of the mounted
Norman warriors. This operation was in the south frequently carried out
between the mainland and Sicily by Greek ships in the pay of the Normans,
and very notably in 1061. Five years later, as the Bayeux Tapestry so
graphically records, the Normans brought their horses with them in their
little ships across the English Channel. It is even tempting to speculate
whether here the Conqueror may not have used techniques learnt from the
Greeks by contemporaries of his own race in Italy, perhaps through the
medium of those men from Apulia and Calabria which the Carmen de
Hastingae Proelio reports as having joined his expedition.

Be that as it may, one general conclusion here seems indicated. Despite
all the differences between them, the foundation of the Norman states of
Capua, Apulia and Calabria, the Norman Conquest of England, the
Norman conquest of Sicily, are all alike to be regarded in the first instance
as the achievement of a military élite of mounted warriors supported by
mercenaries, and using their own techniques of warfare under the direction
of highly competent leaders such as Robert Guiscard, William the Conqueror, Roger the 'Great Count' and Bohemund of Taranto.

III

The interrelation between the various enterprises of the Normans in the
latter half of the eleventh century was, however, reflected still more
notably in the common sentiments they inspired, and more particularly in
the propaganda which contributed to their success. No feature of the
conflict of 1066, for example, is better known than the manner in which
the duke of Normandy then sought to support his cause by an appeal to
moral and ecclesiastical considerations. The murder of the Atheling
Alfred in 1036, it was said, called for divine vengeance. Stigand, a schismatic archbishop, it was added, occupied the throne of St Augustine. The
promise of a venerated king had been set aside, and the violation of an
oath solemnly sworn upon relics demanded the punishment of Heaven on
the perjured usurper. The truth or falsity of the Norman case thus presented is of course not here under consideration. What is to be remarked is

firstly the character of William's propaganda at this juncture, and secondly the extent to which it was accepted in Europe. As is well known, the Norman case was successfully stated at Rome, and in the event William was to fight at Hastings under a papal banner, and with consecrated relics round his neck. His expedition against England had in short been made to appear as a Holy war, so it was to be widely regarded.

This is usually regarded as a triumph of diplomacy, and so it was. But it was a diplomacy exactly adapted to the general Norman situation within western Europe at this time, and only thus is its success to be explained. Erdmann and others have shown how gradual was the process by which a general condemnation of war as evil had been supplanted in the political theology of western Christendom by its sanctification in particular circumstances. There is, however, no doubt that this process reached a critical stage just at the time when the Norman expansion was taking place. In the eleventh century, western Europe seemed to be becoming more conscious of a common and militant purpose. The reforming movement associated with Cluny and its offshoots was imparting fresh vigour into the western Church. At the same time the new feudal aristocracies whose status and privileges depended upon the specialized performance of military service were being established. These movements were distinct, but they combined to produce a climate of opinion favourable to the prosecution of religious war. Sword-blessings, for example, multiplied, and there was an increase of liturgical prayers for victory. Even the modes of popular devotion began to be affected. Veneration continued of course to be paid to Martyrs such as St Sebastian or St Lawrence who had refused to resort to violence in the armed service of Rome. But the temper of the eleventh century was better represented in the growing enthusiasm for St Michael, the warrior archangel or for St Gabriel, 'chief of the angelic guards'. It would, of course, be easy to exaggerate, but the general tendency is evident. The sanctification of religious warfare was becoming a dominant and a unifying sentiment in the west.

Here was an enthusiasm capable of being exploited both by the believing and by the unscrupulous. And the chief beneficiaries were in fact to be the papacy and the Normans, acting often in conjunction. Though earlier precedents might be cited, it was in 1053 that the papacy first emphatically proclaimed a Holy War, and in view of subsequent events, it is one of the paradoxes of history that it was then proclaimed against the Normans. At all events the German and Italian troops whom Leo IX led towards Civitate were blessed by him as they moved into battle; they were granted remission of their sins; and they were promised that if they were slain they would be received into the shining company of the martyrs in Heaven. This might perhaps be regarded as an exceptional episode. But between

1060 and 1083 the papacy was constantly urging one or other group of the secular magnates of the west to war on behalf of the Faith, providing them with consecrated banners under which to fight, and promising beatitude to those who fell in battle. It is true that before the time of Urban II the bestowal of a papal banner might be merely a form of feudal investiture, and the *milites sancti Petri* might be simply vassals of the papacy rather than those who took up arms on behalf of the Faith. None the less, it is also true to say that by the end of the pontificate of Gregory VII there had begun to be formulated from Rome what may perhaps be called a 'theology of armed action'. The *militia Christiana* were no longer exclusively the ascetic 'athletes of Christ', or that army of praying monks whose duties had been set out in the military metaphors of St Benedict. Rather, they represented the armed might of the West mobilized for war with papal approval or under papal leadership on behalf of Christendom.

Partly as a result of the policy of Archdeacon Hildebrand, the Normans early became involved in this development and from it they were to reap the richest rewards. The incongruous alliance between the Normans and the papacy grew gradually during the years that followed the battle of Civitate, and it was to be fully displayed, as against both the western and eastern Empires, at the Synod of Melfi in 1059. There, as will be recalled, within a few months of the proclamation of the *Constitutio Romana* by Nicholas II, the pope invested Richard with the Principality of Capua, and Robert Guiscard with the Duchy of Apulia, and they in return swore to protect the freedom of papal elections, and to champion papal claims against the see of Byzantium. Henceforth, the Normans were to lose no opportunity of exploiting a situation which enabled them to pose in a special sense as *milites Christi*, and the propaganda which they based upon this notion coloured their activities from one end of Europe to the other.

Their success in disseminating these ideas could be illustrated by brief extracts from the life of William the Conqueror by William of Poiters, from the 'History of Sicily' by Geoffrey Malaterra, and from the treatise of Amatus of Montecasino. These were considerable writers, who were filled with a fervent admiration for the Normans to whom they addressed their works, and by and large they reflected the Norman point of view. Nothing is therefore more remarkable than the identity of the terms employed by them to proclaim the religious mission of the Normans. According to his most recent editor, the work of William of Poitiers was permeated by the notion that William the Conqueror waged a holy war.

With even less restraint did Malaterra and Amatus develop the same idea. According to the former, St George, fully armed and mounted on a white horse, led the Normans to their victory at Cerami in 1063. And Amatus stresses the divine assistance accorded to the Normans in their Sicilian wars and describes how their entrance into Palermo was celebrated by a descending flight of singing angels. Anything might perhaps be expected from a writer who could salute men such as Richard of Capua and Robert Guiscard as the 'anointed of the Lord', and cite miracles to prove the divine favour which was extended to them. But other contemporary writers besides Amatus developed the same theme; and the description of the battle of Cerami in 1063 given by Malaterra could be aptly compared with that given by Eadmer of the battle of Hastings in 1066. So heavy were the losses inflicted on the Normans at Hastings, says this writer, that they must have been defeated if God had not Himself intervened. Therefore, concludes Eadmer, the Norman victory at Hastings is to be considered as 'without question a miracle of God'.

It is tempting to dismiss such assertions with impatience or disgust. Robert Guiscard might join the Blessed in Dante's Paradise of Mars, but it is hard to picture him as a *miles Christi*, and in 1098, it may be recalled, Robert the Count, who had been so signally helped by St George against the infidels, brought a large contingent of Saracen mercenaries to assault Capua, and refused permission to St Anselm of Canterbury to attempt their conversion. It might be rash, however, to indulge here too readily in indiscriminate cyncism. The religious motive was undoubtedly at first used by many of the Norman leaders as the thinnest cloak for wanton aggression, and in early days many of their followers were little better than brigands. But evidence might be cited from writers like Anna Comnena, who were no friends of the Normans, to suggest that this same motive grew in some Norman quarters into a sincere sentiment. If this be so, the process, as Professor Lopez points out, might be described as almost the opposite of that which is sometimes alleged to have taken place during the Crusades when religious fervour is frequently stated to have been gradually supplanted by material incentives. In any case, the early exploitation of the notion of the Holy War by the Normans may in part explain their dominant and sometimes unfortunate participation in the opening phases of the World's Debate.

Quite apart from this, it would be unwise to minimize the effect of propaganda relating to the Holy War on the successes of the Normans. The support which William the Conqueror received in 1066 not only from the papacy but from many other quarters in western Europe was due in part to this, and the largest intrusion of Normans into Spain took place two years earlier in connection with the so-called 'crusade' of Barbastro. The Norman conquests in Apulia and Calabria were undoubtedly facilitated by the claim that the Normans were winning back for Rome provinces which had been lost to Byzantium, and in like manner the papacy supported the Normans in Sicily on the understanding that they were not only fighting the Saracens but also restoring the Sicilian church to the Latin rite. Robert Guiscard himself, albeit three times excommunicate, never lost sight of the value of this propaganda. When in 1081 he attacked Durazzo, he posed as a second Charlemagne, and Norman aggression against the eastern Empire was deliberately associated with the revival of papal claims over the lost dioceses of Albania and Greece, and with Roman assertions of jurisdiction over the patriachate of Constantinople. Sentiments derived from the conception of the Holy War, and propaganda inspired by them thus served in their turn to link together all the Norman achievements of the latter half of the eleventh century.

IV

The close association between all the Norman exploits during this period was further strengthened by the fact that they were undertaken by men who were the brothers and cousins of each other, fully conscious of their kinship and conscious also of their common and militant purpose. Indeed, no better illustration of the unified character of Norman enterprise at this time could be found than in the history of particular families, and by way of example it may be permissible to refer briefly to three of them.

Take for instance the family of Tosny. In 1015–16 Ralph II of Tosny in central Normandy is to be found fighting on behalf of Guaimar IV, the Lombard ruler of Salerno, against the Saracens. His son Roger was to visit Spain where he so distinguished himself against the Moslems that he was ever afterwards dubbed in Normandy with the nickname of the Spaniard. Then Roger's son Ralph III of Tosny further extended the activities of the family but this time to the north, for he fought both at Mortemer and at Hastings, and was in due course rewarded with lands in no less than seven English shires. Three generations of the family of Tosny (which remained strongly established in Normandy) thus contributed in the eleventh century to the Norman impact on Italy, Spain and England.

A similar record might be compiled for the family of Crispin. Gilbert Crispin I was established as castellan of Tillières in the reign of Duke Robert I, and his second son William became closely associated with Herluin in the early fortunes of Le Bec. His third son, however, left Normandy at an early date, and his career speedily became the subject of legend. According to Amatus of Monte Cassino he fought at Barbastro in 1064, and later, having lost the city to the Saracens, he departed to Italy where he remained for some years. Then, once more moving on, he entered the service of the Eastern Emperor to whom he proved unreliable. He fought without much enthusiasm against the Turks at Manzikiert in 1071, and died soon afterwards. Meanwhile, his nephew Gilbert had started a notable career in the Church which was to lead him across the Channel in 1085 to become a highly distinguished and respected abbot of Westminster. Between 1060 and 1090, therefore, three members of the family of Crispin, that is to say William, his brother and his son, made their contribution to the history of Normandy, Spain, the eastern Empire and England.

Nowhere, however, was the character of Norman enterprise in this age better exemplified than in the family of Grandmesnil, or to be more precise in the lives of Hugh of Grandmesnil, his brothers and his sons. Hugh himself is one of the most familiar figures in Anglo-Norman history. Prominent in Normandy during the Conqueror's reign as duke, he fought at Hastings, and after being custodian of Winchester he was established at Leicester. He was one of the inner circle of the Conquereor's advisers, and active in the politics of the Anglo-Norman kingdom. By the time of the Domesday Survey he had become one of the largest landowners in all England, and he was to survive until 1095. Long before then, however, his children were making their way not only in Normandy but in many other parts of the Norman world. His second son William is for instance particularly noteworthy in this respect since he left for Italy early in life and having secured in marriage a daughter of Robert Guiscard he acquired for himself very large estates in southern Italy, especially in the neighbourhood of Rossano. In 1081 he accompanied Robert Guiscard to the assault on Durazzo, and at some period in his life he is to be found at Constantinople with an official title at the imperial court. Finally he appears, though this time without honour or distinction, alongside his brothers Yves and Aubrey, at the siege of Antioch in 1099.

Meanwhile, Hugh's younger brother Robert had begun a yet more influential career in the Church. About 1059, as is well known, this man who was then abbot of St Évroul came into conflict with Duke William, and fled to Italy where in due course after considerable adventures he transported many of the monks of St Évroul. Thereafter, his Italian career was to be most notable. When in 1062 the abbey of St Euphemia in Calabria was founded by Guiscard, monks from St Évroul were placed therein with Robert of Grandmesnil as their abbot, and from this time forward his influence spread rapidly with the Norman conquests in the south. Thus the abbey of Venosa was early subjected to St Euphemia, as was also at a later date the abbey of St Michael at Mileto. Over both these houses monks from St Évroul were appointed as abbots, and the movement which had thus been started by Robert of Grandmesnil continued after his death. For in 1091 a monk from St Euphemia was called to preside as abbot over the newly established Sicilian monastery of St Agata at Catania on the slope of Etna, and from St Agata were to derive three more monasteries which might not inaptly be described as the Sicilian great-grandaughters of the distant Norman abbey of St Évroul in the forest of Ouche.

The history of the family of Grandmesnil during the last four decades of
the eleventh century may surely, both in the secular and in the ecclesiastical spheres, offer an admirable example of the unity of Norman
enterprise at that most constructive time. Hugh rose to power and immense
wealth in association with William the Conqueror; Robert and William in
association with Robert Guiscard. But the family interest was integral, and
it was sustained. Based upon Normandy it operated over England, Italy
and Sicily.

No apology need surely be made for alluding to these episodes of
family history, for not only could many others of a similar nature be added
to them, but they all illustrate, more clearly than any literary generalizations, the close interconnection between the various zones of Norman
action during the latter half of the eleventh century. Indeed, the unity of
Norman enterprise at that time was widely recognized. As early as
February 1053, John, abbot of Fécamp, is to be found at Rome stating the
cause of the Normans in Italy to Pope Leo IX, and William the Conqueror,
we are told, was wont to confirm his courage by reflecting on the deeds of
Robert Guiscard. In like fashion, prelates such as Odo, bishop of Bayeux
(who was also earl of Kent), received contributions from their kinsfolk in
Italy to help them rebuild their cathedrals at home, and it was noted with
pride that the chant of St Évroul was heard in Sicilian abbeys. Assuredly
between 1050 and 1100 the Norman world was a reality, and the effort which
created it stretched from Syracuse to Abernethy, from Spain to beyond
Durazzo, from Brittany to Antioch. It is in fact in that setting that must
be placed the Norman Conquest of England. For this vast movement of
inter-related endeavour reached a climax nine centuries ago, when on
Christmas Day 1066 a Norman duke was consecrated King of the English
in the abbey church of St Peter at Westminster.

XII

William the Conqueror: Duke and King

❧❧❧❧❧❧❧❧❧❧❧❦❧❧❧❧❧❧❧❧❧❧

This book is designed to commemorate the nine-hundredth anniversary of the battle of Hastings. The battle is described in detail and its consequences are to be considered both in relation to the ancient English kingdom which was thereby to pass under a new ruler, and in connection with the political and ecclesiastical changes which thereafter ensued. The other papers in this volume thus deal with large questions of general importance to English history, with which the present essay has no concern. But there may be room in such a commemoration for a comment on the personality and career of the central figure in the drama of 1066 – the Norman duke who on the evening of 14 October 1066 stood victor on the downs above Hastings, and who, on the next Christmas Day, was hallowed as king of the English in the abbey church of St Peter at Westminster.

But even if the subject be thus rigidly circumscribed, it none the less presents difficulties. So much has been written on William the Conqueror that it might well be doubted whether anything more could usefully be said about him. He is familiar to schoolboys and scholars; facts and fictions about him are part of the currency of general conversation; and even today he is one of the few figures in the English story about whom it is considered shameful, or eccentric, to profess ignorance. The fact, indeed, deserves some note. England is perhaps unique among the nations in having taken so thoroughly to herself a successful invader from overseas; and she has been content to start the long succession of her numbered kings from a man who began his rule by conquest.

Considering the remote age in which he lived, and the circumstances of his life, it is surely remarkable that this eleventh-century magnate of foreign birth should have entered so deeply into the English consciousness. That he has done so might of itself be cited as testimony to his historical importance. But it has been due also to the fact that the literature concerning him has been not only of long duration but of a very peculiar character. A mass of erudition has been expended upon his life and work; and over the centuries a war of words has raged about him. His career has provided a constant text for political controversies and social sermons, to such an extent that sometimes he has almost seemed to remain a figure in contemporary politics. He has been presented in terms of Whig theory, of sectarian fervour, and of modern nationalism. He has been hailed as one of the founders of British greatness and as the cause of one of the most lamentable of English defeats. He has been pictured as an enemy of Protestantism and as both the author and the subverter of the English constitution. Indeed, it might almost be said that the influence which he has exercised on English growth has been conditioned not only by what he did but also by what men thought, or imagined, or hoped, that he did.

Even today, it is hard to escape from the consequences of these controversies, but it is clear that any description of the Conqueror, and any account of his life, must seek to do so. William, if it be possible, must be pictured against his own eleventh-century background. More particularly must he be placed in his own Norman setting. Not only was he a Norman by birth, but the major part of his life was spent in Normandy. It was as a Norman duke that he came to England, and his conquest was effected by one who had already shown himself the exceptional ruler of an exceptional province. And it was as a Norman king of the English that (for good or ill) he influenced the subsequent development of England. His career did not begin in 1066, nor did it then end, and it will be a primary purpose of this essay to suggest that what he accomplished as king must be closely related to what he had earlier achieved as duke.

William the Conqueror was born in 1027 or 1028, being the bastard son of Robert I, sixth duke of Normandy, by Herleve, a girl of Falaise, and on his father's death in 1035, he became, when still a child, the ruler of a province which was then unique in Christendom. Normandy in 1035 can be regarded as the product of two contrasted traditions, both of which were to affect the whole career of William himself. The first was Scandinavian. It is very usual to ascribe the special characteristics of Normandy to the intrusion of a Scandinavian population into this region of Gaul during the previous century, and to find the starting-point of the history of medieval Normandy in the establishment of Rolf the Viking (Rollo) and his followers in Neustria between 911 and 918 by means of grants made by the Emperor Charles III. Nor is evidence wanting to support such an interpretation. Later chroniclers assert that there was a considerable repopulation of Neustria in the tenth century, and it would seem that the flourishing ecclesiastical life which had formerly distinguished the province of Rouen was severely disrupted by the invaders. The surviving lists of Norman bishops show gaps at this time which are testimony to the disintegration that had occurred, and it is probable that in the third decade of the tenth century not a single monastery remained in the Norman land. Again, despite the politic conversion of Rollo to Christianity, the ruling dynasty itself seems only slowly to have renounced the traditions of its Viking past. Even as late as 996, a French chronicler could refer to the Norman duke as a 'pirate chief', and within twenty-five years of the birth of William the Conqueror his grandfather welcomed in his capital of Rouen a Viking host which had recently spread devastation over a considerable area of north-western France. In short, it would be rash indeed to minimize the Scandinavian factor in the making of the Normandy which William ruled.

On the other hand, it would be equally rash to give it too great a prominence. On many of the great estates of Normandy the events of the tenth century do not seem to have interrupted a tenurial continuity which apparently here proceeded with scarcely more modification than elsewhere in Gaul, and the place-names of Normandy have been held to indicate a society in which men from the north formed only a minority. These, moreover, seem soon to have been absorbed. Adémar of Chabannes, writing about 1030, goes out of his way to emphasize how quickly the new settlers had adapted themselves to the civilization into which they had entered, and we have the contemporary word of Dudo of Saint-Quentin that by 1025 Scandinavian speech was already obsolete in Rouen though it still persisted in Bayeux. At the same time, trade and ideas flowed across the insubstantial land boundaries of Normandy and up and down the great waterway of the Seine. Viking Normandy, in fact, quickly assimilated the surrounding culture of France, and despite the survival of Scandinavian traditions among them, William and his followers when they came to England were French in their speech, in the essentials of their culture and in their political ideas. It was in keeping with the earlier history of Normandy that one of the chief results of the Norman conquest was to deflect the destinies of medieval England away from the Scandinavian north and towards Latin Europe.

William's reign as duke of Normandy was also to be conditioned by the fact that the province over which he presided was itself of ancient delimitation. It was in fact almost precisely the pre-Viking ecclesiastical province of Rouen with its six dependent bishoprics, and this in turn was based upon a division of the old Roman Empire. The ducal ancestors of William had thus been able to build upon established foundations, and they had in fact used many of the older institutions of government, inheriting traditional rights to revenue and to military obligations, inheriting, too, such powers as had been vested in the counts of the Carolingian age, and also authority over constituted local officials such as the *vicomtes*. This was, in fact, to stand William in good stead during his terrible minority, and it helps to explain his survival during the perils of his early years. His succession as a bastard child in 1035 tested the ducal authority to the uttermost, and the horrors of his boyhood have been often and luridly described. His court was a shambles; his guardians nearly all perished by murder; and he had himself frequently to be taken from his home by night to seek refuge in neighbouring dwellings. Elsewhere the province was given over to private wars among the greater Norman families, almost all of whom were involved at this time in violence or disaster. There is no doubt that William's minority was one of the darkest periods in Norman history.

That these calamities were not (as might have been expected) fatal to William, and to Normandy, was certainly due in part to the inherited authority that had come to be vested in the ducal office. It is remarkable, for instance, that during these tumultuous years nearly all the *vicomtes* regularly discharged their duties; the ducal revenues continued to be collected; and the bishops of Normandy seem, in general, to have given their support to the child ruler. It would appear also that the boy duke, or those who acted for him, had a specifically ducal force at their disposal. In short, the traditions of ducal authority and the administrative machinery which might give it effect were sufficiently strong to enable the ducal power to survive the critical decade between 1035 and 1046. How important this was can be judged by reference to the revolt of the western *vicomtes* which broke out in 1047, when the duke needed to be rescued by his overlord, the French king. By that time, however, William had reached maturity, and was beginning to exercise his personal influence on the afflicted duchy he had inherited.

Yet if the battle of Val-ès-Dunes signalized the end of Duke William's minority, it marked also the beginning of six more years of uninterrupted war in his struggle for survival. It is unlikely, for instance, that the strong fortress of Brionne in central Normandy held by his enemy Guy 'of Burgundy' was retaken before the end of 1049, and it is doubtful whether William was able to re-enter his capital of Rouen before 1050. At the same time Geoffrey Martel, count of Anjou, who had risen to a position of dominance in western France, was starting to exercise pressure on Normandy through Maine. As a result, during the winter of 1051-2 Duke William was engaged in his famous campaign which resulted in the sack of Alençon after siege, and in the capture of Domfront. In all this continuous warfare between 1046 and 1052 it should be noted, moreover, that William had the support, active or passive, of King Henry of France. But before 15 August in the latter year Henry transferred his support from the Norman duke to the count of Anjou, and henceforth the king of France, far from being the ally of Duke William, was always to be his most formidable opponent in Gaul. This transformation of political filiations has been described by a great French historian as constituting nothing less than 'a turning point in history', and certainly its results were to be far-reaching. The relations between Normandy, Anjou and the Capetian monarchy were to be affected for more than a century with consequences that were not to be fulfilled until after 1154 when Henry II from Anjou became duke of Normandy and king of England.

These were long-term developments, but the immediate effect of the change was to create a lethal threat to Duke William, whose danger was further enhanced by the fact that it was not only from outside Normandy that he was now menaced. During these same months, two of his uncles, William, count of Arques, and Mauger, archbishop of Rouen, who between them controlled much of eastern Normandy, revolted against their young nephew. William, therefore, once again faced destruction, for there is little doubt that if this coalition from Arques and Rouen, from Anjou and Paris had ever been brought in unison against him, he must have succumbed. In the event, he was able to capture the stronghold of Arques before Normandy, early in 1054, was invaded by a strong force collected from all over France by the French king. It entered Normandy in two sections, and the main contingent was heavily defeated in February 1054 at the battle of Mortemer. It was an important engagement, for at Mortemer the crisis of Duke William's Norman reign was met and passed, and never again was the integrity of his duchy to be threatened as it had been imperilled between 1046 and 1054. The French king's raid in 1057 which was repelled at Varaville was a minor affair, and the deaths of Geoffrey of Anjou and King Henry of France in 1060 did but give final assurance that the perils which had been faced during the previous fourteen years had at last been surmounted.

The severity of the long struggle which occupied all the youth and early manhood of William the Conqueror needs to be borne in mind in estimating his character and assessing his achievement. Indeed, one of the most difficult questions of Anglo-Norman history is here involved. In 1066 William was able to effect the conquest of a great kingdom. But it is by no means easy to explain how he was able to undertake such an enterprise, and still less easy to explain how he was able to bring it to a successful conclusion. In 1054, when he was at last freed from his worst perils, he was some twenty-six years of age; all his life, he had been involved in defensive war; and Mortemer is separated by only twelve years from Hastings. The contrast between the strength of Normandy in 1066 and its weakness at the beginning of William's reign is in fact so remarkable that it is only to be explained firstly by the personality of this young ruler, and secondly by reference to aristocratic and ecclesiastical developments within Normandy which William somehow succeeded in harnessing to his own policy and his own purpose.

It is unnecessary to emphasize the importance to William's achievement of those great Norman families whose names were to become household words in medieval England, and indeed in medieval Europe. This was perhaps the most remarkable secular aristocracy produced in Europe during the earlier Middle Ages, so that it is important to note that it was in 1066 only of comparatively recent establishment. Few, if any, of these families can be traced back before the first quarter of the eleventh century, and many of the greatest of them such as Tosny, Beaumont, Grandmesnil and Montgomery only then acquired their landed wealth, and the territorial names by which they later came to be distinguished. Their advance was, however, thereafter to be extremely rapid, and it presented special problems for Duke William. It is thus of fundamental importance to an explanation of William's later achievement that under his rule as duke the rise of this aristocracy should have been made to contribute not to the disunity of his duchy but to its strength.

For this was not inevitable. Feudal organization developed gradually in Normandy with the tumultuous rise of this new nobility: it was not imposed, as in England, by the administrative policy of a prince. All the more notable, therefore, was it that William managed to enlist the support of these families to his own cause during his hazardous reign as duke. His success in this must be attributed to his own personality. Already in 1051 during the campaign round Domfront we find closely associated with the duke a group of young men (*tirones*) which included William fitz Osbern (later earl of Hereford), William I of Warenne (later earl of Surrey) and Roger II of Montgomery (later earl of Shrewsbury). Again, during the defence of Normandy against the French king in 1054 the war was waged by families who were in each case operating near their own estates: Tosny, for instance, in central Normandy; Mortemer and Giffard in the east. The result was notable; and it was to affect all the future. After the defeat of William, count of Arques, in 1053, there was no major revolt among the Norman aristocracy, and in 1066 the vast majority of the Norman nobility were ready to stake all their newly won fortunes on the success of Duke William's adventure overseas.

Equally important to the development of Normandy under Duke William was an ecclesiastical revival. This, particularly in respect of the Norman monasteries, has attracted so much attention from historians that there is little need to comment upon it further. But it is important to note that this movement, also, was of comparatively late development. The first definite evidence that the Norman bishoprics were being reconstituted comes from a charter of 990, and of the ten principal religious houses that were in existence in Normandy at the time of William's accession only four had been re-established before 1000, and four more had been set up since his birth. The subsequent resuscitation of Norman monastic life was, however, to be astonishingly rapid, and after 1047, the new Norman aristocracy took over from the ducal house the work of patronage; so that by 1066 the Norman land was famed throughout western Europe for the extent and for the quality of its monastic life. Distinct from this, but by no means negligible, was the work of the Norman bishops between 1035 and 1066. Their achievements were in the main – though not exclusively – mundane. Hugh, bishop of Lisieux, and John, bishop of Avranches, were by any standards notable prelates, and the history of Normandy and England would have been very different apart from the careers of Odo, bishop of Bayeux, and Geoffrey, bishop of Coutances. The general result of this ecclesiastical revival was to prove little short of spectacular. An ecclesiastical province, of no abnormal size, which in 1066 could be represented by men of such contrasted distinction as Odo of Bayeux and Geoffrey of Coutances, Maurilius, archbishop of Rouen, John of Avranches, Hugh of Lisieux, Lanfranc, then abbot of St Stephen's, Caen, John, abbot of Fécamp, Herluin, abbot of Le Bec, and the young St Anselm, was in very truth not to be ignored.

The ecclesiastical and aristocratic developments in Normandy during Duke William's Norman reign were, throughout, most closely associated both with each other and with the policy of the duke. The new aristocracy had shared with the duke the sponsorship of the monastic revival, and, with the single exception of Maurilius, archbishop of Rouen, from 1054 to 1067, all the Norman bishops of this time were members either of the ducal house or of the greater Norman families. In this way the aristocratic, the ecclesiastical and the ducal advance in Normandy had become merged into a single political achievement which could perhaps be summarized by saying that in 1065 a man might go from end to end of Normandy without ever passing out of the jurisdiction, secular or ecclesiastical, of a small group of inter-related great families with the duke at their head.

For William had established himself at the centre of this progress. He had identified with his own, the aims of the new aristocracy. In like manner, his influence pervaded the reformed Norman church being expressed in all major appointments, and more particularly in the pro-vincial church councils. But perhaps this inter-related development was expressed most clearly in his ducal courts, which, attended by the secular and ecclesiastical magnates of Normandy, steadily increased in importance after 1054. It was in every way a notable *curia* which, sometime after 1060, confirmed at Bayeux the gifts made by Bishop Odo to his cathedral church, and equally notable was the court which, early in 1066, ratified at Fécamp grants made to the abbey of Coulombes. Most certainly, too, the assembly which met at Caen in July 1066, and which, as stated in the relevant charter, looked out on the comet which was even then illuminating the Norman skies, was a court of which any European ruler might have been proud. It symbolized the rapid and intense concentration of power which had been accomplished in this province of Gaul, and which was itself one of the most notable political phenomena of mid-eleventh-century Europe. From this, indeed, was to derive much of the strength which made possible the improbable success of William's invasion of England.

William's invasion of England was not only facilitated by the developing strength of the province he ruled. It was the outcome of a policy which was of long duration. The establishment of the English Danelaw, and of the Viking dynasty in Neustria, had forged links between England and Normandy from which neither could escape. The momentous marriage in 1002 of Ethelred II to the daughter of a Norman duke had given dynastic expression to this inter-dependence, and the deposition of Ethelred, and Emma's second marriage to Cnut, his supplanter, was of scarcely less importance to Normandy than to England. Nor was it merely the ruling families which were concerned. The political filiations of England with Scandinavia, and the changing position of Normandy within Gaul, were likewise reciprocally involved. Yet if William was here heir to a tradition, he none the less enlarged it. Even during his boyhood the issues that were involved were being given clearer definition. He may well, for instance, have watched the exiled sons of Ethelred II at his father's court. The athelings, Edward and Alfred, took refuge in Normandy very shortly after the establishment of Cnut in England, and their claims to England were kept alive in the duchy. It was during this period for instance that Edward's sister Goda was given in marriage to Dreux, count of the Vexin, who was the ally of the Norman duke; and William of Jumièges, who is usually to be relied upon, asserts that William's father actually planned an invasion of England on Edward's behalf and collected ships for that purpose. The story is unconfirmed, and, though not impossible, must be received with caution. But there can be no doubt that Edward's succession to the English throne in 1042 could be regarded as in some sense a victory for Norman policy. The murder of his brother Alfred in England in 1036 had caused an outburst of indignation in Normandy, and it was to be used at a later date as a cardinal point in Norman propaganda which made Godwine, earl of Wessex, responsible for the crime. Certainly, after Edward's accession, the Norman dynasty, under William, must have felt itself in some measure committed to the cause of the new king in England.

It will be recalled also how conscious Edward the Confessor was of this,

and how ready he was to turn to Norman support both in his dealings
with the great earls of Northumbria, Mercia and Wessex, and in the
hazardous defence of his kingdom against Scandinavian attack. But
certain qualifications should be made with regard to his acts in this respect.
His policy of introducing Normans into England was not wholly original,
for some Normans had followed Emma to England in 1002, and, though
these receded into the background after her marriage with Cnut, they
were precursors of the men who responded to her son's invitation.
Moreover, the new Norman aristocracy was, during these years, too fully
occupied in establishing itself at home to pay much attention to England.
Indeed, of the laymen who came from France to England in this period
few, except Earl Ralph the Timid from the Vexin (the son of Dreux and
Goda), were of the first rank, and no Norman layman at this time seems
to have been given possessions in England of any wide extent. In the
church, however, the situation was different. Norman clerks appear in the
royal household early in Edward's reign, and the introduction of Norman
prelates into England such as Ulf, bishop of Dorchester, William, bishop
of London, and more particularly Robert, abbot of Jumièges who became
archbishop of Canterbury in 1051, was a characteristic feature of the reign.
Nor is there much doubt that, as generally believed, Edward had by 1051
designated Duke William as his heir.

In these circumstances, the unsuccessful rebellion of Earl Godwine in
1051, his triumphant return in 1052 and the succession of Harold to the
earldom of Wessex in 1053, were obviously of direct concern to Normandy
since these earls of Wessex were irrevocably opposed to the Norman
succession in England. But between 1051 and 1054 Duke William could
make no intervention in English affairs, since, as has been seen, he was
during those years involved in one of the major crises of his own reign.
Nor was he able to oppose the plan formulated in England during the
next four years to substitute as the Confessor's heir, the Atheling Edward
(son of Edmund Ironside), who was then an exile in Hungary. After the
atheling's return from exile, and his very suspicious death in England in
1057, the Norman duke must surely have realized that his chief opponent
in England was likely to be Harold Godwineson who, from this time
forward, was evidently contemplating the succession for himself. All the
complex elements in Anglo-Norman relations thus began to be crystallized
into an individual rivalry between two of the most remarkable personalities of eleventh-century Europe.

But William must also have been aware that the impending struggle
would be a triangular contest. It was as well known to him as it is to us
that England had recently formed part of a great Scandinavian empire,
and that there were Scandinavian princes whose claims were pressing and
exigent. Indeed, the threat to Edward himself from this quarter had been

persistent. It is permissible to surmise that, in 1047, only the death of
Magnus of Norway had prevented an invasion of England which might
well have been successful, and in 1058 the son of Harald Hardrada, king
of Norway, attacked England with a large fleet collected from the Hebrides
and from Dublin. The attempt failed in its purpose, but it clearly foreshadowed the greater expedition which Harald Hardrada was himself to
launch in 1066. William's policy towards England was thus always bound
to take account of Scandinavia.

Before 1066 it had, moreover, been given further precision not only by
the developing strength of Normandy (which we have watched) but also
by the duke's changing position in the political structure of Gaul. In
1050 or shortly afterwards William made his famous marriage with
Matilda daughter of Baldwin V count of Flanders. The lady was, it seems,
of diminutive size, but she appears none the less to have been one of the
few persons who were not overawed by her formidable husband, and on
occasion she could act as regent for him. William on his part is stated to
have been notoriously devoted to her so that she may have had some
personal influence on his career. But it was the political implications of
this match which were from the first important. The marriage took place
despite papal prohibition (allegedly on grounds of consanguinity), and for
this reason William's relations with the papacy were to be strained for
nearly a decade, until in 1059 Pope Alexander II sanctioned the marriage,
and William and his wife in return undertook to build the two great
monasteries in Caen which today commemorate them so worthily in stone.
In 1050, however, the marriage was chiefly significant as indicating the
place which the young duke was beginning to win for himself among
the greater fedatories of north-western Europe, and in fact the Flemish
alliance was to persist until after the Norman conquest of England which
it helped to make possible.

It was not, however, until after 1060 that William's position in Gaul
began rapidly to be transformed and in such a manner as might vitally
affect his relations with England. In that year the deaths of King Henry I
and Count Geoffrey of Anjou freed him from his two most formidable
opponents in France, while Philip I, the new king of France who was then
a boy, was placed under the tutelage of the duke's Flemish father-in-law.
In 1063, the death of Count Walter of Maine, who was the Confessor's
nephew, removed a possible claimant to the English succession, and the
acquisition of Maine itself by the duke of Normandy further altered the
balance of political power in northern France to his advantage. The
famous visit which Harold earl of Wessex made to Normandy, as it seems
in 1064, whatever may have been its motives, was to prove of even greater
importance, since the resulting oath sworn by Harold to William was
understood throughout western Europe as pledging the earl to support

the claim of the duke to England, or at all events not to oppose it. Again, the successful Norman expedition against Brittany in the same year minimized the threat of resistance in the west, while the Northumbrian revolt of 1065 indicated what was to be the chief weakness of his principal adversary in England. When, therefore, on 5 January 1066 there occurred the death of the childless king of England, and on the very next day Earl Harold seized the English throne, William's policy towards England was brought to its test at a time peculiarly favourable to its fulfilment.

Political power, thus consistently developed, controlled and extended by a great duke, made it possible for the conquest of an ancient kingdom to be attempted. But it does not of itself suffice to explain *why* the venture was undertaken; nor does it account for its peculiar consequences. The crisis of 1066 is not to be viewed simply as a struggle between three princes contending for a throne; and though a lust for plunder (which was later to be abundantly sated) undoubtedly fired the Norman followers of William, this does not by itself account for the consequences to England of the Norman conquest. Again, if the Norman success in arms derived in large measure from the recent increase of Norman power under Duke William, this alone cannot explain the support which the duke received from outside Normandy, or for the ultimate results of the policy which he was to bring to fruition in England.

The character of the propaganda which William employed in 1066, and which was so materially to assist him thus also deserves examination in this respect. This propaganda, it will be recalled, was informed throughout by moral and ecclesiastical sentiments. The murder of Alfred Atheling in 1036 called (it was said) for divine vengeance on the son of his murderer. Stigand, a schismatic archbishop, occupied the throne of St Augustine. The solemn promise of a venerated king had been abrogated, and a solemn oath sworn upon relics demanded the punishment of Heaven on the perjured usurper. We are not here concerned, of course, with the falsity or truth of these assertions. What is notable is firstly the character of William's propaganda at this juncture, and secondly the extent to which it was accepted in western Europe. As is well known, the Norman case was successfully stated at Rome, and in the event William was to fight at Hastings under a papal banner and with consecrated relics round his neck.

The Norman expedition had in fact been made to appear in the nature of a holy war, and so it was to be widely regarded. This is usually considered as a triumph for William's diplomacy, and this in truth it was. But it was a claim that was particularly attuned to contemporary Norman sentiments, and was indeed probably inspired by them. For the latter half of the eleventh century was emphatically the time when the notion of a holy war was continuously and widely exploited in Norman interests.

Again and again the same theme was stressed. In 1059 the Normans Robert Guiscard and Richard of Capua, becoming vassals of the Holy See, had pledged themselves to its defence. In 1062 Pope Alexander II had given his blessing and a banner to Norman knights fighting in Sicily. In 1064 according to both French and Arab sources, the Normans were especially prominent in the 'crusade of Barbastro' in Spain. In 1066 the same Alexander II gave William his blessing and a banner for the expedition to England. Between 1060 and 1070 the Normans (though with very diverse motives) were achieving in Sicily what was in fact to prove the most important victory of Christians over Moslems in the eleventh century. In 1070 William was to be solemnly proclaimed by papal legates at Winchester, and in 1072 while William was advancing into Scotland, Roger son of Tancred captured Palermo from the Saracens.

These events were, moreover, closely connected, not only in time but also in spirit, for (as must be emphasized) they were conducted by men who were brothers and cousins of each other, and fully conscious of their relationship and their common purpose. William the Conqueror is said to have been wont to refresh his courage by contemplating the achievements of Robert Guiscard, and the name of Grandmesnil was as famous in Apulia as it was to become at Leicester. John, abbot of Fécamp, mediated between Pope Leo IX and Richard of Capua, while Geoffrey, bishop of Coutances, received from his relatives in Italy contributions towards the building of his cathedral at home. The Norman warriors of this age were avid of plunder and stained with brigandage, but they were none the less conscious of belonging to an integrated Norman world which was proud of its armed might, and also of its self-asserted Christian mission. Its exploits had before 1066 already stretched from Spain through Apulia to Constantinople, from Brittany to the Taurus, and they were soon to extend from Abernethy to Syracuse. Here was a vast zone of interconnected endeavour comparable even to that of the fabled Charlemagne in the *Song of Roland*. The sentiments it inspired coloured all Norman policy at this time. And, in a real sense, this far-flung extension of Norman power reached its climax in Sussex in October 1066.

William's expedition to England in the autumn of 1066, the campaign which followed and the battle which was its culmination are to be described elsewhere in this book, as will also be the social and political consequences to England of the Norman conquest. The purpose of the foregoing remarks has been simply to indicate the extent to which William's success in 1066 may be related to what he had earlier achieved in the development of Norman power and policy. And it will now be further suggested that the political developments which took place between 1066 and 1087 under his rule as king may likewise be related to what he had previously achieved as duke. The interconnected movements which under William, as duke, had created the strength of Normandy in 1066 we have discovered to be aristocratic, ecclesiastical and ducal. The chief directions in which Norman influence was exercised in England during the reign of William as king may fairly be described as aristocratic, ecclesiastical and royal.

The most striking social consequence of the Norman conquest was undoubtedly the aristocratic revolution which involved the tragic downfall of the Old-English nobility and its replacement by a new secular aristocracy imported from overseas. The magnitude of the change and the vast spoliation it involved are well documented, and they can be considered quite apart from the vexed question of the origins of feudal organization in England. Those members of the Old-English nobility which in 1066 escaped the slaughters of Fulford, Stamford Bridge and Hastings faced a bleak future as the defeated supporters of a lost cause, and they suffered further misfortunes in the early wars of William's English reign which ended any policy of compromise which the new king might have been disposed to adopt towards them. The result was catastrophic. The collapse of the Old-English nobility was almost complete by the end of William's reign. It has been estimated that in 1086 only about eight per cent of the land of England remained in the possession of this class. It had ceased to be an integral part of English society.

The substitution in its place of an aristocracy which was overwhelmingly Norman in origin has likewise been fully established. But the statement needs some qualification in that, even as the expedition had been widely supported in Europe, so also did many of the new holders of English lands come from outside Normandy. Flemings, for instance, were prominent among them, particularly perhaps in the north, and it was a man from Flanders, Gerbod, who, about 1070 became the first earl of Chester. More important still were the Bretons who had followed the Conqueror to England. The great honour of Richmond (Yorkshire) with its 400 dependent manors was given to a member of the comital house of Brittany, and it was a Breton, Ralph of Gael who, perhaps as early as 1067 was made earl of Norfolk. The significance of the non-Norman element in the aristocracy set up by William in England should therefore not be minimized, but this was none the less always subordinate, and political events were soon to diminish its importance. The hostility of Flanders to the Anglo-Norman kingdom which grew after 1067 immediately detracted from the Flemish influence on England, and Gerbod, earl of Chester, having fought in the battle of Cassel, disappeared from the English scene, and was replaced as earl by Hugh son of Richard, *vicomte* of Avranches. In like manner, the suppression of the rebellion of the earls in 1075 was said to have 'purged' England from Breton influence, and while Ralph of Gael thereafter ceased to be earl of Norfolk, so also did Brian of Brittany then make way in Cornwall for the Conqueror's half-brother Robert, count of Mortain.

The aristocracy imposed upon England by William the Conqueror was in fact to be overwhelmingly representative of just that aristocracy which had arisen in Normandy between 1040 and 1066. By 1086 nearly half the land of England had passed into the possession of this class, and about half of this (namely a quarter of the total) had been given to only eleven men, of whom all but two were Normans who had been identified with the young duke during his early career. And the same is true of the more important personages by whom they were surrounded: the representatives of the comital houses of Eu and Évreux; Roger Bigot from Calvados; Robert Malet from the neighbourhood of Évreux; Robert and Henry the sons of Roger of Beaumont on the Risle. It is an impressive list, but while of course it could be supplemented, it could not be very widely extended. The important secular tenants of English lands in 1086 probably numbered less than two hundred. And from among these the greater men and the greater families stand out to testify to the manner in which the territorial wealth of England had been acquired by the leading members of that aristocracy which had obtained power in Normandy under Duke William.

The cohesion which had earlier been achieved by this group in Normandy, and its association with William, were likewise to be reproduced in England. Indeed the Conqueror's success in retaining his conjoint realm between 1066 and 1087 was due in no small measure to the maintenance of that unity of purpose between William and his magnates which had been attained in Normandy before the Conquest. After 1066 as before, it remained as much to the interest of these men as to the Conqueror himself that dissensions among them should not be allowed to develop. The rebellion of 1075 received no general support from the Norman nobility, and in 1079 elder members of the same aristocracy took common action to recall to their allegiance cadet members of their own families who had supported the revolt of the king's son Robert against his father. It was a violent age dominated by the rivalries of highly competitive families. But a recognition of mutual obligations by the king and his magnates both in England and in Normandy assisted the Anglo-Norman kingdom to survive, and went far to determine its character.

In ecclesiastical affairs also a similar relationship can be discerned between William's reign in England and his previous rule of Normandy. The church in England between 1070 and 1087 under the control of William was to experience great changes, many of which tended to make it conform more closely to the pattern which had previously taken shape in the Province of Rouen. Whether these changes were good or bad is not

of course here in question: nor need it be debated whether the loss of a
fine vernacular culture which was involved was compensated by a closer
relation between England and those intellectual movements in western
Europe which were contributing to the renaissance of the twelfth century.
The connection between the ecclesiastical development of Normandy
and England during the Conqueror's lifetime is, however, apparent.
Between 1066 and 1087 the reformed monasteries of Normandy gave no
less than twenty-two abbots and five bishops to England; and even as
William as duke had controlled the Norman church so also did he now,
in cooperation with his great Archbishop Lanfranc, make himself responsible for the changes in England. All major appointments (most of
which were good) were in practice in his hands, and the bishoprics of
England were very generally in his time to assume the form they were to
retain until the Reformation. Most notable of all was the royal participation in the work of ecclesiastical councils which now began to be a
regular feature of church life in the kingdom as in the duchy. Thus,
William took part in the councils at Winchester in 1070, 1072 and 1076;
at Rouen in 1074; at Lillebonne in 1080, and at Gloucester in 1085. This
was evidently a ruler who in the words of Professor Knowles 'was
resolved of set purpose to raise the whole level of ecclesiastical discipline
in his dominions'.[1]

It was in fact the domination he sought to exercise over the church
which in part explains his ambivalent attitude towards the papacy. He had
come to England with papal support; he could claim with some justice
to be the sponsor of those reforms which with papal approval were
beginning to pervade the western church. But as in Normandy so also
now in England he would not abandon the rights over the church which
he held to be inherent in his office. The opposition was clear cut and
fundamental; it was to be productive of long-enduring controversies. But
its implications during William's lifetime should not be overstressed. In
one respect William's disputes with Gregory VII were concerned with the
means by which might be implemented a policy of ecclesiastical reform
which they shared in common. There was more cooperation than controversy between William and the papacy. Relations might be strained
almost to breaking point, but the pope with whom William contended
could none the less praise his zeal for religion.

In conformity with the earlier growth of Normandy under Duke
William the Norman impact upon England after 1066 was thus in the
first instance to be aristocratic and ecclesiastical. It was, however, to be
more specifically royal, in the sense that it was dependent upon the work
of a duke who had become a king. The coronation of William at Westminster on Christmas Day 1066 was not only the central event of his life:
it foreshadowed the character of his rule in England. By becoming a king,

William assumed all the semi-sacred prestige which the men of the time were disposed to give to the royal office, and this had deep Norman implications since it could be easily related to the religious sanctions which had been so widely claimed for Norman enterprise. At the same time a wider gulf was placed between him and even the greatest of his followers, and he was thereby to be assisted in his endeavour to hold together as a single political entity his dominions on both sides of the Channel. As a sanctified king he could moreover exercise over the church a closer control with a greater appearance of legitimacy. And his position among the secular rulers of western Europe was transformed.

This was, however, only part of the matter. William in 1066 became not only a king: he became more specifically king of the English (*Rex Anglorum*). He was hallowed by a rite substantially identical with that which had been employed in the coronation of English kings from at least the time of Edgar. As a result his Norman policy which we have watched was now brought into contact with a distinct complex of loyalties, some religious, some traditional, but all emotionally compelling. The policy itself thus at once began to be modified, and in the more practical sphere William was enabled to assume all the powers, and much of the prestige, which had formerly been vested in Old-English royalty. It was a mark of his astute appraisal of the situation that, from the start of his rule in England, he claimed to be the legitimate successor of Edward the Confessor. The reign of Harold II was treated as a usurpation – as an interregnum.

Such claims, exercised and developed at the hands of a man who was also a great constructive statesman, were in fact to entail remarkable and unexpected results. William was a conqueror; his advent into England was a cause of spoliation; in the English church and in the higher ranks of secular society it entailed revolutionary change. But, in many respects, William could also be considered as a conservative, and it was a mark of his political genius that he could adapt to his purpose the institutions of the land he had won by invasion. As *Rex Anglorum* he used the royal system of administration. His writs are substantially identical in form with those of Edward the Confessor, though they came soon to be couched in Latin rather than in the vernacular. He employed the sheriff as his chief executive officer in local government though the shrievalty became progressively Norman in composition. He gave fresh vitality to the courts of shire and hundred, and he utilized (with ruthless efficiency) the taxational system that he found in this country. Most of his earliest charters were concerned to insist that the customs which had prevailed in the Confessor's time should be respected, and this injunction was con-sistently to be repeated and very often enforced. In the great trials, which were so marked a feature of his reign, appeal was constantly made to Old-

English law, and it was partly for this reason that the great transference of landed property which the Conquest entailed was carried out without general anarchy. Even in the church, where the changes were very far-reaching, respect was paid to Old-English traditions, particularly with regard to the rights of the See of Canterbury. It was, in short, directly due to William himself – the duke who had become a king – and a king of the English – that the Norman conquest proved almost as important for what it preserved as for what it created.

It is assuredly no part of the purpose of this short essay to describe the constitutional and administrative history of England during the reign of William the Conqueror. But any estimate of William's character and career must take note of the fact that what he wrought in England was accomplished in the midst of incessant warfare. The formation of the Anglo-Norman kingdom which was the immediate result of William's victory altered the balance of political power in western Europe in such a manner as to provoke a continuous and relentless opposition that was bent on its destruction. Paris and Anjou, Scandinavia and Scotland were immediately and directly effected, and William's conjoint realm was in fact only to survive by means of an unremitting military effort which extended over two decades.

Looking back on that prolonged defence, which was so strongly to affect the English future, its chief feature may well seem to have been the inherent inter-dependence of all its parts. The suppression of risings in England was always connected with the persisting threat of attack from Scandinavia or Scotland from Anjou or Maine, and the protection of the northern frontier beyond Yorkshire could never be dissociated from the active hostility which was manifested in France or Flanders or beyond the North Sea. It was, moreover, characteristic of this situation that after 1070 the attack directed against the Anglo-Norman realm should have been ever more closely coordinated by the astute diplomacy of Philip I of France whose object throughout was to disrupt the political union of Normandy and England – which was in fact to be achieved for seventeen years after William's death. The preservation of his rule in England, and the maintenance of the unity of the Anglo-Norman kingdom, must always have seemed to William to involve a single problem; and the related campaigns of the king and his lieutenants had a common purpose, whether they were waged in Northumbria or Maine, or whether they were directed against Sweyn Estrithson of Denmark or Fulk le Rechin of Anjou, King Malcolm of Scotland or King Philip of France.

The point perhaps deserves more emphasis than it always receives, and it could be plentifully illustrated. The claims of Edgar Atheling to the English throne were for instance to be sponsored successively by King

Malcolm and King Philip. The rising of the north in 1069–70 was supported by a fleet from Scandinavia which was to operate off the coast of England for four years. The revolt of Maine began almost simultaneously with the Yorkshire rebellion, and culminated in 1072 with the establishment of Fulk le Rechin at Le Mans. Again, in 1075, the rebellion of the earls in England was led by a Breton earl of Norfolk, and though it was suppressed in England, the war that it initiated was continued in Brittany, and ended with William's defeat at Dol – a reverse which was to rob him of the initiative in France for a decade. Once again, the news of William's repulse before the walls of Gerberoi in 1079 by King Philip and William's son, Robert, had no sooner spread to Scotland than King Malcolm of Scotland raided Northumbria and started the rising which led to the murder of Bishop Walchere and the temporary collapse of Norman authority in the north.

The same pattern of politics was in fact to persist until the end of the reign. It was entirely characteristic of the earlier defence of the Anglo-Norman realm that during the last twenty months of his life, William should have faced not only the threat of a combined attack from Scandinavia and Flanders – from Cnut IV of Denmark and Count Robert of Flanders – but that he should also have been constrained to conduct his final campaign on the south-eastern frontier of Normandy against the king of France. During these months, and in connection with this crisis, he initiated the Domesday Survey, and convoked the Salisbury Moot. But he met his lethal injury at Mantes in the Vexin, and early in the morning of 9 September 1087 he died within sound of the church bells of Rouen.

At the close of this astonishing career it is tempting to contemplate the character of the extraordinary man who made it. To do so is not, however, easy, since such diverse judgements have been passed upon William, and he had no intimate biographer who could examine his motives, or probe his private thoughts. He must be judged by his acts, but his acts are sufficiently illuminating. They leave no doubt of his greatness, but they reveal also a man who was harsh and unlovable – perhaps even personally repellent. Most of his life was spent in war, and war brought out what was brutal in this burly warrior whose physical strength (until diminished by corpulence) was exceptional, and who may have looked something like Henry VIII of England. His savagery in war is well attested. The horrors of Alençon in 1052 were matched by those which he inflicted on Mantes in 1087, and his devastation of the Home Counties in 1066 was a fit prelude to his harrying of the north in 1070. Yet it may be questioned whether William, as a warrior, was more brutal than most of his contemporaries, or that he had a blunter sense of ethics or humanity than many of his successors in war down to the twentieth century. And if many of his acts in this respect cannot be excused, they can at least be explained. The sack of Alençon made certain the bloodless surrender of Domfront; the isolation of London in 1066 was based upon considered strategy; and there were many occasions when William went out of his way (as in Normandy in 1066, and at Exeter in 1068) to prevent plundering by his troops. The horrible devastation of northern England in 1070 is in truth impossible to palliate, but it took place at a crisis when the Anglo-Norman kingdom was threatened from Northumbria and Scotland, from Norway and from Maine. As to the New Forest it might perhaps be remarked that William was not the first – nor the last – king in England to lay waste a countryside for his sport.

As a warrior, William was (perhaps inevitably) stained with blood. As a ruler, his avarice was notorious, and his taxation savage. He needed money for his government, and particularly for the numerous mercenaries he employed. The ruthlessness with which he extracted money from England must be set against the good administration he provided. Here, too, however, a balanced judgement is necessary. If William was 'stern beyond measure', there were many who benefited thereby. It was not for nothing that a panic spread among lesser folk when they heard of his death, for they were aware of the disorders which were likely to follow his passing, and it was an Englishman who knew him, who, at the last, after lamenting his harshness, paid tribute to the good order he maintained. Ruthless in war, he was not a bloodthirsty brute. Strong in rule, he was not a tyrant. Contemporaries found him a man to fear, but also a man to respect.

The basis of his achievement was his genius for leadership. Reference is often made to the good fortune which he sometimes enjoyed, as in the deaths of his two chief rivals in France in 1060, and in certain of the circumstances of 1066. But no reference to luck can possibly be adequate to explain a career of this character, or an achievement of this magnitude. There must have been a wonderful strength of personality in this man who could rise from his bastard beginnings to such power, and who could elicit from the hard-faced men who surrounded him, both in Normandy and England, such a constant measure of support. He was harsh and rapacious, personally pious, courageous in adversity, and indomitably tenacious of purpose. He could suit his policy to opportunity; but his will was inflexible, and his energy was untiring. Thus between 1051 and 1054, when in his middle twenties, he captured Alençon and Domfront, reduced the stronghold of Arques, repelled a great invasion by the French king, held an important ecclesiastical council and deposed an archbishop of Rouen. Again, at a later stage of his career, only a matter of months elapsed between his invasion of Scotland late in 1072 and his campaign in Maine in the next year. He was ever on the move, and if both his vices and his virtues were exceptional, so also were the conditions in which his life was spent. His vigorous leadership pervaded his whole career, and not least the last two years of his life when so much was accomplished. This quality alone made possible not only his survival as duke, but also the existence and preservation of the Anglo-Norman kingdom which he established. As Professor Southern has justly remarked, 'he had an unrivalled mastery of the problems of the secular world – that is to say of other men's wills – in both fighting and ruling unapproached in creative power by any other medieval ruler after Charlemagne'.[2]

It would, in truth, be difficult to deny to William the Conqueror a place among the greatest monarchs of the Middle Ages. He stands four-square, a dominant figure against the background of his own fascinating and tumultuous age. As a warrior he was widely renowned, and probably justly, for if his later campaigns in France were undistinguished, his earlier siege operations in Maine were notable, and in the great enterprise of 1066 his patience, his organization and his generalship were surely of the highest order. But it is above all for his constructive statesmanship that he commands attention; and here his achievement must appear all the more remarkable when it is recalled that his ceaseless preoccupation with the problems of government was coupled with ceaseless campaigning. The results of his rule had enduring consequences which stretched even beyond the confines of his own wide dominions. He adapted his policy to a crisis which, in his time, affected Scandinavia and Italy, France and England; and the development of western Europe in the Middle Ages was substantially affected by what he accomplished. In Normandy he brought a distracted province to a new peak of strength. To England he gave a new aristocracy and a reconstituted church. At the same time, he was concerned to respect the traditions of the country he conquered, and he revitalized many of its ancient institutions. He made his own contribution to the highly individual character of medieval England, and Anglo-Norman history in the eleventh century cannot be appraised without reference to his characteristic acts.

NOTES

1 David Knowles, *Monastic Order in England* (1940), p. 93.
2 R. W. Southern, *Saint Anselm and his Biographer* (1963), p. 4.

XIII

The Hundred Years War

―――――✦❦✦―――――

The Hundred Years War provides some of the best-known episodes in the English national story but, as a unity, it probably looms less largely than it should in our national consciousness. Sluys and Crecy, Poitiers and Agincourt are as battles familiar names; the treaties of Brétigny and Troyes are famous; but the political background of diplomacy and war against which they must be considered remains for most of us somewhat nebulous. The elaborate and successful investigation of English history in the later Middle Ages with which the names of Stubbs and Tout are particularly associated have in the main been concerned with constitutional development and with ecclesiastical controversy. Less progress, however, has perhaps been made in the elucidation of the diplomatic history of the period, and of the difficult problems relating to Anglo-French relations in this age. It would not be difficult to defend the opinion that the best general history of the reign of Edward III is that which Joshua Barnes produced in 1688. The Hundred Years War as a whole still awaits its English historian. And the notable work devoted to this theme by Professor Perroy of the Sorbonne which was translated into English in 1951 thus went some way towards filling a gap in English historical literature.

For it is impossible to dissociate the social and constitutional growth of England during this age from the military history of the period. The development of Parliament at this time was by no means unconnected with the demands made upon the royal revenue by the needs of the war in France. The machinery of the royal administration was likewise affected. The preliminaries to the Hundred Years War thus saw established in England an office of diplomacy directed by an official styled the 'Keeper of the Processes' who has been described as 'a sort of under-secretary of state for foreign affairs'; and a major factor in the English successes has been held to be 'an administrative system singularly elastic and capable of expansion and adaptation to war needs'. Again, the anti-papal legislation of fourteenth-century England was stimulated by the conflict, being fostered by the belief, perhaps unjustified, that the popes at St Avignon were less anxious to promote peace than to further French interests. It has been alleged that Henry V's revival of the struggle was not unconnected with a desire to use the enthusiasm generated by a foreign war to allay discontent at home, and more certainly during the period of the Wars of the Roses the position of the Lancastrian dynasty in England was weakened by the defeats of the English armies in France.

If, however, the Hundred Years War forms an essential part of the history of England, it cannot be considered merely from an English standpoint. For four generations Englishmen and Frenchmen conducted their domestic affairs against the background of a continual struggle in which they all found themselves directly or indirectly involved. It is true that there were pauses in the war, and in particular there was the long truce between 1380 and 1415. But the campaigns of Edward III, Lancastrian attacks under Henry V, and the French recovery form part of a single story which stretches from 1328 to after 1445. Here, moreover, may be found reason for further reflection. Any comparison between the fifteenth and the twentieth centuries would be hazardous, but few will be found to dispute the claim that when a great nation such as France reaches the brink of the abyss, as was the case at that time and in our own, certain ways of behaviour in misfortune, certain reactions against fate, throw mutual light upon each other. In no exact sense does history repeat itself. But the flux in human affairs is constant, and as the spiral unfolds, so are similar problems posed to different men with different capacities and desires. 'The great and exemplary wheels of heaven' revolve, and we who watch them are brought to contemplate afresh the marriage between Time and the Hour.

More superficially, there might be sought other comparisons between the military history of that remote age and our own. The Normandy beachhead which allied troops in the twentieth century made familiar to the world, played an important part in the Hundred Years War. In 1346 Edward III landed at Barfleur in the neighbourhood of the American landings in 1944, and in the subsequent campaign he took in succession Saint-Lô and Laen before proceeding westward through Crecy to Calais. Again, in 1471, Henry V (like General Eisenhower) decided that the mastery of Lower Normandy was the best preparation for the conquest of the Seine valley, and the Treaty of Troyes of 1420 has been compared with the abortive Act of Union proposed by the British Government on 16 June 1940. Such comparisons are, however, more facile than illuminating. The circumstances of the invasions were widely different, and the Treaty of Troyes foreshadowed a union which was much less close than that suggested in 1940.

Nevertheless, if the circumstances of the Hundred Years War must be placed in their medieval setting, it remains true that the history of that war is a primary interest in the history of two peoples whose destinies became inextricably intertwined. The fact that a duke of Normandy in the eleventh century made himself king of England, and the fact that the descendants of that duke won for themselves a large empire in France, produced conditions which were exactly calculated to promote an uneasy alternation between projects of union and periods of acute conflict. The destruction of the Angevin Empire as an effective political unit in the thirteenth century, and the later centralization of administration effected respectively by Edward I and Philip IV, might seem to have weakened the connection between the two countries, but sentiments derived from the earlier age none the less persisted even into the fifteenth century. It was not merely arid legislation, it was not simply astute propaganda which inspired Henry V to claim as his own inheritance Normandy, Maine, Anjou and Touraine, or to assert that his ancestors had been unjustly deprived of these provinces by Philip Augustus. To modern students conscious that the early Renaissance was even then beginning to brighten in Italy, and that the age of nationalism was about to dawn, such sentiments may well seem anachronistic. But to Henry V and to many of his advisers, they were a reality. Normandy was always 'his own' Duchy, and Rouen 'his own' city. Passion is ever a stronger element in politics than the cool assessment of contemporary circumstance, and one of the prime causes of the Hundred Years War must be sought in traditions from a past which was already remote at the time of Agincourt. Before ever Edward III resolved on his French enterprise, before Philip VI, the first Valois, succeeded to his uneasy inheritance, France and England had been brought into an intimate historical relationship from which neither could escape. Of this relationship – close, embarrassing, and enduring – the Hundred Years War was at once a symbol and a solvent.

This was a feudal world, and in its complicated meshes both countries were involved. It is easy – and it is just – to discover the immediate causes of the Hundred Years War in the impossible situation created by the position of an English king who was also duke of Gascony. An independent prince, he was also a French vassal subject in France to a monarchy whose interests were frequently directly opposed to his own. Here indeed was a reason for war much more important than Edward III's much advertised claim to the French throne. The dynastic arguments advanced in connection with this claim may indeed be regarded primarily as a move in propaganda calculated to appeal to possible allies. It takes its place, however, in that tradition of Angevin aspirations which was a legacy from the past, and it was partly for that reason that it was developed by Henry V. More significantly was it designed to appeal to feudal sentiment.

It gave a spurious excuse of legality to any vassals of the king of France who desired to revolt. Such men could thus, while pursuing a self-regarding policy, argue that they were but transferring their allegiance to another and a more legitimate overlord.

These feudal obligations were of the first importance at the beginning of the Hundred Years War, and they influenced much of its course. Even as the papacy could still assert, albeit with waning success, political obligations which overrode the boundaries of modern national states, so also were these divisions blurred by the interests of feudal families with estates on both sides of the Channel. Only very gradually, and never completely, did the Hundred Years War come to be, in the modern sense, a war between 'France' and 'England'. In the first phase of the war, Edward III received support from Robert of Artois, brother-in-law to Philip VI, and sixty years later the whole character of the conflict was modified by the strife in France between the Burgundian and Armagnac factions. The assassination in 1407 of Louis of Orleans by Burgundian partisans, and the consequent enmity between John the Fearless duke of Burgundy and Bertrand count of Armagnac were symptoms of a deep-seated political malaise. The more notorious murder in 1419 of John the Fearless on the bridge of Montereau by Armagnac nobles under the eyes of the future Charles VII opened the way to much more serious consequences. Such events made possible for a time a real alliance between the English and the Burgundians so that the conflict was for long (within France) of the nature of a Civil War. Henry V might conquer 'his own' duchy of Normandy, and reorganize its administration, but it was the Burgundians who in 1418 seized Paris, and when in 1422 the infant son of the victor of Agincourt was recognized and crowned as king of France, he was acknowledged as their natural lord by the citizens and by the University of the French capital.

It is difficult therefore to explain the development of the Hundred Years War by close reference to more modern notions of politics. None the less it might be possible to discern here an early manifestation of these permanent problems relating to the opposed ideals of political order and political liberty. In the first quarter of the fifteenth century there were two regimes in France: in the north a France occupied by a foreign prince whose power rested to a large extent upon the support of a French party; towards the south, a France weaker in strength but perhaps stronger in integrity, under the jurisdiction of the dauphin reigning at Bourges. Here was certainly an opportunity for statesmanship, for the cleavage stretched further than political divisions. The war had disorganized French society; suffering had spread; and contemporaries had watched what a modern historian has described as 'the desolation of the Church'. Simple folk yearned after security. But who could supply it? It is hardly surprising

that Henry V saw the possibilities latent in the situation. Not the least
potent factor in his success was his offer of a new order which might re-
establish justice, restore the administration, and put an end to civil disturbance. It was good propaganda, and effective against a young dauphin
weak in himself and surrounded by venal counsellors.

Today it is fashionable to explain the causes of all wars by reference to
economic rather than political factors, and the Hundred Years War is
certainly to be considered with regard to this general question. The
relations between Edward III and the Flemish towns at the outbreak of
hostilities were undoubtedly influenced by the ramifications of the English
wool trade. Flanders at the beginning of the Hundred Years War was a
French fief; its aristocracy was French in sympathy; but the burgesses in
the important towns were dependent for their prosperity on wool from the
backs of English sheep. It was natural therefore that strong support for the
claims of Edward III should come from Flemish burgesses who were
threatened by an interruption of a commerce which was essential to their
well-being. And it is similarly significant that the first battles in the war
should have been fought in Flanders. Similarly, when in 1411 John the
Fearless duke of Burgundy sought English help against the Armagnacs he
offered to hand over four Flemish towns to English control, and posed as
being able to ensure the safety of Calais where were the headquarters of the
English wool staple. Later, after John's murder at Montereau, his young
successor Philip received the support of the burgesses of Flanders in his
efforts to sustain and develop the same alliance. The Hundred Years War
would have considerable effects on the English wool trade, and the English
war effort was financed to a large extent by English wool merchants.
Furthermore, the desperate expedients to which both Edward III and
Philip VI were reduced to obtain money for war purposes compelled
them and their successors to pay some attention, however unwillingly to
the rival commercial interests of their respective countries.

Nevertheless it would be easy to emphasize unduly the influence of the
commercial classes in England and France on either the outbreak or the
continuance of the war. The hostilities certainly did more harm than
good to the English wool trade, and Edward III's alliance with the
Flemish towns had little appreciable effect on the course of the conflict.
Again, in the early years of the fifteenth century the English crown was
for a time as ready to enter into an alliance with the Armagnacs as with the
Burgundians, and when, after the advent of Henry V as king, the English
fortunes in France became linked with those of the Burgundians, this was
due more to political than to economic causes. Commercial rivalry
undoubtedly played its part in stimulating a conflict of interests, just as the
destructive effects of the war fostered social unrest both in France and
England. But outbreaks such as the Peasant Revolt in England, the

Jacqueries in France, the Harelle at Rouen, and the Cabochian uprising in
Paris might well have occurred even if there had never been a struggle
between the French and the English monarchies. An exclusively economic
interpretation of human history – and of human conflict – will in short
find little support from the study of the Hundred Years War.

Indeed, if attention were to be concentrated on economic considerations,
it might be difficult to provide an adequate explanation of the English
successes in the war. At the outbreak of hostilities, the resources of the
two countries seemed so disproportionate. It may be recalled that when the
war started the population of France was approximately three times that of
England. Her countryside supported a peasantry comparable in numbers
to that of the present day, and while the towns were not of course of the
same relative importance then as now they were quickly increasing in size
and prosperity. Paris during this period was rapidly expanding. Moreover,
the profound changes in international commerce which were characteristic of the thirteenth century had not as yet appreciably affected the
prosperity of France, and the prestige of the French was without rival
in Europe. The Empire was divided. The papacy was in the throes of
schism. France was the acknowledged leader in western Christendom.
Yet it was on this country, thriving and respected, that there fell the
initial disasters of the war. Even so, such was the French strength that it
only needed the single reign of Charles V for France to make a rapid
recovery, and by 1380 France could once again be considered the predominant power in the West. Against such an adversary, England might
well seem to be unevenly matched. She was relatively poor, and relatively
underpopulated, and at the time when hostilities began she had but recently
emerged from a period of civil strife. But it was England and not France
that, until after the time of Henry V, dominated the war in Europe.

An explanation of this apparent paradox may probably be sought not in
the economic but in the more strictly military sphere. France during the
early decades of the struggle refused to adapt herself to new developments
in the art of war. Her feudal army, although strong and respected, had
few ideas of tactics save the unsupported cavalry charge. The English, on
the other hand, during the recent Scottish war had learnt at Stirling
Bridge and Falkirk that in favourable circumstances infantry could be
more than a match for the mounted knight. Their leaders had moreover
comprehended the only conditions upon which such success might be
obtained. The footmen must be equipped with a long-range weapon,
trained in its use, and themselves confident of its power. At Crecy the
decision was obtained because the expert bowmen in the English force
were able to stand on the defensive against a cavalry charge in the sure
knowledge that if they kept their line, and controlled the rapid delivery of
their arrows, the cavalry charge would be broken up before ever it got

home. At Poitiers the French had so far learnt this lesson that they fought on foot, but even so the device proved ineffective against the long-range weapon of the archers. At Agincourt once again the English victory was due to the disciplined action of a new type of specially trained foot soldier ignorant alike of feudal traditions and feudal courtesies.

Here, and not in any comparison of the fighting capacity of individuals, is to be found the explanation of the English victories in the Hundred Years War. Too much emphasis has been given to the fact that the defeated French armies in the great battles were more numerous than those of the victors. An army fighting on its own territory against an expeditionary force will always have a large following of untrained and relatively ineffective supporters. It was the earlier recognition of the importance of a long-range weapon in the hands of disciplined foot soldiers which gave the English their first successes. As soon as it was realized that a cavalry charge by itself could do little against such tactics, the advantage of the English in France began to dwindle.

Charles V taught his commanders – and particularly Du Guesclin – to avoid large set battles and to suffer pillage rather than to court defeat, and the futility of the later expeditions of Edward III in France testified to the success of this policy. Agincourt illustrated the disastrous result of a reversal to the outworn tactical method, and the wisdom of Charles V was later to be demonstrated afresh. In truth, while the English could afford large-scale raiding expeditions, they could not afford the men or the money to hold down a hostile countryside. Henry V was only successful in this because he could rely on the support of a large French party, and confine his own attention primarily to the difficult task of occupying Normandy. When, after 1435, the Burgundian faction had left the English alliance, the task of the English in France became impossible. The end was then in sight, and was hastened by the decline of the long-bow as the dominant long-range weapon. Before the close of the war, the tactical advantage had passed to the French. Formingny, though on a smaller scale, may in this sense be regarded as Crecy, in reverse. There, too, a small disciplined force of infantry relying on the controlled fire of primitive artillery succeeded in overcoming a much larger army. The supreme tactical factor in the Hundred Years War was thus from a new angle demonstrated afresh.

The chief weakness of the French kingdom throughout the war lay in its recurrent disunion. The strength of its opponent was to be found in a centralized system of administrative control. During the fourteenth century feudal conditions in France were giving place to a social order in which the magnates of the land, having acquired quasi-independent princedoms, were seeking to control the royal administration in their own interests. In particular, the power of various members of the royal house – close relatives of the reigning kings – was a perpetual source of disturbance which reached its climax in the Burgundian–Armagnac feud. The careers of Louis count of Anjou, of Louis duke of Orleans, of John duke of Berry and of the Burgundian dukes are sufficient to illustrate the disastrous effects of such divisions. The administrative machine was in its turn dislocated, and for long periods the monarchy found itself served by a crowd of competing officials whose chief concern was not to give effect to the policy of the king but rather to aid the patrons to whom they looked for promotion. Between 1328 and 1422 only one French king, namely Charles V, was able to control the situation. His 'marmosets' may have been venal, and they certainly were unpopular, but they fostered the interests of the monarchy and strengthened its policy. Generally speaking, however, the French monarchy throughout this period suffered from an inherent weakness caused by competing interests within the royal administration.

Such conditions were not of course peculiar to France. A constant feature of English history during this age was likewise a struggle within the royal administration between the professional servants of the king and the great magnates of the land, who as the king's 'natural counsellors' sought to obtain control over the household administration. That struggle in fact goes far to explain the disturbances at the end of the reign of Edward III, and the failure of Richard II to build up the royal power afresh on more autocratic foundations. None the less, the 'over-mighty subject' was, as a rule, kept in check in England until the end of the reign of Henry V, or at least he was made to cooperate to a reasonable extent with the king. Not until the time of Henry VI did the rivalry of aristocratic factions reproduce in England some of the considerations associated with the struggle between the Burgundians and the Armagnacs in France. Then indeed did the English war effort become weakened at the same time as defeats abroad lowered the prestige of the monarchy at home. Before the last phase of the Hundred Years War, however, the administrative machine established by Henry II and developed by Edward I served the English monarchy reasonably well. Despite the development of a 'bastard feudalism' which contributed to 'lack of Governance', there remained in England during the whole of the fourteenth century a far more intimate relationship between Westminster and the shires than was to be found between the French royal administration and the French provinces. There was also a closer connection between the English baronage and the royal court. And down to the end of the first quarter of the fifteenth century there persisted in England an enduring consciousness of 'the community of the realm'.

In part this was due to previous history; to the absence in England of anything corresponding to the greater French fiefs; and to the previous absence in England of such political divisions as had been created for instance by the Angevin empire in France. But in part also was it due to the fact that between 1328 and 1422 France was far less fortunate than England in her kings. On both personal and public grounds it is possible to criticize Edward III and Richard II, Henry IV and Henry V. But taken together, and viewed in respect of their contrasted characteristics, they represent a succession of more than average ability. Very different was the case in France. Philip VI was, it is true, faced by exceptional difficulties, but he showed himself irresolute and reckless, neither exciting respect nor deserving it. John the Good was imbued with the sentiments of chivalric honour, but having obtained royalty he showed himself unworthy of it, and temperamentally he was a natural defeatist. Charles VI, with a taint in his blood, was still immature at the age of twenty-four; and though he never grew up it was his tragedy to grow old. After his lapse into imbecility in 1392, the great French monarchy remained for thirty years in gilded disgrace under the charge of a madman. Even Charles VII, under whom delivery was to come, was personally unimpressive. Lethargic, ill-natured and morose, he displayed few qualities of leadership, and the successes of his later years were due more to others than to himself.

From this melancholy sequence one man alone stands out. Charles V has perhaps been over-praised by some of his admirers, but if he was not great, he was certainly not negligible. An intellectual rather than a warrior, he was introspective, given to petty device, something of a quibbler and not guiltless of bad faith. But he did possess both a sense of royal dignity and a consciousness of the duties it implied. In his self-questioning and legal subtleties he may seem sometimes to have doubted his present if not his future, but his sense of duty and his resourceful tenacity served his country well, and he was the right king for a debilitated and dismembered France. Yet even Charles V cannot by himself reverse the adverse judgement which must be passed upon the kings of the House of Valois during this age. It is significant that while on the English side the popular hero of the Hundred Years War remains a Lancastrian king, the acclaim of France is still and properly given not to a monarch but to a girl from Lorraine.

Students of the Hundred Years War may indeed be tempted to consider the validity of those current interpretations of history which are based upon purely mechanistic principles. If economic factors will not by themselves explain the causes of this conflict, it remains equally difficult to discount the influence of individual character upon its course. Subsequent legend and popular sentiment have of course tended to enhance unduly the importance of certain figures in the war. It is probable for instance that too much has been made to depend on the personality of Du Guesclin, whose successes depended as much upon the sagacity of his master as on his own obstinate valour. Nor is it surprising that their fortuitous association with the Maid has irradiated beyond historic reality the exploits of such as Dunois and la Hire. Many of the minor personalities of the war, and indeed such spectacular mediocrities as John of Bohemia, may now certainly be allowed to pass into oblivion by the student of historical causation. None the less, the personal factor remains of importance. The prestige of Edward III in the middle of his reign was an asset to his cause, and Charles V made his individual contribution to the recovery of France after the Treaty of Brétigny. With the fifteenth century, moreover, personal influences can be more clearly discerned. When all allowances have been made for the exaggerations of contemporaries and the panegyrics of posterity, it would be hard to deny that the story of the Hundred Years War would have been very different apart from the personal qualities and the individual characters of Henry V and Joan of Arc.

Henry V is known to most Englishmen through the medium of Shakespeare's dramatic pageant. It is therefore encouraging to learn that while many reservations must be made, the Henry of Shakespeare is a true figure of history. Here of course is a portrait illuminated by Elizabethan sentiment in respect particularly of the relations between the Crown and the Church, and of the national aspirations of sixteenth-century England. At the same time, dramatic necessities led to over-emphasis. But if some of the glowing tints need to be toned down, the final summary leaves essentially unimpaired the notion of a dominant king strong in the enthusiasms he evoked, and fortified by the support of the people over whom he ruled. Slight of build, diseased, unlovable, Henry V was in fact at once calculating and courageous, superstitious and sincere. He was revoltingly cruel. He adhered unflinchingly to his purposes through the manifold chicaneries which he did not scruple to employ. A politician of outstanding ability, a military commander of considerable capacity, Henry V had above all the qualities of a great leader in that he could present to those he led a picture of himself very different from the private reality it masked.

> The king's a bawcock, and a heart of gold,
> A lad of life, an imp of fame;
> Of parents good, of fist most valiant:
> I kiss his dirty shoe, and from heart-string
> I love the lovely bully.

The real man was very different from the popular conception of him, but Henry V knew how to exploit this crude appeal. He had a personal magnetism, and displayed a wide humanity even if he did not feel it. The magnificent and familiar speeches which Shakespeare puts into his mouth – the harangue at Harfleur, the exhortation before Agincourt – are authentic in spirit if fictitious in fact. They reflect and in part explain the conscious influence exercised by this king over his English contemporaries in order to persuade them of the justice of his cause, and to exercise their devoted service in order to make it prevail. Only thus was he enabled to persuade any of his subjects 'to sell the pasture to provide the horse', and to impart confidence to tired troops by 'a little touch of Harry in the night'.

The infectious authenticity latent in Shakespeare's portrait of Henry V makes it the more necessary to recall that this was a medieval and not a Tudor sovereign. Henry V was far less a prophet of modern nationalism than the embodiment of an older theory of monarchy which exalted the position of the king at the same time as it emphasized the special obligations attaching to the royal office: duties involving the maintenance of secular order; duties relating also to the protection of the Church. Even as he clung to the Angevin claims over his French dominions, so also was he inspired by the older notion of kingship which would have been understood by St Louis.

> Upon the King! let us our lives, our souls,
> Our debts, our careful wives, our children and
> Our sins lay on the King; – we must bear all.
> O hard condition! twin–born with greatness,
> Subjected to the breath of every fool
> Whose sense no more can feel but his own wringing!
> What infinite heart's ease must kings neglect
> That private men enjoy.

The picture is of course unduly heightened, but many of the king's known utterances would in part support it. For this was the man who, in the fifteenth century, harboured as his greatest desire the wish to lead a united Europe in a crusade to Palestine, and who, morbidly conscious both of his duties and his sins, despairing held up as an ideal to himself and his subjects to be 'the mirror of Christian kings'. Probably he was fortunate not to survive his successes: he was only thirty-five when he died.

To pass from Henry V to Joan of Arc – from the English hero of the Hundred Years War to the French heroine – involves an abrupt transition. But here too it is necessary to distinguish sharply between the contemporary influence and the posthumous fame of a dominant figure. The character of the Maid, and the full reports that have survived of both her trials, have produced a literature which is astonishing both in its diversity and in its bulk. It is indeed a difficult task to pass judgement upon it. Perhaps it would be safe to suggest that it was only Joan's immediate circle that at first felt the full force of her personality, and that elswhere in France during her lifetime her fame spread only fitfully and slowly. Many of those who in fact were most in her debt seem at the time to have been scarcely aware of her wonderful venture. And her final sacrifice was certainly received with deplorable indifference both by the king she exalted and by many of his subjects. Even the rehabilitation of 1456 takes on the character of a political manœuvre designed to buttress the title of Charles VII, and it may be doubted whether if she had not suffered martyrdom, and if that martyrdom had not been copiously recorded, much would have been known about her, or about her personal contribution to the history of the Hundred Years War.

None the less, when all such considerations have been weighed, the essential and traditional reputation of Joan remains unscathed. In her case, as in the case of every martyr, it is impossible to separate the story of her life from the passion of her death; and her posthumous influence was an integral part of her achievement. It is given to few thus to fire the imaginations of men, and if the French recovery she heralded did not for a time assume the surging sweep of a storm, nevertheless her sacrifice fore-shadowed decisive victory. Many who owed so much to her were in-different to her fate, but some among her enemies seem already to have been conscious of what she brought about. The venemous calumnies circulated by Burgundian chroniclers to sully Joan's memory show that in government circles the Maid's early success created such dismay that (as they thought) only the stake at Rouen could efface its memory. And if the contemporary public was, as if inevitably, scarcely affected by something that did not immediately concern its own comfort, the memory proved ineffacable. Joan left her acts behind her. For the first time the Lancastrian arms had been halted on their road to victory, and the French king had been given the prestige of a unique coronation. Joan of Arc's intervention in the War was in fact decisive. 'And the page she wrote contrary to all expectations in the history of France deserves to be remembered as one of her finest.'

She escapes classification. She remains unique. It is a fact of history, and not an unimportant one, that the flames surrounding her scaffold at Rouen have shone through five centuries in the European memory. And for that reason alone it would be true to say that the war in which she was engaged would have been very different both in course and in its results had she never lived and died. Today, for both French and English, the most enduring figure in the Hundred Years War is Joan the Maid.

The posthumous fame of both Henry V and St Joan may prompt the question how far the Hundred Years War can be considered as a national conflict. Certainly it was not so at its beginning when the feudality of the two kingdoms went to battle against each other according to the set courtesies of chivalric custom and often chose their side with little regard to the demands of any national feeling. Undoubtedly the devastation of the English in France, and the ravaging by Norman sailors of the south coast of England, introduced a sterner element into the struggle, but the war never assumed the character of a modern national conflict in which whole populations are engaged. In the time of Edward III, for example, the English peasant knew little of the wars of princes. Again, during the reign of Richard II there could exist in the highest circles an amicable relationship between the two powers. Western Christendom was still cherished as a reality in the sentiment of both peoples, and the English were still content to learn from Gallic culture. Chaucer, for example, served under Edward III in the French wars, and he had been himself a prisoner. Yet throughout his works it is difficult to detect any trace of dislike for Frenchmen as such. As the years passed he drew more on Italian than on Gallic inspiration, but he none the less gave vivid expression to the sense of belonging to a common civilization in which both England and France were partners.

With the progress of the war, however, its character slowly changed, and it was eventually to produce an altered relationship between France and England. It is significant that even from the start many men in England were suspicious that a pope born within the kingdom of the French king could not be trusted to be impartial in the struggle. And the conflict could hardly have continued so long had there not been some popular support for it in both countries. As the decades passed, the English began to take a patriotic pride in the exploits of the armies in France, while Frenchmen began to look for a deliverer who might rid them of an intolerable foreign oppression. There is already a different temper to be detected in the fifteenth century from what had existed in the time of Edward III. Henry V can most certainly not be regarded as an apostle of Nationalism, but his career would none the less foster in England the growth of national feeling. Joan the Maid was infused by an inspiration very different from those which are kindled by modern nationalistic states, but her life and her death were made to give a sanction to much that was soon to come. By the middle of the fifteenth century such phrases as 'good Frenchmen' and 'true Frenchmen' appear in the chronicles as opposed to 'Français reniés' and 'Français anglais'. It was a new sentiment and one which was pregnant with future consequence.

For these reasons it is legitimate to regard the Hundred Years War as one among the many solvents of the medieval political order, and as marking the beginning of a new era in the history of Anglo-French relations. Indeed it might almost be suggested that in this respect its most notable results were to lie in the sphere of political sentiments and ideas. Both countries, of course, felt the conesquences of the prolonged strain. In England the final failure involved the house of Lancaster and precipitated the Wars of the Roses. In France the countryside of several provinces long bore terrible witness to the ferocity of the savage campaigns.

But the dynasty of York lost little time in reconstituting the royal authority, and France soon started on the road to recovery. Nevertheless, after the Hundred Years War neither French nor English ever thought about each other in quite the same way as they had done before, and never again were they to be conscious in quite the former manner of belonging to the same overriding political system. Feudalism as a cohesive force within, and between, the two peoples had been destroyed. Passing also were those ideas of political and social solidarity among the western peoples which the men of an earlier generation had respected though never realized. A new wind was beginning to blow from across the Alps. Less than half a century separated the death of Joan the Maid from the birth of Machiavelli, but the distance between them is not to be measured in years.

It is thus that in both France and England the real beneficiaries of the Hundred Years War were to be the monarchy and the middle class. For these would unite together eventually to destroy the older aristocracies, and together they would build for their own advantage a new sovereignty upon the ruins of the older order. The transformation in the art of war implied the end of feudalism, and in its place there arose a monarchy of a new type, strongly centralized, and claiming an absolute jurisdiction over all in the kingdom. Such monarchies would come to recognize few limits to their authority in matters either secular or ecclesiastical. Francis I and Henry VIII are already foreshadowed in the acts and in the diplomacy of Edward IV and Louis XI. The modern absolute state built upon nationalism, omnipotent and amoral, was arising, and it held the future in its keeping. But perhaps those who in our own days have watched some of the consequences of its acts may be tempted to reconsider the circumstances of its origin. The twentieth century has twice seen the armies of France and England joined together in a common cause, and the future of the civilization from which they both sprang may well now depend in large measure upon a mutual understanding between the two participants in the Hundred Years War.

XIV

The Domesday Survey[1]

—————◆❖◆—————

Towards the close of his reign King William the Conqueror (as the Peterborough chronicler informs us) 'sent his men into every shire all over England and caused it to be ascertained how many hundred hides were in the shire and what land the King had and what dues he ought to have from the shire – and how much each landholder in England had in land and stock and how much money it might be worth'.[2] These commissioners in their turn received sworn verdicts concerning these things from selected jurors. And finally the verdicts themselves, embodied in 'returns', were re-arranged by the royal clerks, and at last digested into the two great volumes which now repose in Chancery Lane. The whole process of inquiry we may call the Domesday Survey, and the two volumes which resulted therefrom have been known since the twelfth century as Domesday Book.

Domesday Book describes all England south of the Tees and the Westmoreland fells, and since the account contained therein is almost as remarkable for its efficiency as for its scope, it is hardly surprising that very much of English medieval research should have taken the form of a commentary upon this unique text.[3] Domesday scholarship has thus itself a long history which falls into three well-marked phases divided by Farley's great edition of 1783 and the appearance of Round's *Feudal England* in 1895. Before the last quarter of the eighteenth century, Domesday Book was kept under three locks at Westminster, and to consult it the student had to pay a fee of six shillings and eightpence, with fourpence extra for every line he transcribed.[4] Consequently it was little wonder that students shrank from a labour that was so expensive, or that competent critics became convinced that a proper edition of the text was essential to the development of historical scholarship. Robert Harley himself at the beginning of the eighteenth century 'often talked' of publishing Domesday Book engraved on copper plates,[5] but the need, felt by all scholars, was not satisfied until 1783, when, on the instructions of a Royal Commission spurred to its work by such as Philip Carteret Webb,[6] an edition of Domesday Book was produced printed in 'record' types which were specially cut for the purpose and later destroyed in the great fire at Westminster in 1834. This edition was so excellent that it has never been superseded, and its merits were directly due to one man, whose reputation has been shamefully neglected by generations of scholars who have profited by its work. Abraham Farley finds no place in the *Dictionary of National Biography*; but he had 'almost daily recourse' to Domesday Book 'for more than forty years';[7] and he produced one of the most accurate and reliable transcripts in the whole history of English scholarship. The edition for which he was responsible opened a new era in Domesday investigation which did not culminate until the appearance in 1895 of Round's *Feudal England*, a book which not only supplied a critical summary of all previous work on Domesday and added new discoveries of its own, but also prepared the way for future investigations. For these reasons an historical revision concerned with Domesday Book depends even today at every turn on the work of Abraham Farley and John Horace Round; for the former gave us what is still our sole indispensable printed text, and the latter indicated the lines upon which future research might most profitably proceed.

The forty-one years which have elapsed since the publication of Round's book have here been marked by an intensive application of his method of Domesday criticism. For the essence of Round's achievement in this field was his discovery that a wholly new light could be thrown upon Domesday by a detailed comparison of that record with other correlative texts, and the main feature of more recent Domesday study has been the discovery and criticism of new documents with which Domesday can be similarly compared. Round had at his disposal but two such texts: the *Inquisitio Comitatus Cantabrigiensis*, which related to Cambridgeshire and was derived (perhaps imperfectly) from the Domesday returns; and the *Inquisitio Eliensis*, which was made by a writer from the Church of Ely who composed, in part from those same returns, an account of the lands belonging to his monastery. But now, as a result of extensive investigation, we have not merely two but many more such surveys to aid us in our criticism of Domesday. At Canterbury, for example, there is a record which certainly was constructed in some measure out of the Domesday returns;[8] Abbot Baldwin of Bury St Edmunds also compiled in a similar fashion a like survey of his lands[9] which he called his Feudal Book, and before the eleventh century had closed similar surveys had also been drawn up at Evesham,[10] Abingdon[11] and Peterborough.[12] Some of these texts[13] have now been edited and criticized; others, like the Canterbury surveys and the Exon Domesday, still urgently demand a thorough examination: whilst others again, like the Evesham documents, still remain in manuscript. But the body of this evidence has grown so large that it reacts upon every department of Domesday criticism. Domesday, we now know, is not a record in isolation. It is surrounded, so to speak, by a number of satellite surveys. And Domesday research tends more and more to proceed by means of an application to Domesday of correlative texts which have been recently discovered or freshly appreciated.

The value of such a method of procedure has been shown not only when Domesday is brought into relation with other documents derived from the Domesday returns, but also when its evidence has been appraised in strict relation to that supplied by other independent texts. The social structure of the North Mercian Danelaw was only fully exposed when the statistics of Domesday were criticized in the light of the long series of twelfth-century charters which there link up King William's great survey with the thirteenth-century monastic extents.[14] And in East Anglia the account given by Domesday acquires a wholly new significance when it is examined in connection not only with charter evidence,[15] but also with surveys such as Abbot Leofstan drew up in the reign of Edward the Confessor[16] or Abbot Samson in the reign of Henry II.[17] Domesday stands between two distinct epochs in English history. It describes the conditions of the peasantry as they were on the eve of the Norman Conquest. But it was composed after the new feudal order had been established among the higher ranks of society for some twenty years. Here is its unique value as historical evidence. But it was in its essence a statistical record, and its figures can only be given actuality if they are studied in close connection with other evidence. And this is the more true in that the Norman clerks were describing an alien society in alien terms; they were using Latin phrases to describe Anglo-Saxon usages; and the incomparable evidence of Domesday will only be fully utilized when we have discovered what were the Anglo-Saxon equivalents for the words which its compilers used. A complete understanding of these matters is still far to seek.[18] But already the new comparative material has begun considerably to affect our knowledge of the complicated process which at last produced Domesday Book as we know it today – that is to say, our knowledge of (i) the Inquisition by the royal commissioners, (ii) the 'returns' which they received and (iii) the compilation of the final digest, or Domesday Book itself.

The inquisition which was afterwards to result in the completed Domesday Book took place in 1086;[19] and the best description of what happened thereat is to be found in a well-known passage in the *Inquisitio Eliensis*:

This is the description of the inquiry concerning the lands which the King's barons made according to the oath of the sheriff of the shire and of all the barons and their Frenchmen and of the whole hundred-court –

the priests, reeves and six villeins from every village. In the first place (they required) the name of the manor; who held it in the time of King Edward and who holds it now, how many hides are there, how many ploughs in demesne, and how many belonging to the men, how many villeins, cottars, slaves, freemen, and sokemen: how much woodland, meadow and pasture, how many mills and fisheries; how much has been added to or taken from the estate, how much the whole used to be worth and how much it is worth now: and how much each freeman and sokeman had or has there. All this thrice over: with reference to the time of King Edward, and to the time when King William gave the land and to the present time; and if more can be got out of it than is being drawn now.[20]

The information later embodied in Domesday Book itself shows that this was in fact exactly the scope of the inquiry. But it is not quite so certain that we have here a full description of the methods employed by the commissioners. The contemporary writer who compiled the Feudal Book of Abbot Baldwin gives a slightly different account of the whole proceeding when he observes that 'by the order of King William a description was made of the whole of England according to the oaths which were sworn by almost all the inhabitants thereof whereby each man proffered a true statement concerning his own land and substance and also concerning that of his neighbours'.[21] And in 1907 W. H. Stevenson brought to light, from a manuscript work of Robert Losinga based upon the chronicle of Marianus Scotus, a passage which contains perhaps the most remarkable contemporary description of the Domesday Inquisition:[22]

In the twentieth year of his reign by the order of William, King of the English, there was made a description of the whole of England (that is to say) of the lands of the several provinces thereof and of the possessions of all the great men. This was done in respect of ploughland and habitations, and of men both bond and free, both those who dwelt in cottages and those who had their homes and share in the fields; and in respect of ploughs and horses and other animals; and in respect finally of the services and payments due from all men in the whole land. Other investigators followed the first; and men were sent into provinces which they did not know and where they were themselves unknown in order that they might be given the opportunity of checking the first description and if necessary of denouncing its authors as guilty to the King.

The combined testimony of the available evidence now in fact suggests that the Domesday inquest was neither so rapid nor so uniform in character as has sometimes been supposed; and the fact, now clearly established, that many of the great prelates of England used the mechanism of the Domesday inquest to construct their own surveys[23] tempts speculation whether they may not themselves on occasion have been actively concerned with conducting it on their own vast estates. At all events, the great inquest was carried out in the main by royal commissioners making their inquiries normally (but not perhaps always) in the hundred courts, and their findings were checked in each county by a second set of commissioners who were deliberately sent by the king into districts where they had no personal interest.

The information elicited by the commissioners was embodied in the Domesday 'returns'; and if we possessed a group of these, or even one of them, the task of the historian of medieval England would be much simplified. As early as 1734 David Casley, who had been sub-librarian to Bentley in the Royal Library, triumphantly announced that he had discovered a batch of these returns among the Cottonian Manuscripts.[24] But, as Ayloffe pointed out,[25] he was mistaken in his conclusion, and no subsequent searcher has had better success. Nor do we know exactly what these returns contained. At the time when Round wrote, the only criteria for judging the nature of the 'returns' were Domesday Book itself and the two surveys with which he collated it; and he was led to conclude firstly that the surveys represented the returns fairly closely, and secondly that where the surveys added independent information of their own, this was derived not from the Domesday returns, but from personal knowledge.[26] But the similar record now available from Bury St Edmunds (which was certainly also based upon the Domesday inquest) now raises the whole problem in a much more acute form. For the Bury text, in place of a few minor additions such as were to be found in the Ely and Cambridgeshire surveys, adds whole lists of peasant names to take the place of the bare numerical totals to be found in Domesday itself.[27] And it seems therefore extremely probable that the Domesday returns may have been much fuller than has hitherto been supposed, and that they may have contained much information which the royal clerks later considered it unnecessary to include in their final digest.

Whatever was their content, these 'returns' supplied the material for Domesday Book itself. But the labour of constructing that Book even after the inquest had taken place must still have been extremely extensive. Not only was there an enormous mass of material to be dealt with, but it had all to be re-arranged. For while the 'returns' were made hundred by hundred and perhaps village by village, Domesday Book itself was constructed on a feudal plan – that is to say, according to the estates held in each shire by the tenants in chief of the lord king. Such a task was inevitably protracted, and the royal clerks evidently improved their methods as they gradually proceeded with it. For 'volume II' of Domesday Book, containing the account of Norfolk, Suffolk and Essex, was most probably completed before its companion, and it is marked by inferior workmanship and by far less compression.[28] From all points of view it is clear that the compilation of these two volumes must under the circumstances have taken a considerable time, and it therefore deserves an especial emphasis that the evidence now at our disposal tends to postpone our dating of Domesday Book. The earliest reference to the finished book which has hitherto been discovered comes from a charter issued by Queen Matilda[29] either between 1108 and 1109 or between 1111 and 1113.[30] And a clerk writing between 1125 and 1130 speaks of the completed volume which was to be kept in the Winchester Treasury.[31] On the other hand, a charter of the abbey of St Benet of Holme, which may be dated 1094 or even just possibly 1099–1100, refers to the returns, which were for some time preserved, and not to the completed survey, in such a way as strongly to suggest that the latter was not then in existence.[32] The Feudal Book of Abbot Baldwin, which was itself completed in the reign of Rufus, alludes to the Domesday inquest, but never to Domesday Book itself.[33] And the Canterbury survey, which was derived from the Domesday returns, actually records as the existing tenant of an estate the father of the man who appears at the same place in Domesday Book.[34] The dating of Domesday Book is a matter beset with difficulties. But until further evidence is forthcoming it would certainly be unwise to place its final completion before the early years of the reign of Henry I.

The record which was thus at last finished is of such importance that no historian of medieval England can neglect it with impunity. The investigator of Anglo-Norman history finds himself scarcely less indebted to Domesday than the student of Old English society, and, thanks to the labours of Darby and his colleagues, we are now beginning to appreciate afresh its incomparable value for the study of historical geography. Indeed, so high is the reputation of this text that there has always been a danger of isolated passages in a record so reverenced being made to support false inferences, or of more being demanded of Domesday than even that comprehensive survey could reasonably be expected to supply. The optimism of Samuel Pepys, who searched in Domesday 'concerning the sea and the dominion thereof',[35] has been shared by many of his successors, and Freeman based very much of his criticism of the survey on an erroneous interpretation of two detached entries.[36] The mention of such illustrious examples makes it excusable even today to utter a caution. King William did not institute his great inquiry for the benfit of later students of history; nor were his clerks who dealt so admirably with an intractable mass of material themselves infallible. It is thus dangerous to argue from an isolated Domesday entry, and always unsafe to generalize from a particular instance of its technical terminology. And the accumulated evidence supplied by this invaluable source can never be properly utilized unless it be constantly remembered what were the motives underlying this eleventh-century survey, and what was the resulting character of Domesday Book itself.

Domesday was a 'geld book';[37] and the details which it enumerates were all related primarily to one main object: 'the exact record of the local distribution of the King's geld or Danegeld, the one great direct tax levied over the whole of England'.[38] The meticulous care exercised by the surveyors with such an object in view was made a reproach to the king by the Peterborough chronicler, and we know that for a similar reason riots broke out in several places as a result of the proceedings of the royal commissioners.[39] The relation of Domesday to the royal taxation has received in modern scholarship perhaps even more emphasis than is its due. But it is none the less important always to bear in mind that this was essentially a financial document, for 'many subtle pitfalls'[40] are prepared for those who seek to construct a picture of English society solely from its evidence and in disregard of the special practical purpose for which that survey was made.

But while Domesday was a geld book, it may in many important respects be considered as a feodary[41] also. It is true that it tells us little of feudal organization as such, but it tells us a great deal about individual barons and their estates,[42] and it thus emphasizes (a fact which is often ignored in modern discussions of an abstract 'feudalism' which never existed) that such organization implied to the men of the time particular arrangements in particular places. Domesday Book throughout presupposes the existence of the feudal order, and its statistics are all arranged upon a plan which assumes that the fundamental relationship in English society has now become that between the king and his immediate tenants. Moreover, detailed information about this relationship was almost as important to the king as were facts about the geld itself. For the reorganization of English society in the late eleventh century was not carried out, as so many modern writers would have had us believe, by the king in constant opposition to a fractious 'baronage', but, on the contrary, through the vigorous cooperation of an extremely able group of men with the king at their head. The successful settlement of England after the Norman Conquest always depended directly upon the maintenance of an active association between the king and that miscellaneous class which appears in Domesday as his tenants-in-chief.[43] In consequence it was vital that the individual implications of that relationship should be known to the king; and it was in Domesday that he could seek and could find this essential information.

Finally, Domesday Book cannot today be regarded only as a financial statement or only as in part a feodary. It was also the result of a great judicial inquiry that was directly connected with the very extensive litigation[44] that inevitably followed a conquest by a king who strove at all costs to uphold tradition. Very many of the documents with which Domesday has now to be related strongly emphasize the important fact that the Domesday Inquest was evolved somewhat easily out of the litigation which preceded it. At Ely, at Canterbury,[45] at Worcester,[46] and probably at Evesham[47] and Abingdon,[48] a continuous series of legal investigations led up to the events of 1086. In these the same method of the sworn inquest was used[49] in the same courts of shire and hundred, and the men who conducted the great trials of the reign of William the Conqueror often themselves became at last the Domesday commissioners. Geoffrey of Coutances, for example, presided over the famous Kentish trial of 'Pennenden Heath'; he heard the Worcester suits; he conducted the great Ely trial which followed the last English rising; and in 1080 he presided again over another important Ely trial at Kentford. Geoffrey of Coutances was in turn one of the chief Domesday commissioners carrying out in 1086 work strictly similar to that which he had often done before.[50] The completed Domesday Book also bears unmistakable traces of being connected with the disputes of ownership and possession which followed the Conquest. Individual entries often discuss and reconcile contested claims; and the important sections of the Book which describe the *clamores* in Yorkshire, Lincolnshire and Huntingdonshire, or enumerate the *invasiones* in Norfolk and Suffolk[51] all testify to the need which in 1086 must have been felt of making an end of the legal controversies of two confused and contentious decades. 'The Domesday Inquisition must, in short, be placed in its contemporary legal setting; it was a judicial eyre among others; and it embodied the results of numerous *placita* which it summarized and attempted finally to settle by the extensive use of a judicial process to which William I had already accustomed England. Domesday Book itself cannot be adequately utilized unless it be regarded as the product of a long series of judicial events which, themselves of long duration, were the direct consequence of the Norman Conquest and of the policy of the Norman King.'[52]

Modern Domesday criticism has thus been marked by certain broad general features. Dependent on the earlier work of Farley and Round, it has largely relied upon the discovery and appreciation of texts closely related to Domesday which, by comparison with the larger survey, could be made to throw a flood of new light upon it. By such means our knowledge of what took place at the Domesday Inquest of 1086, and of the 'returns' which were made thereat, has been substantially modified. And we are now also led to stress certain new features of the compilation of the Domesday Book itself, and to emphasize more strongly than heretofore the feudal and the judicial nature of that record. Domesday Book will always remain a cardinal source for the history of England in the Middle Ages; and the manifold uses to which historians, legal antiquaries and geographers have put this unique text, form no part of our present subject. It must suffice to suggest that their work must here always depend upon a correct understanding of the genesis and of the character of the most important statistical record ever produced in any medieval kingdom.

NOTES

[1] The sole indispensable printed text of Domesday is still that issued by the Record Commission in 1783. Translations of Domesday are included in the *Victoria County Histories*, and the introductions which precede them, though of unequal merit, are often (as in the case of Essex and Worcestershire) of the greatest value: they form perhaps the best means by which the student can in the first instance be made familiar with the scope and with the method of Domesday Book.

Among the older works on Domesday, some are still of great value. The Appendix and Glossary which form the conclusion of Robert Brady's *Introduction to the Old English History* (1684) contain information not easily obtained elsewhere. P. C. Webb's two tracts on Domesday (1756) are more than antiquarian curiosities, and Robert Kelham's *Domesday Book Illustrated* (1788) was a notable publication. The indices contained in Henry Ellis's *General Introduction to Domesday Book* (1833) are indispensable to the researcher.

In the latter years of the nineteenth century a number of outstanding works on Domesday appeared. The edition of the *Inquisitio Comitatus Cantabrigiensis* produced by N. E. S. A. Hamilton for the Royal Society of Literature in 1876 is of the greatest importance; Maitland's *Domesday Book and Beyond* (1897) is a classic which should be read in connection with James Tait's review thereof in *Eng. Hist. Rev.*, vol. xiv, p. 768; while Vinogradoff's *English Society in the Eleventh Century* (1908) is a monument of patient research into the evidence of Domesday. But of all the works produced about this time J. H. Round's *Feudal England* (1895) has best stood the test of modern criticism.

Among more recent works on Domesday, F. M. Stenton's *William the Conqueror* (1908) contains in its concluding chapter what is still probably the best introduction to Domesday for the general reader. In his edition of *Danelaw Charters* (1920) the same writer showed how best the evidence of Domesday could be collated with that derived from other sources, whilst in his *English Feudalism* (1932) he appraised the value of Domesday as a source of English feudal history. W. J. Corbett in *Camb. Med. Hist.* (vol. v, pp. 506–16) gives an admirable general account. *Feudal Documents from the Abbey of Bury St Edmunds*, edited by me for the British Academy in 1932, contains a critical edition of Abbot Baldwin's Feudal Book, together with an introduction which seeks to show the extent to which general Domesday criticism is affected by the evidence of that text. My essay 'Odo Lanfranc and the Domesday Survey' in *Historical Essays Presented to James Tait* (1933) attempts to appraise the relation of the Domesday inquest to contemporary litigation.

The edition of A. Ballard's *The Domesday Inquest*, published in 1923, gives 'A Bibliography of Matter relating to Domesday Book published between the years 1906 and 1923'. And the following among recent special studies may be mentioned as bearing either on the process by which Domesday Book was constructed or on the methods by which its evidence may be interpreted: H. C. Darby, Chapter V of *Historical Geography of England* (1936); H. M. Cam, 'Manerium cum Hundredo' (*Eng. Hist. Rev.*, xlvii,

353–76); D. C. Douglas, 'Fragments of an Anglo-Saxon Survey from Bury St Edmunds' (*Eng. Hist. Rev.*, xliii, 376–83); D. C. Douglas, 'Some Early surveys of the Abbey of Abingdon' (*Eng. Hist. Rev.*, xliv, 618–25); J. E. A. Jolliffe, 'Hidation of Kent' (*Eng. Hist. Rev.*, xliv, 612–18); F. M. Stenton, Introduction to *The Lincolnshire Domesday and the Lindsey Survey* (Linc. Rec. Soc., vol. xix); F. M. Stenton, 'St Benet of Holme and the Norman Conquest' (*Eng. Hist. Rev.*, xxxvii, 225–35); W. H. Stevenson 'A Contemporary Description of the Domesday Survey' (*Eng. Hist. Rev.*, xxii, 72–84).

2 Ed. Rolls Series, ii, p. 186.

3 Cf. Stenton, *English Feudalism*, p. 7.

4 Nicolson, *English Historical Library* (1736), p. 213; Thoresby, *Diary*, ii, p. 30.

5 Hearne, *Collections*, x, p. 101.

6 Cf. P. C. Webb, *A Short Account of Domesday with a View to its Publication* (1756).

7 Ellis, *Introduction to Domesday*, i, p. 360.

8 Canterbury Muniment Room: MS. F. 28. This text, usually known as the 'Domesday Monachorum', is still unedited and uncriticized. Parts of it were printed by William Somner in his *Antiquities of Canterbury* (1640 and ed. Nicholas Battely, 1703), and in the new *Monasticon* (iii, pp. 100 *sqq.*). A. Ballard printed extracts from this MS. for the purposes of illustrating another text (Brit. Acad. 'Records', vol. iv) and a translation appeared in *Vict. County Hist.*, *Kent*, vol. ii, pp. 253 *sqq.*, together with an inadequate introduction. A critical edition of this most important text is a major need of Domesday scholarship.

9 Ed. D. C. Douglas (British Academy 'Records', vol. ix).

10 Cott. Vesp. B. vol. xxiv. Cf. W. Tindal *History . . . of Evesham* (1794), pp. 49–78.

11 Douglas, 'Some Early Surveys of the Abbey of Abingdon' (*Eng. Hist. Rev.*, xlix, pp. 618 *sqq.*).

12 Cf. Stenton, *Types of Manorial Structure in the Northern Danelaw*, pp. 6 *sqq.*

13 For a discussion of these see Douglas, *Feudal Documents*, pp. lxx–lxxi.

14 Stenton, *Danelaw Charters* (British Academy 'Records', vol. v).

15 Douglas, *Social Structure of Medieval East Anglia* (1925), pp. 205–58.

16 Douglas, 'Fragments of an Anglo-Saxon Survey from Bury St Edmunds', *Eng. Hist. Rev.*, xliii, pp. 376–83.

17 *Feudal Documents*, pp. cli–clxxi.

18 But cf. Professor Stenton's establishment of the identity of the old English *mannrædenn* with the Domesday *invasiones* (*Eng. Hist. Rev.*, xxxvii, p. 230), and his successful identification of the Old English *cnaulæcung* with *recognitio* as it is used in the frequent *pro recognitione* of Domesday (*Eng. Hist. Rev.*, li, pp. 97–104).

19 There was for a time some confusion about this date, mainly owing to erroneous statements in Matthew Paris, the Annals of Waverley and Henry of Huntingdon. The colophon of the Little Domesday which expressly states that the inquest throughout the whole of England took place in 1086 outweighs all other evidence. And its testimony was remarkably confirmed by the narrative of Robert of Hereford discovered by W. H. Stevenson and printed by him in 1907 (*Eng. Hist. Rev.* xxii, p. 74).

20 *Inq. Com. Cant.*, ed. Hamilton, p. 97. Translation in Stenton, *William the Conqueror*, p. 459.

21 Douglas, *Feudal Documents*, p. 3.

22 Stevenson, *Eng. Hist. Rev.*, xxii, p. 74.

23 Douglas, *op. cit.*, p. lxxx.

24 David Casley, *Catalogue of MSS of the King's Library* (1734), Appendix.

25 J. Ayloffe, *Calendars of the Ancient Charters* (1774), p. xviii. The MS. to which Casley was led was Cott. MS. Vitell. C viii at fols 143–56. And in my opinion it might repay a more thorough examination than it has received in modern times.

[26] Round, *Feudal England*, p. 130.

[27] Douglas, *op. cit.*, pp. lvii–lix.

[28] Round, *op. cit.*, pp. 139–42.

[29] Abingdon Cartulary (Rolls Series), ii, pp. 115, 116. This should now be compared with the doubtful references to Domesday in an early Abingdon Survey (cf. *Eng. Hist. Rev.*, xliv, p. 623) and with the curious charter of Henry I which J. Bentham printed in his *Antiquities . . . of Ely* (1771), Appendix No. xix.

[30] Round, *op. cit.*, p. 143.

[31] F. Liebermann, *Ungedruckte Anglo-Normannische Geschichtsquellen*, p. 22.

[32] *Mon Ang.*, iii, p. 86; C. Johnson, *Vict. County Hist.*, *Norfolk*, ii, p. 3; J. R. West, *The Register of the Abbey of St Benet of Holme*, i, p. 6.

[33] Douglas, *op. cit.*, p. lxvi.

[34] Compare the following:

Domesday Monachorum, fol. 13b.	D. B. fol 8b.
Willelmus de Taum tenet Dele pro I sull. et I iug.	Filius Willelmi Tahum tenet de episcopo Delce pro uno solin et uno iugo

The estate is probably Little Delce near Rochester.

[35] Round, *op. cit.*, p. 230.

[36] Freeman, *Norman Conquest*, iv, pp. 723 *sqq.*; v. p. 42; *Methods of Historical Study*, pp. 186, 187. Cf. Vinogradoff, *English Society*, p. 220.

[37] Maitland, *Domesday Book and Beyond*, Essay I.

[38] Stenton, *William the Conqueror*, p. 460.

[39] Stevenson, *Eng. Hist. Rev.*, xxii, p. 77.

[40] Stenton, *op. cit.*, *loc. cit.*

[41] Contrast Maitland, *Domesday Book and Beyond*, p. 5.

[42] Cf. Stenton, *English Feudalism*, pp. 9 *sqq.*

[43] Cf. Robert Brady, *Introduction to the Old English History*, Appendix; Ellis, *Introduction to Domesday*, i, pp. 316–515.

[44] On this matter see Douglas, *Feudal Documents*, pp. lxxvi–lxxx; *Odo Lanfranc and the Domesday Survey*, passim.

[45] Douglas in *Essays in Honour of James Tait*, pp. 47 *sqq.*

[46] Round in *Domesday Commemoration Essays*, ii, pp. 540–6.

[47] W. Tindal, *History . . . of Evesham*, p. 75.

[48] *Eng. Hist. Rev.*, xliv, pp. 618 *sqq.*

[49] Brady, *op. cit.*, p. 191.

[50] Round, *op. cit.*, p. 543; Douglas, *op. cit.*, **p.** 57.

[51] Cf. Stenton, 'St Benet of Holme and the Norman Conquest' (*Eng. Hist. Rev.*, xxxvii, p. 230).

[52] Douglas, *op. cit.*, p. 57.

Select Bibliography of David C. Douglas

1927
The Social Structure of Medieval East Anglia (The Clarendon Press, Oxford),
288 pp.
'A Charter of Enfeoffment under William the Conqueror', *Eng. Hist. Rev.*,
vol. xliii, April 1927
Review of M. V. Clarke, *The Medieval City State*, in *History*, vol. 12, July 1927

1928
The Norman Conquest, Historical Association Leaflet, No. 73
'Fragments of an Anglo-Saxon Survey from Bury St Edmunds', *Eng. Hist.
Rev.*, July 1928
Review of E. G. A. Holmes, *The Albigensian or Catharist Heresy*, in *History*,
January 1928
Review of E. J. Martin, *The Trial of the Templars*, in *History*, July 1928

1929
The Age of the Normans (Nelson, London), 256 pp.
'Some Early Surveys from the Abbey of Abingdon', *Eng. Hist. Rev.*, October
1929
Reviews of J. Chartrou, *L'Anjou de 1109 à 1151*, in *History*, July 1929
    E. Barrow, *The Growth of Europe through the Dark Ages*, in *History*,
        July 1929
    W. H. Turton, *The Plantagenet Ancestry*, in *History*, October 1929

1932
Feudal Documents from the Abbey of Bury St Edmunds (British Academy, London),
pp. cxii, 248, 3 plates
Review of F. M. Stenton, *English Feudalism*, in *Econ. Hist. Rev.*, October 1932

1933
'Odo Lanfranc and the Domesday Survey', *Essays Presented to James Tait*,
pp. 42–7
'John Richard Green', *The Times Literary Supplement*, 9 March 1933
'The Saxon Nymph', *TLS*, 28 September 1933
Reviews of J. E. A. Jolliffe, *Prefeudal England*, in *TLS*, September 1933
    H. E. Mulhfeld, *A Survey of the Manor of Wye*, in *TLS*,
        28 December 1933

1934
Reviews of George Sitwell, *Tales of My Native Village*, in *TLS*, 22 February
      1934
      A. Hamilton Thompson, *A Calendar of Charters Belonging to the
         Hospital of William Wyggeston, Leicester*, in *TLS*, 25 October 1934
      V. H. Galbraith, *An Introduction of the Public Records*, in *TLS*,
         29 November 1934

1935
'The Development of Medieval Europe', in E. Eyre (ed.), *Western Civilization*
  (Oxford University Press), iii, pp. 1–350
'Thomas Hearne', *TLS*, 6 June 1935
'William Dugdale, the "Grand Plagiary" ', *History*, December 1935

1936
'The Domesday Survey', *History*, December 1936
Reviews of G. G. Coulton, *Five Centuries of Religion*, vol. III, in *TLS*, 7 March
      1936
      B. A. Lees, *Records of the Templars in the Twelfth Century*, in *Eng. Hist.
         Rev.*, April 1936
      H. Pirenne, *Economic and Social History of Medieval Europe*, in *TLS*,
         22 August 1936
      James Tait, *The Medieval English Borough*, in *TLS*, 29 August 1936

1937
'The Medieval Village', *TLS*, 11 May 1937
Review of V. H. Galbraith, *The St Albans Chronicle*, in *TLS*, 20 February 1937

1938
Review of G. G. Coulton, *Medieval Panorama*, in *TLS*, 4 November 1938

1939
English Scholars (Jonathan Cape, London), 382 pp.
'The Development of English Medieval Scholarship between 1660 and 1730',
  R. Hist. Soc. *Trans.*, 4th series, vol. ix, pp. 21–39
'The Norman Conquest and English Feudalism', *Econ. Hist. Rev.*, May 1939

1940
Review of Marc Bloch, *La Societé féodale*, in *History*, December 1940

1942
'E. A. Freeman', *TLS*, 21 March 1942
'Rollo of Normandy', *Eng. Hist. Rev.*, October 1942

1943
'Companions of the Conqueror', *History*, September 1943
Review of F. M. Stenton, *Anglo-Saxon England*, in *Spectator*, 30 December
  1943

1944

The Domesday Monachorum of Christchurch Canterbury (Royal Historical Society,
London), 128 pp., 13 plates

'The Ancestors of William Fitz Osbern', *Eng. Hist. Rev.*, January 1944

1946

'The Norman Conquest and British Historians', David Murray Lecture to the
University of Glasgow

'The Earliest Norman Counts', *Eng. Hist. Rev.*, May 1946

'Clio's Greatest Gift', *TLS*, 15 August 1946

Review of C. V. Wedgwood, *Velvet Studies*, in *TLS*, 23 November 1946

1947

'The Rise of Normandy', Raleigh Lecture to the British Academy

Reviews of E. Perroy, *La Guerre de Cent Ans*, in *TLS*, 31 May 1947

      E. F. Jacob, *Henry V and the Invasion of France*, in *TLS*, 14 June
        1947

      P. Styles, *Sir Simon Archer*, in *Eng. Hist. Rev.*, April 1947

1948

Reviews of G. O. Sayles, *Medieval Foundations of England*, in *TLS*, 7 February
      1948

      J. W. F. Hill, *Medieval Lincoln*, in *TLS*, 18 December 1948

1949

'The Beginning of England', *TLS*, 30 April 1949

Reviews of H. E. Butler, *The Chronicle of Jocelyn of Brakelonda*, in *TLS*,
      27 May 1949

      W. Ullmann, *Medieval Papalism*, in *TLS*, 7 October 1949

1950

'Some Problems of Early Norman Chronology', *Eng. Hist. Rev.*, July 1950

Reviews of M. Legge, *Anglo-Norman in the Cloisters*, in *TLS*, 19 May 1950

      M. Letts, *Sir John Mandeville*, in the *Listener*, 27 July 1950

      F. S. Schmidt, *S. Anselmi . . . Opeea*, in *TLS*, 3 September 1950

      G. G. Coulton, *Five Centuries of Religion*, vol. iv, in *TLS*,
        13 October 1950

      O. Chadwick, *John Cassian*, in *TLS*, 1 December 1950

      F. M. Powicke, *Walter Daniels' Life of Ailred of Rievaulx*, in *TLS*,
        8 December 1950

1951

English Scholars (second edition, revised; Eyre & Spottiswoode, London),
    292 pp., 8 plates

Introduction to E. Perroy, *Hundred Years War* (Eyre & Spottiswoode,
    London)

'English Medieval History', *TLS*, 24 August 1951

Reviews of M. D. Knowles, *Episcopal Colleagues of Thomas Becket*, in *TLS*,
　　　　27 April 1951
　　　　L. C. Loyd, *Sir Christopher Hatton's Book of Seals*, in *Eng. Hist.
　　　　Rev., April 1951
　　　　V. H. Galbraith, *Historical Research in Medieval England*, in *TLS*,
　　　　29 June 1951
　　　　J. O'Meara, *The Topographia Hibernica of Giraldus Cambrensis*, in
　　　　Eng. Hist. Rev., January 1951

1952

'Medieval Paris', in *Golden Ages of the Great Cities*, pp. 86–104 (Thames &
　　Hudson)
Reviews of M. Chibnall, *Select Documents of the English Lands of the Abbey of
　　　　Bec*, in *Eng. Hist. Rev.*, January 1952
　　　　J. B. Villars, *Les Normands en Méditerranée*, in *TLS*, 1 February
　　　　1952
　　　　F. L. Ganshof, *Feudalism*, in *TLS*, 13 June 1952
　　　　S. Runciman, *History of the Crusades*, vol. ii, in *Listener*,
　　　　11 December 1952
　　　　F. E. Harmer, *Anglo-Saxon Wills*, in *Bulletin* of the Institute of
　　　　Historical Research

1953

English Historical Documents, vol. ii, ed. David Douglas and G. W. Greenaway
　　(Eyre & Spottiswoode), 1014 pp.
'Edward the Confessor, Duke William of Normandy and the English
　　Succession', *Eng. Hist. Rev.*, October 1953
General Editor, *English Historical Documents*, vol. viii, ed. A. Browning
　　(Eyre & Spottiswoode)
Reviews of S. B. Chrimes, *Introduction to the Administrative History of England*,
　　　　in *TLS*, 13 February 1953
　　　　R. W. Southern, *The Making of the Middle Ages*, in *TLS*, 8 May
　　　　1953
　　　　D. Knowles and R. N. Hadcock, *Medieval Religious Houses*, in *TLS*,
　　　　25 September 1953
　　　　G. H. Williams, *The Norman Anonymous of 1100 AD*, in *Journal of
　　　　Ecclesiastical History*

1954

Reviews of Christopher Dawson, *Medieval Essays*, in *TLS*, 15 January 1954
　　　　Victoria County History: Oxford, vol. iii (Oxford University Press),
　　　　in *Listener*, 12 August 1954
　　　　S. Runciman, *History of the Crusades*, vol. iii, in *Listener*, 1954

1955

'Robert de Jumièges, archeveque de Canterbury et la conquete de l'Angleterre
　　par les Normands', in *Jumièges . . . Congrès . . . de XIIIe centenaire*

General Editor, *English Historical Documents*, vol. i, ed. D. Whitelock and vol.
  ix, ed. M. Jensen (Eyre & Spottiswoode)
Reviews of R. Lopez and I. W. Raymond, *Medieval Trade in the Mediterranean*,
          in *TLS*, May 1955
      F. M. Stenton, *Latin Charters of the Anglo-Saxon Period*, in *TLS*,
          27 May 1955
      R. L. Graeme Ritchie, *The Normans in Scotland*, in *Eng. Hist. Rev.*,
          1955
      W. A. Pantin, *The English Church in the 14th Century*, in *TLS*,
          6 May 1955
      T. J. Oleson, *The Witanagemot in the Reign of Edward the Confessor*,
          in *TLS*, 26 August 1955

1956
General Editor, *English Historical Documents*, vol. xii (1), ed. G. M. Young
  and W. D. Handcock (Eyre & Spottiswoode)
Reviews of C. Johnson and H. A. Cronne (eds), *Regesta Regum Anglo-*
          Normannorum, vol. II, in *TLS*, 13 April 1956
      R. C. Smail, *Crusading Warfare 1097–1193*, in *Listener*, 16 August
          1956
      P. Rickard, *Britain in Medieval French Literature*, in *TLS*,
          22 December 1956
      K. R. Potter (ed.), *Gesta Stephani*, in *Eng. Hist. Rev.*, April 1956
      R. Fawtier, *The Capetian Kings of France*, in *TLS*, 14 March 1960
      R. Barraclough (ed.), *Social Life in Early England*, in *TLS*,
          27 May 1960
      H. G. Richardson, *The English Jewry under the Angevin Kings*, in
          TLS, 9 April 1960

1957
'The Norman Episcopate before the Norman Conquest', *Cambridge Historical
  Journal*
General Editor, *English Historical Documents*, vol. x, ed. D. B. Horn and
  M. Ransome (Eyre & Spottiswoode)
Reviews of Winston S. Churchill, *A History of the English Speaking Peoples*,
          vol. i, in *Eng. Hist. Rev.*, January 1957
      G. S. Barrow, *Feudal Britain*, *in TLS*, 25 March 1957
      E. Jamison, *Admiral Eugenius of Sicily*, in *TLS*, 5 April 1957
      R. H. C. Davis, *History of Medieval Europe*, in *Listener*, 17 October
          1957
      L. Fox (ed.), *English Historical Scholarship in the Sixteenth and
          Seventeenth Centuries*, in *Eng. Hist. Rev.*, October 1957

1958
'Les Evêques de Normandie 1035–1066', *Annales de Normandie*, May 1958
'Gloucestershire and the Norman Conquest', *Transactions* of the Bristol and
  Gloucestershire Archaeological Society

Reviews of F. M. Stenton (ed.), *The Bayeux Tapestry*, in *Eng. Hist. Rev.*,
      April 1958
      R. Vaughan, *Matthew Paris*, in *TLS*, 21 March 1958
      Georgina Mason, *Frederick of Hohenstauffen*, in *Listener*, 3 April 1958

1959
General Editor, *English Historical Documents*, vol. xi, ed. A. Aspinall and
  E. A. Smith (Eyre & Spottiswoode)
Reviews of N. K. Chadwick, *Studies in the Early British Church*, in *TLS*,
      20 March 1959
      R. Lennard, *Rural England 1086–1135*, in *TLS*, 24 July 1959
      M. D. Rops, *The Church in the Dark Ages*, in *TLS*, 31 July 1959

1960
'The Song of Roland and the Norman Conquest of England', *French Studies*,
  xiv, pp. 99–116
'The First Ducal Charter for Fécamp', in *L'Abbaye de Fécamp . . . Ouvrage . . .
de XIIIe centenaire*

1961
'Marc Bloch: A Master-Historian', *TLS*, 23 June 1961
Reviews of G. W. S. Barrow, *The Acts of Malcolm IV King of Scotland*, in
      TLS, 27 January 1961
      W. L. Warren, *King John*, in *TLS*, 7 April 1961
      J. C. Holt, *The Northerners*, in *TLS*, 17 November 1961
      V. H. Galbraith, *The Making of Domesday Book*, in *TLS*,
      22 December 1961

1962
Reviews of *Medieval Studies presented to Aubrey Gwyn*, in *TLS*, 2 February 1962
      D. Mathew, *The Norman Monasteries and their English Possessions*, in
      TLS, 7 October 1962
      P. Kibre, *Scholarly Privilege in Medieval England*, in *TLS*, August
      1962
      H. R. Loyn, *Anglo-Saxon England and the Norman Conquest*, in
      TLS, 23 July 1962

1963
Reviews of J. Wallace Hadrill, *The Long-Haired Kings*, in *TLS*, 18 January
      1963
      H. J. Richardson and G. Sayles, *The Governance of Medieval
      England*, in *TLS*, 19 April 1963
      C. Warren Hollister, *Anglo-Saxon Military Institutions*, in *TLS*,
      25 January 1963
      R. W. Southern, *Saint Anselm and his Biographer*, in *TLS*,
      2 August 1963
      D. Knowles, *The Historian and Character* in *TLS*, 10 August 1963

C. Brooke, *The Saxon and Norman Kings*, in *TLS*, 30 August 1963
M. Fauroux (ed.), *Recueil des Actes des ducs de Normandie*, in *Eng. Hist. Rev.*, October 1963
Marc Bloch, *Mélanges historiques*, in *TLS*, 21 June 1963

1964
William the Conqueror: the Norman Impact upon England (London: Eyre & Spottiswoode; USA: University of California Press – May. History Book Club of America – June. Second revised impression – November.)
Reviews of V. H. Galbraith, *An Introduction to the Study of History*, in *TLS*, 12 March 1964
    F. S. Fussner, *The Historical Revolution*, in *Eng. Hist. Rev.*, April 1964
    Giorgio Falco, *The Holy Roman Republic*, in *TLS*, 20 November 1964
    H. G. Richardson and G. Sayles, *The Administration of Ireland 1072–1377*, in *TLS*, 20 November 1964

1965
Reviews of G. W. Barrow, *Robert Bruce and the Community of the Realm in Scotland*, in *TLS*, 11 January 1965
    The Chronicle of Bury St Edmunds, in *Journal of Ecclesiastical History*, April 1965
    C. H. S. Fifoot (ed.), *The Letters of Frederick William Maitland*, in *TLS*, 1 April 1965
    C. W. Hollister, *The Military Organization of Norman England*, in *TLS*, 22 April 1965
    J. C. Holt, *Magna Carta*, in *TLS*, 1 July 1965
    D. M. Stenton, *English Justice between the Norman Conquest and the Great Charter*, in *TLS*, 23 December 1965

1966
Wilhelm der Eroberer: der Normannische Angriff Auf England (Stuttgart)
'William the Conqueror: Duke and King', in Whitelock, Douglas et al., *The Norman Conquest: its Setting and Impact* (Eyre & Spottiswoode), pp. 45–76
'The Domesday Tenant of Hawling', *Transactions* of the Bristol and Gloucestershire Archaeological Society
'Le couronnement de Guillaume le Conquérant', *Etudes normandes*, October 1966
Reviews of F. Barlow, *William I and the Norman Conquest*, in *TLS*, 17 February 1966
    D. J. Hull, *English Medieval Pilgrimages*, in *TLS*, 12 June 1966
    F. West, *The Justiciarship in England*, in *TLS*, 1 December 1966

1967
"Les reussites normandes, 1050–1100', *Revue historique*, March 1967

General Editor, *English Historical Documents*, vol. v, ed. C. H. Williams
  (Eyre & Spottiswoode)
Review of C. E. and R. Wright (eds), *The Diary of Humfrey Wanley*, in
  Review of English Studies, October 1967

1968
Reviews of R. H. C. Davis, *King Stephen*, in *TLS*, 11 January 1968
  C. R. Cheney, *Hubert Walter*, in *TLS*, 4 April 1968
  E. F. Jacob, *Archbishop Chichele*, in *TLS*, 4 April 1968
  W. Urry, *Canterbury under the Angevin Kings*, in *TLS*, 25 April 1968
  P. H. Sawyer, *Anglo-Saxon Charters*, in *TLS*, 18 April 1968
  H. A. Cronne and R. H. C. Davis (eds), *Regesta Regum Anglo-
    Normannorum*, vol. III, in *TLS*, 6 June 1968

1969
The Norman Achievement (London: Eyre & Spottiswoode), 272 pp., 12 pp. plates
William the Conqueror (Methuen University Paperbacks)
General Editor, *English Historical Documents*, vol. iv, ed. A. R. Myers (Eyre &
  Spottiswoode)

1970
Reviews of F. M. Stenton, Preparatory to 'Anglo-Saxon England' in *TLS*,
    23 July 1970
  E. A. Cronne, *The Reign of Stephen*, in *TLS*, 14 August 1970
  F. Delaney, *British Autobiography in the Seventeenth Century*, in
    Review of English Studies, August 1970

1971
The Norman Conquest and British Historians (second edition, Glasgow University
  Press)
Reviews of *The Manuscripts of Henry Savile of Banke*, in *Eng. Hist. Rev.*,
    March 1971
  G. S. Barrow and W. W. Scott, *The Acts of William I King of
    Scots*, in *TLS*, 13 August 1971
  B. P. Wolffe, *The Royal Demesne in English History*, in *TLS*,
    12 November 1971

1972
The Norman Achievement (revised edition, paperback, Fontana)
Review of E. J. Kealey, *Roger of Salisbury*, in *TLS*, 21 November 1972

1973
Reviews of Marc Bloch, *The Royal Touch*, in *TLS*, 15 June 1973
    C. H. Gibbs-Smith, *The Bayeux Tapestry*, in *TLS*, 21 October 1973

1974
Reviews of J. Deer, *Papstum und Normannen*, in *Eng. Hist. Rev.*, October 1974
    R. Delorte, *Life in the Middle Ages*, in *TLS*, 1 November 1974

1975
General Editor, *English Historical Documents*, vol. iii, ed. Harry Rothwell
   (Eyre & Spottiswoode)

1976
The Norman Fate 1100–1154 (Eyre Methuen), 272 pp., 8 pp. plates

1977
William the Conqueror (new edn, hardback and paperback, Eyre Methuen)
General Editor, *English Historical Documents*, vol. xii (2), ed. W. D. Handcock
   (Eyre & Spottiswoode)

Index